Grade Aid

for

Cook and Cook

The World of Children

prepared by

Carolyn Morgan
University of Wisconsin—Whitewater

Boston   New York   San Francisco
Mexico City   Montreal   Toronto   London   Madrid   Munich   Paris
Hong Kong   Singapore   Tokyo   Cape Town   Sydney

Copyright © 2007 Pearson Education, Inc.

All rights reserved. No part of the material protected by this copyright notice may be reproduced or utilized in any form or by any means, electronic or mechanical, including photocopying, recording, or by any information storage and retrieval system, without written permission from the copyright owner.

To obtain permission(s) to use material from this work, please submit a written request to Allyn and Bacon, Permissions Department, 75 Arlington Street, Boston, MA 02116 or fax your request to 617-848-7320.

ISBN-13: 978-0-205-51364-2
ISBN-10:   0-205-51364-6

Printed in the United States of America

10 9 8 7 6 5 4 3 2 1   11 10 09 08 07

TABLE OF CONTENTS

Chapter Number	Chapter Title	Page Number
Preface	Using This Study Guide	
1	Exploring Child Development	1
2	Heredity and the Environment	29
3	Prenatal Development and Birth	61
4	Physical Development in Infants and Toddlers	87
5	Cognitive Development in Infants and Toddlers	113
6	Socioemotional Development in Infants and Toddlers	139
7	Physical Development in Early Childhood	170
8	Cognitive Development in Early Childhood	192
9	Social and Emotional Development in Early Childhood	218
10	Physical Development in Middle Childhood	242
11	Cognitive Development in Middle childhood	267
12	Social and Emotional Development in Middle Childhood	297
13	Physical Development in Adolescence	326
14	Cognitive Development in Adolescence	354
15	Social and Emotional Development in Adolescence	386
Appendix	Practice Tests and Crossword Puzzle Answers	414

PREFACE

USING THIS STUDY GUIDE

Welcome to the fascinating field of child development! I hope this study guide helps you to master the material in your text, *The World of Children*, by Joan and Greg Cook. My intention in developing this guide was to give you practice in working with the content of your text while providing you with opportunities to expand your critical thinking skills in ways that you will hopefully find intrinsically interesting.

As you look through the guide, you'll see that each of the fifteen chapters, corresponding to your text, is divided into three distinct sections. The **Before You Read** section will help you get your bearings in regard to the upcoming chapter. It includes a brief chapter summary and a listing of key learning objectives. I would strongly suggest that you read the learning objectives before you read the corresponding text material. This will help you more easily identify the text authors' main points. You might also choose to actively seek the answers to the learning objectives as you read the text, or you might elect to use the learning objectives as a final review prior to your exam. Creating a written summary of information relevant to the learning objectives will generate a thorough set of text notes from which to study. Regardless of your approach, when you have mastered the learning objectives, you will have a firm grasp of the text material.

The **As You Read** section contains a variety of activities that were designed to be used "on-line." That is, the activities will probably be most effective if you work through them as you are reading the text. At the very beginning of this section, you will see a list of key concepts from the chapter. It will be to your benefit to learn the definitions of these concepts early in your studying. That way, you will be able to more clearly understand your instructor's class discussion and actively engage with the text itself. Whenever you have to struggle with the basic vocabulary, your ability to understand the meaning of the material is diminished. Therefore, it is essential to learn how to "talk the talk!" As you look through this section of the study guide, you'll see that several kinds of activities are found in most chapters. For example, you'll see a recurring activity called "Being the Teacher." In these activities you'll be asked to take on the role of teacher and outline a lecture or other presentation on a specific chapter topic. This type of active study and preparation is essential to mastery, so it will be beneficial to use this strategy often and well. There is no better way to learn than to teach!

Once you've read your text material and worked your way through the activities, then you're ready to see if you're prepared for an actual exam. In the **When You Have Finished** section, you'll find two ten-item multiple choice quizzes, followed by a more comprehensive practice test containing twenty multiple choice questions and three essay questions. It might be most helpful to take a quiz and then check the accuracy of your answers using the key provided in the Appendix before tackling the other quizzes. In this way, you can identify areas of the chapter that may need your further attention. Each quiz contains examples of different types of test questions common to most multiple choice exams (e.g., factual, conceptual, and applied). A wise student will go even further by thinking of other potential questions your instructor might ask!

The **When You Have Finished** section contains two additional parts. For each chapter you'll find a crossword puzzle using key terms from that chapter. Here is another opportunity to consolidate your knowledge of these concepts by using them. The second part of this section is entitled "Working the Web." Here you'll find descriptions of (and addresses for) five to ten Web sites that are relevant to the chapter. These Web sites were selected for their interest level, as well as for the information they convey, and they can be used in a number of different ways. For example, if there is a particular part of the text on which you need further instruction, see if there is a corresponding Web site that can give you greater clarity. If a certain aspect of a chapter intrigues you, see what other relevant information is out there. For many of the Web sites, critical thinking questions have been included to help you extend your understanding of the importance of child development theory and research. Finally, if you're preparing for a debate or class presentation, many of these Web sites can be highly useful in providing current statistics, visual aids, and downloadable activities. There's an enormous amount of information on the Internet just waiting to be critically evaluated and thoughtfully applied!

I sincerely hope that you find this study guide both useful and engaging.

Best wishes in all of your studies!

Carolyn Morgan, Ph.D.
Associate Professor of Psychology
University of Wisconsin, Whitewater

1 EXPLORING CHILD DEVELOPMENT

Before You Read

In this chapter, you'll encounter a broad overview of the field of child development. The basic questions and issues that have shaped the field are described, with a particular emphasis on understanding the relative contributions of nature and nurture to human development. The major theories of child development are summarized, and you'll have the opportunity to compare and contrast these theories in terms of how they enhance our understanding of social, cognitive, and physical development. You'll then become acquainted with the research strategies typically used by researchers in child development, including descriptive, correlational, and experimental techniques. Specific emphasis is placed on the research methods used to assess developmental patterns, including cross-sectional, longitudinal, and hybrid designs. After tackling basic research design issues, you'll read about the importance of ethical considerations when working with children and adolescents. The chapter concludes by addressing how child development research can be used by individuals working with young people in diverse roles and in making positive social policy changes affecting children.

Chapter Learning Objectives

After reading this chapter, you should be able to do the following:

- Define child development and identify related research areas.

- Describe the three components of child development (i.e., physical, cognitive, and socioemotional) and give examples of each.

- Discuss the importance of nature and nurture in child development.

- Describe behavior genetics and identify three ways in which researchers in this field study child development.

EXPLORING CHILD DEVELOPMENT

- Define "theory." Describe five functions of theories.

- Construct a table comparing and contrasting the main theories of child development.

- Discuss how an individual's views of the way children change will differ depending on the theoretical perspective he or she adopts.

- List and define at least four different descriptive research methods.

- Interpret correlations in terms of their directionality and strength.

- Identify the advantages and disadvantages of using correlational research.

- Describe the experimental method and explain how it differs from correlational research.

- Explain how cross-sectional, longitudinal, and hybrid designs differ in their assessment of development.

- Discuss ethical issues that arise in conducting research with children. Summarize the most important ethical principles guiding this research area.

- Define "social policy" and explain how it can be influenced by research in child development.

- Explain different ways in which parents and professionals can use child development research to guide their interactions with children.

- Discuss different career opportunities available in the field of child development.

EXPLORING CHILD DEVELOPMENT

As You Read

Key terms and concepts are essential to your understanding of the chapter. Your ability to logically discuss and analyze pertinent information is dependent upon your knowledge of these concepts. Terms can be found in boldface throughout the chapter and definitions are listed in a glossary of terms at the end of the chapter. Flashcards may be helpful for memorizing definitions. Begin using the terms as you study, incorporating them into your vocabulary.

behavior genetics	ecological systems theory	physical development
behaviorism	ethology	psychoanalytic theories
child development	experiment	scientific method
classical conditioning	hypotheses	socioemotional development
cognitive development	information-processing approach	social learning
cognitive-development theory	longitudinal method	social policy
correlational method	nature	sociocultural theory
cross-sectional method	neuropsychology	theory
descriptive methods	nurture	
dynamic systems theories	operant conditioning	

⊙ DEFINING THE FIELD

What Develops?

Define and give examples of physical, cognitive, and socioemotional development. Describe at least two ways in which these different facets of development influence one another.

What Drives Development? Nature *and* Nurture

1. Explain the Nature - Nurture controversy as discussed in your text.

EXPLORING CHILD DEVELOPMENT

2. Why is the Nature-Nurture debate important in understanding human development?

3. Think about differences in human aggression, empathy, intelligence, and athletic ability for a moment. Based on classes taken during your school career and in your own reading/research, how do you regard the relative importance of nature and nurture in determining these human characteristics?

4. Reread John Watson's famous quote on page 10 of your text. Explain how his comments are indicative of the Nurture position on child development.

5. How might a behavior geneticist in the early twenty-first century respond to Watson's assertion?

EXPLORING CHILD DEVELOPMENT

6. Indicate whether each of the terms below is most closely associated with the nature or nurture perspective.

Term	Nature or Nurture	Term	Nature or Nurture
heredity		internal influences	
ecology		external influences	
the world		learning	
genetics		ethology	
biology		experience	

⊙ THEORIES OF CHILD DEVELOPMENT

What is a Theory, and Why are Theories Useful?

1. Define "theory."

2. Why are theories necessary to the study of child development?

3. How can you distinguish a theory from a hypothesis?

EXPLORING CHILD DEVELOPMENT

4. Indicate whether the following sentences or questions are examples of hypotheses. Give a brief explanation of your answer.

Statement/Question	Hypothesis?	
At birth, humans are moral creatures. Explanation:	Yes	No
On average, are boys stronger than girls? Explanation:	Yes	No
Human life begins at conception. Explanation:	Yes	No
Folic acid reduces neural tube defects. Explanation:	Yes	No
Smoking cigarettes causes cancer. Explanation:	Yes	No
Is there an afterlife? Explanation:	Yes	No

Theories and Theorists

1. Each of the statements below is connected to a particular theory or perspective in the field of child development. Match the letter of the theory or perspective with the corresponding statement. Theories and perspectives may be used more than once.

    A. psychoanalytic theory
    B. psychosocial theory
    C. behaviorism
    D. social-learning theory
    E. cognitive-developmental theory
    F. information-processing approach
    G. sociocultural theory
    H. ethology
    I. neuropsychology
    J. ecological systems theory
    K. dynamic systems theory

    _____ This theory focuses on the adaptive significance or survival value of specific behaviors.

EXPLORING CHILD DEVELOPMENT

_____ Within this framework, children's development occurs with a complex set of systems and interacting social layers.

_____ This theory describes the developmental significance of social, private, and inner speech.

_____ According to this theory, it is essential to carefully control the environmental conditions to which children are exposed.

_____ This perspective uses relatively new technologies such as CT, PET, and fMRI to conduct research.

_____ This theory has been criticized for placing too much emphasis on the unconscious mind.

_____ Researchers using this perspective have examined how children learn math and science.

_____ Within this perspective, models from mathematics and physics are used to explore how social systems interact and change over time.

_____ This stage theory describes four major phases of change in how children think and understand the world.

_____ This theoretical perspective developed from Piaget's pioneering work on cognitive development.

_____ Within this theory, it is argued that children learn by observing and imitating other people.

_____ This perspective contains a subarea known as sociobiology, which focuses on the evolutionary development of social behaviors.

_____ According to this theory, young children use feedback from their parents to curb their instincts for gratification.

_____ This perspective integrates information from psychology and biology to study the nervous system.

_____ This theory developed as a critical response to Freudian psychoanalytic theory.

EXPLORING CHILD DEVELOPMENT

_____ Within this theory, development proceeds through a series of eight crises.

_____ This theory developed from behaviorism and asserts that reinforcement and punishment are not always needed to alter children's behavior.

_____ Within this stage theory, resolution of a crisis occurs when a specific identity is adopted.

_____ This theory emphasizes the important effects of language and culture on children's cognition.

2. Unscramble the following last names of theorists and researchers involved in the study of child development. Use the hints below if you have trouble unscrambling some of the names. When you have completed all of the names, unscramble the letters in parentheses to reveal the "hidden" term.

   a. KYVYSGTO   (_)_ _ _ _ _ _
   b. ATEGIP   (_)_ _ _ _ _
   c. VVOALP   _ _ _ (_)_ _
   d. RNOEIKS   (_)_ _ _ _ _ _
   e. NFRBBORENNERNE _ _ (_)_ _ _ _ _ _ _ _ _ _
   f. DNABARU   _ _ _ (_)_ _ _
   g. DFUER   _ _ (_)_ _

   Hidden Term: _ _ _ _ _ _ _

   Hints:
   a. social and private speech
   b. assimilation and accommodation
   c. classical conditioning
   d. eight major life crises
   e. layers of social systems
   f. observation, imitation, and modeling
   g. unconscious psychological conflicts

   Hidden Term Hint: "to change over time"

8

EXPLORING CHILD DEVELOPMENT

USING THE SCIENTIFIC METHOD: RESEARCH IN CHILD DEVELOP-

Descriptive Research Methods

Identify the four descriptive research methods described in your text, giving one Advantage and one disadvantage for each.

Method	Advantage	Disadvantage
A.		
B.		
C.		
D.		

Correlational Research Methods

1. Correlation Conundrum
   Folklore tells us that babies are brought by storks. Now, we might contend that our predecessors weren't very bright because, clearly, storks don't cause human births. However, our ancestors did see a naturally occurring relation between the presence of storks and fluctuations in the number of human births. Can you "conceive" of what this relationship might have been?

2. Rank the following correlations from weakest (place a "1") to strongest (place a "9").

   ___ -.73   ___ -.98   ___ -.22

   ___ .23   ___ .51   ___ .17

   ___ .09   ___ 1.00   ___ .67

EXPLORING CHILD DEVELOPMENT

3. Give two examples of positive correlation.

   A.

   B.

4. Give two examples of negative correlation.

   A.

   B.

5. Identify the primary advantage of correlational research methods.

6. Identify the primary disadvantage of correlational research methods.

7. Look through recent newspapers or magazines and find an article about child development that <u>misinterprets</u> correlational research. Specifically, look for a description of a study that uses correlation, but implies a cause-and-effect relation. Describe the study below and explain what it can and cannot tell us about child development.

Experimental Research Methods

EXPLORING CHILD DEVELOPMENT

1. Briefly outline the rationale or logic of an experimental design. In other words, describe how the use of independent variables, dependent variables, and random assignment allow researchers to determine causation.

2. State one major advantage and one major disadvantage of the experimental method.

    Advantage:

    Disadvantage:

Methods for Assessing Development

1. Read each of the statements below and underline the word(s) in parentheses that will make the statements correct.

    (Cross-sectional/longitudinal) designs are used to compare children of different ages with one another at the same time.

    (Cross-sectional/longitudinal) designs are used to compare measurements of the same group of children across time.

    (Cross-sectional/longitudinal) designs can be used to observe how behaviors, attitudes, and other characteristics change or remain the same in a single group of children.

    (Cross-sectional/longitudinal) designs are helpful because studies using these designs can be completed in a relatively short period of time.

    A weakness of (cross-sectional/longitudinal) designs is that if the original comparison groups differ in specific ways, the differences could affect the outcome of the research.

    (Cross-sectional/longitudinal) designs are more limited by a concern for cohort effects.

    In (cross-sectional/longitudinal) designs, it is difficult to get child participants to remain in the study for its entire duration.

    (Cross-sectional/longitudinal) designs are more limited by the concern over differential dropout.

2. In this study, fifty 4-year-olds and fifty 8-year-olds were randomly assigned to one of two groups. One of the groups watched one thirty-minute episode of *Sesame Street* each day for one week, while the other group watched thirty minutes of *Road Runner* cartoons. At the end of the week, all of the children were given a test of creativity.

   What type of research design is being described?

   What is the independent variable?

   What is the dependent variable?

   How are individual differences in the children's initial creativity controlled for in this study?

3. Consider the following hypothesis:

   <u>Children who watch a lot of violent television interact more aggressively with peers than children who watch less violent television.</u>

   Briefly describe a study to test the above hypothesis using the following research methods:

   A.   Correlational-cross-sectional

   B.   Correlational-longitudinal

EXPLORING CHILD DEVELOPMENT

4. Identify a research method that could be used to examine each of the following questions.

   _____A. Does participation in Head Start programs increase children's IQ?

   _____B. At what age do children develop the ability to feel empathy for others?

   _____C. Do boys and girls differ in their verbal skills?

   _____D. Does the use of computers in preschool increase children's math ability in 3rd grade?

   _____E. When do babies learn to count?

   _____F. How many pieces of information can 5-, 6-, and 7-year-olds remember?

   _____G. Can babies hear when they are in the womb?

   _____H. Do 3- and 5-year-olds differ in their understanding of death?

   _____I. Are male and female infants treated differently?

Ethics in Research with Children

1. First, outline six major ethical guidelines associated with child development research as described in your text.

2. Next, identify the role of the Institutional Review Board (IRB) in the research process.

EXPLORING CHILD DEVELOPMENT

3. Now, imagine for a moment that you are a member of an IRB. Discuss the ethical concerns that arise in each of the following research proposals.

Dr. Myers proposes to examine gender and age differences in obedience among 4-, 6-, and 8-year-old girls and boys. He plans to have each child in his experiment interact with an unfamiliar adult who will tell the child to play with a certain toy or ask the child nicely to play with a certain toy. After the adult has given her command or request, the child will be left alone in a playroom for five minutes and unobtrusively observed to see if and for how long they play with the specified toy.

Dr. Cottle proposes to study the long-term effects of parents' marital status on children's ability to make friends. She wants to obtain a large sample of families who have had a new baby within the past three months and follow them over a period of fifteen years. The study will involve yearly surveys for the parents regarding the quality and stability of their marriages and their perceptions of their children's ability to maintain friendships. Once the children enter school, measures of their interaction with peers will be obtained through teacher report and naturalistic observation.

EXPLORING CHILD DEVELOPMENT

⊙ **APPLICATIONS OF CHILD DEVELOPMENT RESEARCH AND CAREERS RELATED TO CHILDREN**

Practical Applications of Child Development Research

1. On your next visit to the local bookstore, take some time to browse the childcare or child development section. Choose a book and skim through it. To what extent does the book appear to be grounded in the child development theories described in your text? To what extent is the book based on actual research?

2. *Numerically Speaking* of Social Policy
   The Social Policy Perspectives section of Chapter 1 gives you some important information regarding the current status of children in the United States. Fill in the correct numerical value to complete each sentence below.

   Every day in the United States the number of:

   A. children who are living in poverty is _____.

   B. children arrested for violent crimes is _____.

   C. babies born to mothers who had late or no prenatal care is _____.

   D. babies born with low birth weight is _____.

   E. children who are confirmed as abused or neglected is _____.

EXPLORING CHILD DEVELOPMENT

Careers Related to Children

Being the Teacher
    Prepare an outline for a presentation on career options for people interested in working with and helping children.

EXPLORING CHILD DEVELOPMENT

When You Have Finished

◉ WORKING THE WEB

1. Think for yourself! Learn more about how to evaluate the accuracy of information contained in a variety of Web resources, including advocacy, informational, and personal Web sites at www.widener.edu/659/ and www.library.cornell.edu/olinuris/ref/webcrit.html. Be sure you critically evaluate the Web sites discussed in this grade aid.

2. An excellent way to begin the study of child development is to get a broad overview of what we know about the status of children in the United States. To examine a comprehensive report entitled America's Children: Key National Indicators of Well-Being, 2002, go to childstats.gov. Here you will find statistical information regarding the impact of such factors as economic security, health, education, social environment, and family structure on children's outcomes. Another helpful source of statistical information is the Child Trends DataBank (www.childtrendsdatabank.org/), which covers such topics as reading skills, dropout rates, accidental deaths, child maltreatment, sexual behaviors, media influences, and prevalence of children staying home alone.

3. Information on the U.S. Census Bureau's American Community Surveys can be found at www.census.gov/acs/www/index.html. After you've read Chapter 1, ask yourself the following questions:
   - What type(s) of research methods does the census use?
   - What size samples were involved and how were they selected?
   - How was the data collected and how was it used?
   - Can this information be used to make meaningful social policy decisions?

4. As the authors of your text note, researchers in many fields work together to learn more about child development. To familiarize yourself with some of these research fields and how they work together, take a look at the following Web sites:
   Society for Research in Child Development at www.srcd.org/
   American Educational Research Association at www.aera.net/
   Academy of American Pediatrics at www.aap.org/
   National Associaiton for Child Development at www.nacd.org/
   National Association of School Psychologists at www.nasponline.org/
   American Psychological Association at www.apa.org/
   How many others can you identify?

EXPLORING CHILD DEVELOPMENT

5. The Child and Family WebGuide (www.cfw.tufts.edu) is an outstanding information source for parents. Its mission is to describe, evaluate, and provide access to the "best links about infants, children, and teens." This is another excellent place to begin your Internet study of child development.

6. Throughout your text, the authors discuss the important and varied relationships between research in child development and social policy. The sheer number of organizations devoted to social policy as it influences children and families is staggering. To get an idea, first go to the Almanac of Policy Issues (www.policyalmanac.org/). Then take a look at some specific social policy Web sites:

crcw.princeton.edu	Center for Research on Child Well-being
www.clasp.org/	Center for Law and Social Policy
www.yale.edu/21c	School of the 21st Century

    To what extent do different organizations appear to emphasize and utilize research in child development to inform their social policy initiatives?

7. Are you considering a career in childcare or education? If so, go to the Vocational Information Center at www.khake.com and click on "Childcare" to link to the Early Childcare and Education Career Guide. Pick several careers and follow the links to gather information on required skills and training, salary, licensure, and typical activities. What do you see as the advantages and disadvantages of these different careers?

EXPLORING CHILD DEVELOPMENT

⊙ PRACTICE TEST #1

Multiple-Choice Questions
For each question, circle the best answer from the choices given.

1. Which of the following is NOT one of the primary facets of development? (p. 5)

a. behavioral
b. cognition
c. physical
d. socioemotional

2. Nurture refers to (p. 6)

a. interactive forces that impact development.
b. environmental forces that impact development.
c. cognitive forces that impact development.
d. biological forces that impact development.

3. _____ are able to organize varied facts in a coherent manner. (p.8)

a. Cognitions
b. Hypotheses
c. Behavior genetics
d. Theories

4. In the emergence of theories of child development, which of the following theories did NOT develop after behavioral/social learning theory? (p. 9)

a. cognitive theory
b. neuropsychology
c. ecological systems theory
d. psychoanalytic theory

5. Psychoanalytic theories focus on the structure of _____? (p. 9)

a. personality
b. the brain
c. social learning
d. the environment

EXPLORING CHILD DEVELOPMENT

6. Which of the following is the best example of a conditioned response? (p. 13)

a. A cat salivates in response to the smell of tuna.
b. A dolphin hears his trainer's "clicker".
c. A dog runs to the front door when he hears a car pull in the driveway.
d. A bird instinctively knows how to build a nest.

7. Accommodation is (p. 15)

a. when an infant incorporates new information into an existing mental scheme.
b. when an infant adjusts a mental scheme to allow for new information.
c. another name for a mental scheme.
d. none of the above.

8. A PET scan (p. 17)
a. is a computer-enhanced, three-dimensional X-ray of the brain.
b. involves the injection of radioactive markers into the bloodstream and then tracing them through the brain as the person engages in tasks.
c. detects changes in the rate of metabolism in smaller areas of the brain.
d. none of the above.

9. According to _____, development emerges from complexity. (p. 18)

a. psychoanalytic theories
b. biological theories
c. social learning theories
d. systems theories

10. Bronfenbrenner is a theorist who is most often associated with the (p. 18)

a. biological theory.
b. social learning theory.
c. ecological systems theory.
d. cognitive developmental theory.

EXPLORING CHILD DEVELOPMENT

⊙ PRACTICE TEST #2

Multiple-Choice Questions
For each question, circle the best answer from the choices given.

1. Which of the following layers is considered the "widest level" of Urie Bronfenbrenner's ecological systems theory? (p. 19)

a. microsystem
b. mesosystem
c. exosystem
d. macrosystem

2. Attractor states are the (p. 20)

a. effects of systems over time.
b. values, customs, and laws, of a culture.
c. connections among elements in the larger social environment.
d. stable patterns of preferred behavior or dominant psychological attitudes.

3. The method of research by which individuals collect data by making systematic observations is called (p. 22)

a. a structured observation.
b. the scientific method.
c. observational learning.
d. the correlational method.

4. Which of the following is NOT a descriptive method of research? (p.23)

a. naturalistic observation
b. structured observation
c. correlation
d. case study

5. The correlational method is when (p. 24)

a. researchers investigate whether an observed behavior is related to another trait or characteristic.
b. a person's knowledge could influence the outcome of research.
c. the researcher creates a suitable situation and observes behavior in it.
d. a person creates a detailed description of his or her observations.

EXPLORING CHILD DEVELOPMENT

6. Which of the following is NOT an experimental research method? (p. 27)

a. experimental method
b. case study
c. path analyses
d. naturalistic observation

7. An independent variable is the (p. 27)

outcome that researchers measure.
variable that researchers manipulate.
hypothesis that determines the variables of the experiment.
determined cause and effect of an experiment.

8. Which of the following methods of research compares the observations across ages by taking repeated measurements from the same people across time? (p. 29)

a. cross-sectional method
b. longitudinal method
c. experimental method
d. correlational method

9. Unforeseen consequences is an ethical principle that states that (p.31)

a. when an experiment results in any negative consequences for a child, a researcher must do whatever is necessary to correct the situation.
b. when the data that an experiment would collect would not have enough value to subject the participants to any adverse effects, the researcher must not conduct the experiment.
c. both a. and b.
d. neither a. nor b.

10. Social policy is (p. 34)

a. when researchers try to use child development research to affect laws, regulations, and programs.
b. when researchers try to use laws, regulations, and programs to affect child development research.
c. when politicians attempt to change child development research to line up with laws, regulations, and programs.
d. when laws, regulations, and programs guide what type of child development research can be done.

EXPLORING CHILD DEVELOPMENT

⊙ COMPREHENSIVE PRACTICE TEST

Multiple-Choice Questions
For each question, circle the best answer from the choices given.

1. Professionals from psychology, sociology, anthropology, social work, biology, medicine, economics, and other related fields all work together to describe and understand _____. (p. 4)

a. psychoanalytic theories
b. child development
c. operant conditioning
d. behavior genetics

2. Height and weight gain in children are considered examples of (p. 5)

a. physical development.
b. cognitive development.
c. socioemotional development.
d. behavioral development.

3. Which of the following is NOT an example of nurture? (p. 6)

a. poverty
b. malnutrition
c. sexual maturation
d. lack of adequate medical care

4. A theory is an explanation of (p. 8)
a. facts.
b. hypotheses.
c. inferences.
d. psychology.

5. According to Freud, which of the following components of the mind lies completely below the level of conscious awareness? (p. 9)
a. psyche
b. id
c. ego
d. superego

EXPLORING CHILD DEVELOPMENT

6. Freud proposed that during the _____ stage of psychosexual development, children have unconscious sexual desires for their opposite-sex parents. (p. 11)

a. anal
b. phallic
c. latency
d. genital

7. Who was the "father of American behaviorism"? (p. 12)

a. Sigmund Freud
b. Erik Erikson
c. John Watson
d. Albert Bandura

8. Pavlov, a Russian physiologist, discovered his principles of classical conditioning while doing experiments on the _____ in dogs. (p. 13)

a. sense of smell
b. cognitive ability
c. genetic inheritability
d. digestive system

9. In operant conditioning terms, _____ is any characteristic in the environment that serves to increase the probability that a person will repeat a behavior in the future. (p. 14)

a. reinforcement
b. punishment
c. conditioned response
d. unconditioned response

10. Which of the following theories was created by the Swiss psychologist, Jean Piaget? (p. 15)

a. psychoanalysis
b. cognitive developmental theory
c. operant conditioning
d. observational learning

EXPLORING CHILD DEVELOPMENT

11. The sociocultural theory states that (p. 15)

a. children actively adjust their own understandings as they learn about the world.
b. children learn by observing and imitating the behavior of others in their society or culture.
c. language and culture influence the growth of thought in children.
d. identity is formed as children pass through a series of crises.

12. Which of the following theories often emphasize the roles of basic processing efficiency and change in a child's knowledge base? (p. 16)

a. psychoanalytic theories
b. information-processing approach
c. sociocultural theory
d. cognitive developmental theory

13. One important biological theory is _____, which examines the adaptive significance or survival value of behaviors. (p. 17)

a. ethology
b. behavior genetics
c. neuropsychology
d. sociocultural theory

14. _____ can detect changes in the rate of metabolism in smaller areas of the brain. (p. 18)

a. computerized tomography
b. functional magnetic resonance imaging
c. positron emission tomography
d. electroencephalogram

15. Which of the following theories uses models from mathematics and physics to understand complex systems of development? (p. 20)

a. behavior genetics
b. dynamic systems theory
c. ethology
d. information-processing approach

EXPLORING CHILD DEVELOPMENT

16. A researcher watches children interact with each other on the playground at school and records what they do, when, with whom, and other details. Which type of research is exemplified? (p. 23)

a. scientific method
b. structured observation
c. naturalistic observation
d. observer bias

17. A positive correlation coefficient indicates that (p. 24)

a. the scores on two variables tend to run in the same direction.
b. the scores on two variables tend to run in different directions.
c. the score on two variables have no relationship to each other.
d. the scores on two variables prove that the increase on one variable caused the increase on the other variable.

18. Path analyses are valuable for studying (p. 25)

a. the effects of an unstudied variable on the variables included in an experiment.
b. the effects of the relationships between multiple variables.
c. the outcome of tests of the hypotheses.
d. the manipulation of the experimental variable.

19. Differential dropout poses an especially serious problem for (p. 29)

a. cross-sectional method research.
b. correlational research.
c. case studies.
d. longitudinal method research.

20. In order to keep confidentiality, researchers must (p. 31)

a. never meet the research participants.
b. not ask personal questions of research participants.
c. not reveal research participants' names to anyone not involved in the experiment.
d. never ask research participants to give their names, but only ask them to identify themselves by their social security number.

EXPLORING CHILD DEVELOPMENT

Short-Answer Questions

Answer each question in the space provided.

1. According to Sigmund Freud, the mind contains three basic components. Name and describe these components.

2. Your textbook described a number of major developmental theories. Choose three theories to explain. Be sure to include the major theorist(s) from each theory, as well as a coherent summary of the contribution of each theory to an understanding of child development.

3. Define the term descriptive research methods. Then, name and define two examples of types of research that fall into this category.

EXPLORING CHILD DEVELOPMENT

⊙ CROSSWORD PUZZLE

Across

2. biological forces that govern development
3. the IRB is concerned with this
4. a specific inference
6. _____ policy uses research to affect laws and programs
7. cognitive developmental theorist
9. development related to changes in how children think
10. Pavlov's _____ conditioning
11. theories allow us to _____ behavior

Down

1. Watson was the father of American _____
3. study of survival value of behaviors
5. method measuring same children across time
8. explains how facts fit together

Puzzle created with Puzzlemaker at DiscoverySchool.com

2 HEREDITY AND THE ENVIRONMENT

Before You Read

This chapter focuses on helping you understand more about how genes interact with the environment to produce complex human characteristics and behaviors. You'll start by reading a basic description of genes' composition, how they work, and how they are transmitted from one generation to the next. You'll then read about the human reproductive process and the importance of meiosis and mitosis in development. The text explores issues and questions surrounding genetic diseases and chromosomal abnormalities, as well as controversies in regard to the genetics of sexual orientation, alcoholism, and aggression. Prenatal screening and genetic testing are described. An extensive discussion of the numerous ways researchers have conceptualized G x E interactions, including range of reaction, canalization, niche-picking, and probabilistic epigenesis, will help you become more familiar with the current ways of thinking about these interactions within the field of behavior genetics. The chapter ends with an overview of research examining the heritability of cognitive skills and personality. Here you'll learn more about how twin and adoption studies are used to estimate genetic and environmental contributions to various complex human characteristics and behaviors.

Chapter Learning Objectives

After reading this chapter, you should be able to do the following:

- Describe how DNA, genes, and chromosomes determine our genetic code.

- Describe the Human Genome Project. Summarize some of its most important findings, identify areas of future research, and outline potential ethical issues.

- Identify alternative techniques for conception.

- Compare the processes of mitosis and meiosis and describe the two functions of meiosis.

- Describe how the dominant-recessive relationship between genes explains certain inherited characteristics.

HERIDITY AND THE ENVIRONMENT

- Compare and contrast three recessive gene disorders and explain why recessive gene diseases are less common than dominant gene diseases.

- Explain how X-linked (or sex-linked) traits and diseases are inherited.

- Describe how chromosomal abnormalities cause Down syndrome, Klinefelter syndrome, trisomy X, Turner syndrome, and sex reversal.

- Compare and contrast methods of prenatal screening and genetic testing.

- Discuss how the G x E interaction determines human traits.

- Compare and contrast how reaction range, canalization, niche-picking, and probabilistic epigenesis are used to help explain the G x E interaction.

- Describe how the field of behavior genetics explains development.

- Define heritability and discuss the meaning of heritability estimates.

- Distinguish between shared and nonshared environments and give examples within a family.

- Compare and contrast two methods that have been used to estimate human heritability.

- Summarize what is known about the heritabilities of cognitive skills and personality.

HERIDITY AND THE ENVIRONMENT

As You Read

Key terms and concepts are essential to your understanding of the chapter. Your ability to logically discuss and analyze pertinent information is dependent upon your knowledge of these concepts. Terms can be found in boldface throughout the chapter and definitions are listed in a glossary of terms at the end of the chapter. Flashcards may be helpful for memorizing definitions. Begin using the terms as you study, incorporating them into your vocabulary.

adoption studies	fertilization	nonshared environment
allele	G x E interaction	phenotype
amniocentesis	gene	probabilistic epigenesis
canalization	genotype	range of reaction
chorionic villus sampling (CVS)	heritability	sex chromosomes
chromosomes	Human Genome Project	shared environment
dizygotic (DZ) twins	meiosis	twin studies
DNA	mitosis	ultrasonography (ultrasound)
dominant-recessive relationship	monozygotic (MZ) twins	X-linked (sex-linked) traits
Down syndrome	niche-picking	zygote

⊙ GENES AND HUMAN REPRODUCTION

Genes and the Magical Four-Letter Code

1. Match the terms with their descriptions, by placing the correct letter in the blank.

Terms

____ chromosomes   ____ autosomes   ____ sex chromosomes
____ adenine   ____ guanine   ____ male chromosomal pattern
____ nucleotide bases   ____ DNA   ____ female chromosomal pattern
____ gene   ____ genome   ____ gametes
____ mitosis   ____ meiosis   ____ monozygotic
____ allele   ____ dizygotic

Description

A. "copy division"   G. strands of DNA   M. full genetic code for a species
B. pairs with thymine   H. identical twins   N. a segment of a DNA strand
C. fraternal twins   I. XX   O. two twisted strands of protein
D. XY   J. XY and XX   P. A, T, G, and C
E. "reduction division"   K sex cells   Q. twenty-two pairs same in males and
F. alternate gene versions   L. pairs with cytosine   females

31

HERIDITY AND THE ENVIRONMENT

2. *Numerically Speaking* of Genetics

   Fill in the blanks with the correct numerical values.

   A. There are _____ chromosomes in each human cell.

   B. Humans have _____ sex chromosomes.

   C. There are _____ kinds of DNA molecules, called nucleotides.

   D. In each human cell, there are approximately _____ pairs of nucleotide bases.

   E. There are approximately _____ genes aligned along the _____ chromosomes in each human cell.

   F. In the human genetic code, approximately _____ pairs of nucleotide bases must be ordered properly to form _____ genes aligned along _____ pairs of chromosomes.

   G. Only about _____ percent of the nucleotide base pairs provide active instructions.

   H. In mitosis, a cell copies its own chromosomes as it divides to form _____ cells.

   I. Each sperm or ovum contains _____ chromosomes.

   J. At fertilization, there is a single cell with _____ chromosomes.

   K. MZ twins have the same _____ chromosomes.

   L. MZ twins occur in about 1 in every _____ births.

   M. DZ twins develop from _____ eggs.

   N. DZ twins occur about 1 in every _____ births among Asians, 1 in _____ births among Caucasians, and 1 in _____ births among African populations.

   O. The symptoms of Huntington disease do not usually appear until age _____ or later.

   P. The gene for Huntington disease has been identified on chromosome _____ and occurs in about 4 to 8 out of every _____ births.

   Q. Nearly 1 in every _____ Caucasians carries the recessive gene for cystic fibrosis.

HERIDITY AND THE ENVIRONMENT

R. SCD occurs in about 1 in _____ African American babies and is caused by a gene on chromosome _____.

S. Tay – Sachs disease is usually fatal by the age of _____.

T. If both parents are carriers of the recessive gene that causes Tay – Sachs, there is a _____ percent chance that their children will inherit the disease.

U. In Down syndrome, there are _____ chromosomes at location _____.

3. Reread the section in your text concerning the Human Genome Project and use the information to answer the following questions.

   A. When did the Human Genome Project begin and why?

   B. What do you think might be the potential ramifications of this project?

   C. What moral and ethical questions arise out of our enhanced understanding of human genetics?

   D. In what specific ways might the Human Genome Project affect the lives of you and your family?

Adapted from *Development: Journey Through Childhood and Adolescence* CD-ROM by Dr. Kelly Welch.

HERIDITY AND THE ENVIRONMENT

Human Reproduction and Cell Division

1. Using Figure 2.5 in your text, briefly summarize the steps involved in mitosis. Explain why mitosis is referred to as "copy division."

2. Using Figure 2.6 in your text, briefly summarize the steps involved in meiosis. Explain why meiosis is referred to as "reduction division."

3. Identify the two functions of meiosis.

    A.

    B.

HERIDITY AND THE ENVIRONMENT

4. Alternative Methods of Human Conception
   Using the following descriptors, correctly identify and label each alternative technique for human conception.

Label	Descriptor
_____	Ova and sperm are collected and then injected into the fallopian tube for fertilization and further development.
_____	Ova and sperm are placed in a petri dish for fertilization and early cell divisions. Later, several embryos are placed in the mother's uterus.
_____	Embryos are frozen and later thawed, then placed in the mother's uterus.
_____	Sperm and ova are combined. Then, the embryos are placed in the uterus of another woman who grows and delivers the baby.
_____	Sperm are collected from the biological father and then injected into the biological mother's reproductive system for fertilization.

◉ HOW TRAITS AND GENETIC ABNORMALITIES ARE INHERITED

Dominant –Recessive Traits

If: A = dominant   And: Gene for arched feet is dominant (A)
     a = recessive   Gene for flat feet is recessive (a)

1. Explain what would need to occur for a child to inherit flat feet.

HERIDITY AND THE ENVIRONMENT

2. Fill in the box diagram below to illustrate potential outcomes for the offspring of Parent 1 and Parent 2.

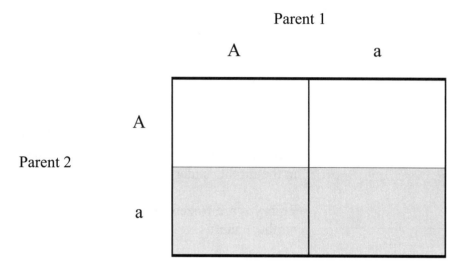

Identify each cell in the box above as to whether the outcome would be arched feet or flat feet.

3. John and Mary are soon-to-be parents of different children. They both know that they carry the gene for fragile-X syndrome and they are concerned about passing this disorder to their child. Fill in the two diagrams below showing why Mary's child might have the disorder, but John's child would not.

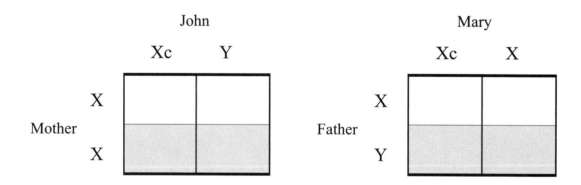

Explain the diagram using words.

HERIDITY AND THE ENVIRONMENT

4. Huntington disease is the most common example of a genetic disorder controlled by a dominant gene. Fill in the following diagrams to illustrate the different likelihoods of offspring inheriting the disease.

H = dominant gene for Huntington disease
h = recessive gene for no Huntington disease

0% Likelihood of inheriting HD   50% Likelihood of inheriting HD

75% Likelihood of inheriting HD   100% Likelihood of inheriting HD

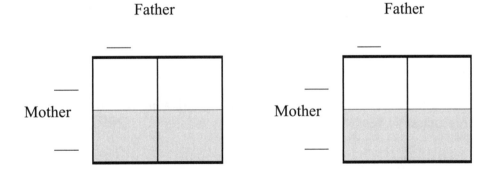

HERIDITY AND THE ENVIRONMENT

5. Each of the following statements regarding recessive gene diseases is FALSE. Your job is to change some part of each statement in order to make it TRUE.

   A. Recessive gene diseases are more common than dominant gene diseases, because only one recessive gene is necessary for a person to inherit the disease.

   Change(s):

   B. Researchers do not yet know specifically which recessive genes are responsible for certain diseases.

   Change(s):

   C. The most common recessive disease among Asian populations is cystic fibrosis.

   Change(s):

   D. There is no simple test for the presence of sickle cell anemia in newborns.

   Change(s):

   E. The most common recessive disease worldwide is Tay – Sachs disease.

   Change(s):

   F. Sickle cell disease creates breathing difficulties due to the excess production of mucus.

   Change(s):

   G. Because SCD is fatal in childhood, individuals with the disease do not live to reproductive age.

   Change(s):

   H. Cystic fibrosis causes mental retardation, blindness, and loss of muscle control.

   Change(s):

HERIDITY AND THE ENVIRONMENT

6. Explain why Tay – Sachs, a recessive gene disease, continues in the population of Ashkenazi Jews even though individuals with the disease die by the age of two or three years and do not live long enough to reproduce.

7. Within each of the cells of the box below, write in the chromosomal pattern that would emerge and identify the sex of the child. Then place an "I" in the box indicating the chromosomal pattern that would lead a child to display the inherited characteristic. Place a "C" in the box indicating the pattern that would lead a child to carry, but not display, the characteristic.

Xc = carrier gene

Father

	X	Y
Mother X	Sex =	Sex =
Mother Xc	Sex =	Sex =

HERIDITY AND THE ENVIRONMENT

8. Fill in the blanks to make each of the following statements regarding X-linked traits correct.

   A. Genes operating on the sex chromosomes cause X-linked (or _____) differences between _____ and _____.

   B. _____ are much more likely than _____ to suffer from X-linked recessive diseases because the ____ chromosome is very small and does not contain a lot of genetic material.

   C. When males inherit the recessive gene for _____ on their _____ chromosome, they will suffer from abnormal blood clotting because their _____ chromosome does not carry the dominant gene to mask the disease.

   D. To suffer from classic hemophilia, females would need to inherit the recessive gene on both _____ chromosomes.

   E. In addition to classic hemophilia, males are more likely than females to suffer from _____,

   _____, and

   _____.

   F. With dominant disease genes on the ____ chromosome, females have _____ chances to inherit the disease, whereas males only have one chance.

   G. Females are more likely than males to inherit _____ disease genes on the _____ chromosome. Three examples of this type of disorder are _____, _____, and _____.

   H. _____, which occurs in about 1 in _____ males and 1 in _____ females, is one of the leading inherited causes of mental retardation among males.

9. Explain why Rett syndrome is only seen among females.

HERIDITY AND THE ENVIRONMENT

Chromosome Abnormalities

1. How are fragile-X syndrome and trisomy 21 similar to, and different from one another? Be specific and complete in your response.

2. Each of the following "facts" about Down syndrome is FALSE. Change some part or parts of each statement to make it TRUE.

    A. Down syndrome occurs when children are born with an extra 23rd chromosome.

    Change(s):

    B. Down syndrome is due to the absence of a chromosome at location 23.

    Change(s):

    C. Individuals with Down syndrome typically have IQs ranging from 70 – 85.

    Change(s):

    D. Down syndrome is the third leading inherited cause of mental retardation among males.

    Change(s):

    E. In all Down syndrome cases, the extra chromosome is due to an error that occurs during mitosis.

    Change(s):

    F. After the mother reaches 45, the risk of Down syndrome is so high that abortion is usually recommended.

    Change(s):

    G. More than half of all babies with Down syndrome are born to mothers who are younger than 16 years of age.

    Change(s):

HERIDITY AND THE ENVIRONMENT

3. Identify the disorder, frequency of occurrence, and major physical and mental problems associated with each of the following patterns of sex chromosomes.

Chromosomal Pattern	Name of Disorder	Frequency of Occurrence	Major Problems
XY (reversal)			
XX (reversal)			
X			
XXX			
XXY			
XYY			

Prenatal Screening and Genetic Testing

A pregnant woman believes that her unborn child may have birth defects. Describe three tests that are available to medical personnel working with this woman. Include in your description the actual test procedure, the uses and limitations of each test, and the time period during pregnancy in which the test can be safely used.

1. Name of test:

   Procedure:

   Uses of test:

   Limitations:

   Time Frame:

HERIDITY AND THE ENVIRONMENT

Prenatal Screening and Genetic Testing (continued)

2. Name of test:

    Procedure:

    Uses of test:

    Limitations:

    Time Frame:

3. Name of test:

    Procedure:

    Uses of test:

    Limitations:

    Time Frame:

HERIDITY AND THE ENVIRONMENT

⊙ HOW GENES AND ENVIRONMENTS INTERACT

1. Explain what is meant by the phrase "G x E interaction."

2. Distinguish between "genotype" and "phenotype."

3. Identify four ways in which genes and environment can interact.

    A.

    B.

    C.

    D.

4. Read each of the following statements carefully, then underline the word(s) in parentheses that will make the statement correct.

    A. According to the idea behind (range of reaction/canalization), the genotype establishes boundaries or constraints on the phenotype.

    B. The idea behind (range of reaction/canalization) is that a child's genes can protect, or provide a buffer against, environmental variations.

    C. According to Sandra Scarr, as children grow older and have more freedom to choose their own activities, their genes can act in an (evocative/active) manner on the environment.

    D. Birds with teeth and fruit flies with two sets of wings are two potential examples of (canalization/probabilistic epigenesis).

    E. The view of (canalization/niche-picking) stresses the protective role of genetics as well as genetic determinism.

HERIDITY AND THE ENVIRONMENT

    F.   The (canalization/experiential canalization) view stresses the role of the environment in limiting developmental outcomes.

    G.   According to Scarr, niche-picking is another name for the (passive/ active) manner in which genes can interact with the environment.

    H.   According to Gottlieb, the basic idea behind (experiential canalization/ probabilistic epigenesis) is that the environment can play a crucial role in the activation of specific genes.

    I.   A fascinating implication of (range of reaction/probabilistic epigenesis) is that changes occurring in an organism's environment may change which genes are expressed.

⊙ BEHAVIOR GENETICS: Measuring the Heritability of Traits

1. Give two examples of shared and nonshared environments.

    Shared   A.

                      B.

    Nonshared   A.

                      B.

2. Identify the different contributions shared and nonshared environments make to human behavior.

HERIDITY AND THE ENVIRONMENT

3. Fill in the blanks in the following sentences to make them TRUE.

A. The study of how genetic and environmental factors influence observable differences among people is known as _____.

B. _____ is a mathematical estimate of the degree to which genes influence the presence of a specific characteristic.

C. These estimates can range from _____ to _____, with _____ values indicating a stronger influence of _____ on the characteristic.

D. Estimates over _____ are generally considered to be relatively high and indicative of a strong genetic influence.

E. _____ types of environments must be considered when attempting to understand observable differences among people.

F. _____ environmental effects produce similarities among individuals, whereas _____ environmental effects produce differences among people.

G. Parenting style within a family may represent either a _____ or _____ aspect of the environment.

How is Heritability Estimated?

1. Explain the logic behind the following two statements:

   A. Twin studies are used to estimate heritability.

   B. Adoption studies are used to estimate heritability.

HERIDITY AND THE ENVIRONMENT

2. Describe how selective placement, assumption of equal environments, and the correlation between genetics and environments each limits research findings to estimates of heritability rather than actual heritability values.

   A. Selective placement

   B. Assumption of equal environments

   C. Correlation between G and E

3. Each of the following statements regarding the heritability of cognitive skills and personality is FALSE. Change some part or parts of each statement to make it TRUE.

   A. Correlations between IQ scores of dizygotic twins are higher than the correlations between IQ scores for monozygotic twins.
   Change(s):

   B. Researchers generally agree that the heritability of IQ is about .25.
   Change(s):

   C. Heritability estimates for most cognitive skills tend to decrease with age indicating a weaker genetic influence as individuals get older.
   Change(s):

   D. Research indicates that approximately 75 percent of the variation in personality characteristics is due to genetics.
   Change(s):

   E. Heritability estimates for most personality characteristics tend to decrease with age indicating a weaker genetic influence as individuals get older.
   Change(s):

HERIDITY AND THE ENVIRONMENT

    F.   A limitation of recent studies on the heritability of personality characteristics is their reliance on self-report or parent-report measures.

         Change(s):

    G.   Differences in children's temperaments do not arise until children enter school.

         Change(s):

4. Explain Jerome Kagan's assertion that some aspects of culture may reflect genetic as well as environmental factors.

5. To some extent, the cut offs for determining whether a particular heritability estimate is high, medium, or low are arbitrary. Using the following fabricated heritability ranges, identify three traits or behaviors that fall within each range.

    Low = .00 to .29   Moderate = .30 to .49   High = .50 and higher

Low heritability estimates	Moderate heritability estimates	High heritability estimates
A.	A.	A.
B.	B.	B.
C.	C.	C.

HERIDITY AND THE ENVIRONMENT

Heritability of Complex Characteristics

1. Travis has been searching the Internet for information regarding the genetic inheritance of IQ and personality traits. As a result of his search, he has concluded that there is really very little he and his partner can do that will affect the intelligence or personality of their future children. How would you respond to Travis's assertion after reading your text material regarding heritability of complex characteristics?

2. According to your text, what has research shown regarding the heritability of intelligence? From a social policy perspective, what difference could it make whether the heritability of intelligence is high or low? Explain how a politician's beliefs regarding the extent to which IQ is influenced by nature or nurture might influence his or her social policy decision-making.

HERIDITY AND THE ENVIRONMENT

When You Have Finished

⊙ WORKING THE WEB

1. Before reading this chapter, take the brief "Our Genetic Future" survey at www.pbs.org/wgbh/nova/genome/survey.html and print a copy of your responses. After reading the chapter, read the survey again and see if any of your opinions have changed.

2. If you're interested in creating your own genetic trait family tree, go to www.childrenheartinstitute.org/educate/fmlytree/fmlytree.htm for instructions and a copy of a family tree to complete.

3. Learn more about the classic Minnesota Twin Study at their own Web site (www.psych.umn.edu/psylabs/mtfs/). Here you'll find background information and summaries of research findings regarding these continuing studies. Of special interest is a new section under construction entitled "What's Special About Twins to Science?"

4. Subscribe to *The DNA Dispatch*, a free electronic newsletter, and stay current on developments in genetic policy at www.geneforum.org. The motto of Geneforum, the organization that publishes the newsletter, is "building an informed citizenry for the Gene Age."

5. Parents who want to know if their twins are fraternal or identical can take the Twin Zygosity Questionnaire at http://statgen.iop.kcl.ac.uk/bgim/. This technical Web site with lots of interactive opportunities offers an online introduction to Behavior Genetics research. Check out the interactive module illustrating the ways that nature and nurture can influence trait variation.

6. Thinking about a career in behavior genetics? This Web site (www.faseb.org/genetics/) has a nice selection of links to information on genetics-related careers and training programs.

7. Go to http://ibgwww.colorado.edu/ for an excellent example of a multidisciplinary institute at the University of Colorado, Boulder that is dedicated to the study of behavior genetics. Here, you can read about the ongoing Colorado Adoption Project and Longitudinal Twin Study.

8. Preparing for an ethics debate? An fine database containing information related to the legal, social, and ethical aspects of human genetics is found at www.humgen.umontrealca/en/.

9. If you qualify, you can participate in a pilot study regarding genetic privacy, genetic discrimination, and informal decision-making regarding genetic issues at www.geneticalliance.org. This Web site is an excellent resource for individuals and families dealing with genetic-related issues such as discrimination and disease.

HERIDITY AND THE ENVIRONMENT

⊙ PRACTICE TEST #1

Multiple-Choice Questions
For each question, circle the best answer from the choices given.

1. Strands of DNA molecules are known as (p. 44)

a. adenine.
b. RNA.
c. genes.
d. chromosomes.

2. The nucleotide base molecule, cytosine, always pairs with (p. 45)

a. adenine.
b. thymine.
c. mitosine.
d. guanine.

3. The Human Genome Project was a multinational effort among governments and scientist to (p. 46)

a. map the order of every nucleotide base.
b. locate the position of every gene.
c. both a. and b.
d. neither a. nor b.

4. An allele is (p. 49)

a. a chromosome.
b. a type of gene.
c. a thymine molecule.
d. a damaged molecule.

5. The alternate technique of conception which involves the injection of sperm into the mother's reproductive system for fertilization is called (p. 49)

a. artificial insemination.
b. in vitro fertilization.
c. in vivo fertilization.
d. cryopreservation.

HERIDITY AND THE ENVIRONMENT

6. A zygote is the term used to refer to the (p. 50)

a. human egg cell.
b. human sperm cell.
c. first divisions of a fertilized egg cell.
d. first divisions of a fertilized sperm cell.

7. Another name for the human sex cells is (p. 51)

a. zygotes.
b. gametes.
c. mitosis.
d. meiosis.

8. Dizygotic twins are formed when (p. 53)

a. one zygote divides to make two zygotes.
b. two zygotes combine to make one zygote.
c. two egg cells are fertilized by two separate sperm cells.
d. one egg cell is fertilized by two separate sperm cells.

9. Chromosome 4 has been identified as containing the gene for (p. 56)

a. fragile X.
b. cystic fibrosis.
c. sickle cell disease.
d. Huntington disease.

10. Down Syndrome is a genetic disorder that occurs when (p. 60)

a. there is an extra chromosome present in the genetic code.
b. there is a missing chromosome in the genetic code.
c. there is an extra gene in the DNA.
d. there is a missing gene in the DNA.

HERIDITY AND THE ENVIRONMENT

⊙ PRACTICE TEST #2

Multiple-Choice Questions
For each question, circle the best answer from the choices given.

1. Having an extra chromosome usually leads to pregnancy loss or death of the infant within the first few months of life EXCEPT in the case of (p. 61)

a. the 21st chromosome.
b. the X chromosome.
c. the Y chromosome.
d. all of the above.

2. Klinefelter syndrome has which of the following characteristics? (p. 61)

a. tall stature
b. webbed neck
c. small testicles
d. remains fertile

3. Ultrasonography is a procedure that is used to detect genetic abnormalities in a fetus by (p. 62)

a. extracting fetal cells from the amniotic fluid.
b. producing images of the fetus in the womb.
c. extracting cells from the placenta around the fetus.
d. constructing a karyotype.

4. The interacting effects of genetics and the environment on the development of traits and characteristics is known as (p. 65)

a. the karyotype.
b. the GxE interaction.
c. canalization.
d. a range of reaction.

5. A genotype is (p. 66)

a. an observable trait.
b. a recessive or unobservable trait.
c. an inherited genetic code.
d. the range of possible phenotypes.

HERIDITY AND THE ENVIRONMENT

6. When children's genetic tendencies evoke certain responses from parents, a child's genes are playing a(n) _____ role. (p. 68)

a. passive
b. active
c. evocative
d. probabilistic

7. The term that refers to the emergence of a trait, characteristic, or behavior over the course of development is (p. 69)

a. epigenesis.
b. probabilistic.
c. niche-picking.
d. canalization.

8. Higher heritability estimates means that there is a (p. 71)

a. stronger environmental influence on a trait.
b. stronger genetic influence on a trait.
c. stronger shared environment.
d. stronger nonshared environment.

9. Which of the following traits has the highest heritability estimate? (p. 73)

a. general intelligence
b. perceptual speed
c. belief in God
d. anxiety

10. _____ is a child's activity level and pattern of response to stimulation. (p. 76)

a. Hyperactivity
b. Canalization
c. Temperament
d. Intelligence

HERIDITY AND THE ENVIRONMENT

⊙ COMPREHENSIVE PRACTICE TEST

Multiple-Choice Questions
For each question, circle the best answer from the choices given.

1. The "side rails" of this structure are made of sugar and phosphate molecules. (p. 45)

a. chromosomes
b. alleles
c. DNA
d. RNA

2. The four varieties of nucleotide base molecules make up the (p. 45)

a. DNA rails.
b. DNA stairs.
c. RNA rails.
d. RNA stairs.

3. Scientists announced the completion of the Human Genome project in what year? (p. 46)

a. 1987
b. 1990
c. 2003
d. 2005

4. A female fetus has which of the following sets of sex chromosomes? (p. 46)

a. XX
b. XY
c. XXX
d. XYY

5. When in vitro fertilization is used to combine the sperm and eggs from a mother and father and then place the created embryo into the uterus of another woman who delivers the baby, this is called (p. 49)

a. cryopreservation.
b. surrogacy.
c. in vivo fertilization
d. mitosis.

HERIDITY AND THE ENVIRONMENT

6. During _____, the DNA strand unzips and creates a new complementary strand. (p. 51)

a. cell division
b. mitosis
c. meiosis
d. reduction division

7. During meiosis, doubled pair that exchange genetic information before separating are called (p. 52)

a. monozygotic twins.
b. dizygotic twins.
c. tetrads.
d. gametes.

8. When a sperm and egg cell unite, a single cell with _____ chromosomes results.

a. 23 chromosomes.
b. 35 chromosomes.
c. 46 chromosomes.
d. 92 chromosomes.

9. The sex chromosome reside on the _____ pair of chromosomes. (p. 54)

a. 1st
b. 15th
c. 21st
d. 23rd

10. A dominant-recessive relationship is a relationship between (p. 56)

a. genes.
b. zygotes.
c. chromosomes.
d. gametes.

HERIDITY AND THE ENVIRONMENT

11. Cystic fibrosis is controlled by genes on chromosome (p. 57)

a. 4.
b. 7.
c. 21.
d. 23.

12. Which of the following is the most common genetic disorder worldwide? (p. 57)

a. Tay-Sachs
b. Cystic Fibrosis
c. Huntington disease
d. Sickle-cell disease

13. Traits that differ in rate of occurrence between males and females, caused by dominant and recessive alleles on the X and Y chromosomes are called (p. 59)

a. Y-linked traits.
b. sex-linked traits.
c. both a. and b.
d. neither a. nor b.

14. Children with Down syndrome have _____. (p. 60)

a. one chromosome at location 21
b. three chromosomes at location 21
c. one chromosome at location 23
d. three chromosomes at location 23

15. _____ is the name of the disorder in females where an individual has an extra X chromosome. (p. 61)

a. Trisomy 21
b. Trisomy 23
c. Triple X
d. Trisomy X

HERIDITY AND THE ENVIRONMENT

16. Chorionic villus sampling can be performed beginning around the _____ week of pregnancy. (p. 63)

a. 8th
b. 12th
c. 15th
d. 20th

17. Canalization is (p. 66)

a. the range of possible phenotypes.
b. the range of possible genotypes.
c. the genetic limits on the effects of the environment.
d. the environmental limits on the effects of genetics.

18. Niche-picking is (p. 68)

a. the genetic limits on the effects of the environment.
b. the tendency toward activities that fit our genetics.
c. genetic determinism.
d. all of the above.

19. The statement that "it is the individual's environment that controls which parts of the genome are activated" is an example of the theory of _____. (p. 69)

a. probabilistic epigenesis
b. niche-picking
c. canalization
d. range of reaction

20. The experiences and aspects of the environment that differ across people is called (p. 71)

a. heritability.
b. nonshared environment.
c. niche-picking.
d. canalization.

HERIDITY AND THE ENVIRONMENT

Short-Answer Questions
Answer each question in the space provided.

1. Discuss the similarities and differences between mitosis and meiosis.

2. Define GxE interaction. Name and define at least two of the four ways to think about the GxE interaction that are defined in your text.

3. Define heritability. Explain the range of heritability estimates and what those values mean.

HERIDITY AND THE ENVIRONMENT

⊙ CROSSWORD PUZZLE

Across
2. a mathematical estimate of the degree of genetic influence for a trait or behavior
4. the observable inherited trait
9. the union of the father's sperm with the mother's egg
10. an alternative version of a gene

Down
1. strands of DNA that contain genetic codes
3. a segment of DNA that provides an instruction for a structure, function, or trait
5. the inherited genetic code
6. procedure used to detect chromosomal and genetic abnormalities in the fetus
7. occurs during the formation of gametes
8. also known as "copy division"

"Puzzle created with Puzzlemaker at DiscoverySchool.com"

3 PRENATAL DEVELOPMENT AND BIRTH

Before You Read

This chapter covers human development from conception through the birth of a baby. As you'll see, your text authors emphasize two major points throughout the chapter. First, most babies develop normally and are born healthy. Second, the chances of having a healthy baby can be increased greatly by avoiding known environmental risk factors (i.e., teratogens) and making healthy life choices. You'll learn about the normal course of prenatal development, the stages of birth, the options that exist regarding labor and delivery methods, and the effects of pain medication on the baby. You'll also read about potential problems that can arise during prenatal development and the birth process.

Chapter Learning Objectives

After reading this chapter, you should be able to do the following:

- Explain the process of fertilization and identify where conception usually occurs.

- Outline and summarize the major events in each stage of prenatal development.

- Name and describe the two patterns of development and growth of the embryo.

- Compare and contrast the terms "premature," "preterm birth," and "low birth weight."

- Summarize information regarding the most common teratogens and their associated risks.

- Define "critical period" and identify the periods of prenatal development during which the developing baby is most vulnerable to teratogens.

PRENATAL DEVELOPMENT AND BIRTH

- Summarize research regarding the role that fathers may play in prenatal development.

- Describe the three stages of birth and identify potential complications (e.g., malpresentation, fetal distress).

- Summarize the characteristics of a healthy newborn.

- Explain the use of the Apgar test, including when and how often it is given, its purpose, and its scoring system.

- Describe factors in the successful transition to parenthood.

- Outline available birthing options and discuss the advantages and disadvantages of each.

- Discuss the pros and cons of using pain-relieving drugs during labor and delivery.

- Describe four primary roles that partners can play during labor and delivery.

PRENATAL DEVELOPMENT AND BIRTH

As You Read

Key terms and concepts are essential to your understanding of the chapter. Your ability to logically discuss and analyze pertinent information is dependent upon your knowledge of these concepts. Terms can be found in boldface throughout the chapter and definitions are listed in a glossary of terms at the end of the chapter. Flashcards may be helpful for memorizing definitions. Begin using the terms as you study, incorporating them into your vocabulary.

afterbirth	fetal alcohol syndrome (FAS)	ovulation
Apgar test	fetal distress	premature
cephalocaudal pattern	fetal stage	prenatal development
caesarean section (C-section) births	germinal stage	prepared child birth
critical period	implantation	preterm birth
differentiation	low birth weight	proximodistal pattern
dilation	malpresentation	teratogen
embryonic stage	miscarriage	
fetal alcohol effects (FAEs)	organogenesis	

⊙ PRENATAL DEVELOPMENT

Mitosis and Meiosis Review

It is not uncommon for students to have difficulty distinguishing mitosis (see Chapter 2) and meiosis. To help in this regard, underline the word that accurately completes each of the following sentences.

1. (Mitosis/Meiosis) occurs when a cell copies its chromosomes as it divides to form two cells.

2. After fertilization, all of the cell divisions that occur during prenatal development will be through (mitosis/meiosis).

3. The end product of (mitosis/meiosis) is a complete copy of the genetic material in all 46 chromosomes in each cell.

4. Gametes are specialized sex cells that form through the process of (mitosis/meiosis).

5. The exchange of genetic material referred to as "crossing-over" occurs in (mitosis/meiosis).

PRENATAL DEVELOPMENT AND BIRTH

Conception

1. You'll notice quite a few new terms in this chapter. To help keep them straight, identify the meanings of important word components in the chart below.

Root, Prefix, or Suffix	Meaning
an	
cephalo	
caudal	
derm	
distal	
ecto	
endo	
meso	
micro	
natal	
proximo	
tera	

2. Fill in the blanks below to complete a brief summary of the process of conception.
   Within the normal female reproductive system, there are _____ ovaries, each of which contains several _____ eggs, also called _____. During the period in which a woman is able to reproduce, a single egg, or _____, will mature approximately every _____ days. When an ovum has matured, it will be released from the ovary in a process known as _____. When two or three ova are released simultaneously, _____ twins or triplets can be conceived. After ovulation has occurred, the ovum is pulled into the _____ tube where _____ normally occurs. During sexual intercourse, a man may ejaculate as many as _____ million sperm cells. However, only a few _____ sperm cells will make it into the fallopian tube containing the ovum. During fertilization, the usual occurrence is for the _____ chromosomes from one of the father's sperm cells to combine with the _____ chromosomes from the mother's single ovum to create _____ fertilized egg cell. At this point, the ovum's outer membrane becomes _____ to other sperm. After fertilization, prenatal development will occur through the processes of _____ and _____.

PRENATAL DEVELOPMENT AND BIRTH

Stages of Prenatal Development

1. First, identify the three major stages of prenatal development, the duration of each stage, and the label given to the developing organism during that stage.

	STAGE	DURATION	LABEL FOR ORGANISM
1.			
2.			
3.			

2. Now, identify the stage of prenatal development in which each of the following events occurs. Include the specific timing of the event if known.

STAGE/TIMING	EVENT
_____	The neural tube forms.
_____	The ectoderm, mesoderm and endoderm form.
_____	The first cell differentiation takes place.
_____	The trophoblast and blastocyst form.
_____	First arm and leg movements appear.
_____	The organism becomes vulnerable to toxins.
_____	The brain and spinal cord begin to form.
_____	Eyes begin to form and heart tissues "flutter."
_____	Implantation occurs.
_____	The placenta becomes functional.
_____	The risk of pregnancy loss drops rapidly.
_____	The embryo does not yet have a circulatory system.
_____	The organism grows dramatically in size.
_____	The sex can be detected with ultrasound.
_____	Miscarriage due to major abnormalities is likely.
_____	Organogenesis is complete.
_____	The brain produces 100,000 new cells per minute.
_____	The startle and sucking reflexes first appear.
_____	Trophoblast differentiates into placenta, umbilical cord, and amniotic sac.

PRENATAL DEVELOPMENT AND BIRTH

⊙ TERATOGENS: HEATLH RISKS FOR THE BABY

1. Take the Prenatal Challenge!

   Your textbook authors assert that you should be able to identify more than a dozen potential prenatal risk factors after reading this chapter. See how well you do!

Teratogen	Most Likely Period of Risk	Possible Effects
A.		
B.		
C.		
D.		
E.		
F.		
G.		
H.		
I.		
J.		
K.		
L.		

PRENATAL DEVELOPMENT AND BIRTH

2. Indicate which of the following statements are true and which are false. If false, alter the statement in some way to make it true.

   A. About 1/3 of all birth defects are related to environmental factors. T/F

   B. The placenta is not an effective barrier against harmful substances. T/F

   C. ZDV is used to reduce the transmission of herpes from mother to fetus. T/F

   D. Researchers have examined newborn fecal matter for the presence of teratogens. T/F

   E. Greater damage occurs with greater exposure or doses of teratogens. T/F

   F. Babies born with HSV usually contract it through the umbilical cord. T/F

   G. Up to 30 percent of premature births may be due to vaginal infections. T/F

   H. Chromosomal abnormalities are due to the effects of teratogens. T/F

   I. The effects of teratogens may not be obvious at birth. T/F

   J. Low birthweight is the most common effect in newborns exposed to cocaine. T/F

   K. About 50 percent of the United States population is infected with HIV. T/F

   L. A baby can be completely protected from the effects of syphilis. T/F

   M. Nicotine and carbon monoxide are the only toxins in cigarette smoke. T/F

3. Describe the three conditions used to identify the presence of fetal alcohol syndrome.

   A.

   B.

   C.

PRENATAL DEVELOPMENT AND BIRTH

4. Self-Reflection on Teratogens
   List all of the substances you have ingested in the last seventy-two hours. If you were pregnant, which of these substances would be of concern? How might the length of time you've been pregnant influence the effects of the substances you've ingested?

5. *Numerically Speaking* of Alcohol, Cocaine, and Cigarettes
   Fill in the blanks with the correct numerical value.

   A. According to one national survey, _____ percent of all pregnant women drink alcohol during their pregnancies.

   B. Regular binge drinking is defined as the consumption of _____ or more alcoholic drinks per occasion, at least _____ times per week.

   C. In the United States, the incidence of FAS is estimated as being approximately _____ out of every _____ live births.

   D. Noticeable attention deficits and hyperactivity have been reported with babies whose mothers consumed only ___ drinks on average per week.

   E. In a nationwide survey, around ____ out of every _____ women reported using cocaine during pregnancy.

   F. Researchers found that _____ percent of privately insured babies tested positive for cocaine exposure compared to _____ percent of Medicaid or underinsured babies.

   G. About _____ % of pregnant women smoke cigarettes.

   H. More than _____ different harmful chemicals are present in cigarette smoke.

6. Be the Teacher
   Prepare a presentation to a high school health class on the effects of teratogens on prenatal development. What would you say to a group of 16 to 18-year-olds about teen pregnancy and exposure to environmental toxins?

PRENATAL DEVELOPMENT AND BIRTH

Maternal Age

Summarize what we know about the effects of maternal age on prenatal development.

    A. Teenage mothers:

    B. Mothers who are 40 years of age and older:

Critical Periods in Prenatal Development

1. Define "critical period."

2. Identify the points during prenatal development at which the risk for birth defects is lowest and highest.

3. Explain why the risks for birth defects fluctuate so much during prenatal development.

PRENATAL DEVELOPMENT AND BIRTH

Fathers' Role in Prenatal Development

Describe at least three ways in which fathers are responsible for the prenatal health of their children.

1.

2.

3.

⊙ THE PROCESS OF BIRTH

Stages of Birth

Label each of the three major stages of birth. Then, match each of the following events with the stage of birth in which it occurs.

Stages of Birth

Stage 1 - _____   Stage 2 - _____   Stage 3 - _____

Event	Stage
This stage begins with the onset of regular uterine contractions.	_____
Contractions are intense and between 2 and 5 minutes apart.	_____
The cervix gradually opens during this stage.	_____
This stage ends with the delivery of the baby.	_____
The baby moves through the birth canal.	_____
The longest stage, lasting 6 to 14 hours.	_____
Effacement occurs during this stage.	_____
The uterus expels the placenta in this stage.	_____

PRENATAL DEVELOPMENT AND BIRTH

Birthing Complications

1. Fill in the blanks to complete the following sentences.

   A. The optimal fetal position for delivery is _____.

   B. The complication that arises when the fetus is positioned in a less-than-optimal position for delivery is called _____, which occurs in approximately _____ percent of births.

   C. In a _____ position, the buttocks or feet are lowest in the uterus.

   D. In a _____ position, the fetus is lying sideways inside the uterus.

   E. Two procedures used to determine the position of the fetus are _____ and _____.

   F. If the fetus does not appear to be positioned safely, medical personnel may opt for a _____ rather than a _____ delivery.

   G. A fetus that experiences a lack of oxygen, change in heart rate, or change in respiration is said to be in _____.

   H. The condition in which a fetus is deprived of oxygen is called _____.

2. A fetus can be deprived of oxygen for a number of reasons, including

   A.

   B.

   C.

   D.

   E.

PRENATAL DEVELOPMENT AND BIRTH

The Newborn Baby

1. Your best friends are anxiously awaiting the birth of their first child. The mother expects her child to be an absolutely gorgeous "Gerber-baby look-alike," and the father is ready for a playmate! Describe for these soon-to-be parents the typical appearance and abilities of a newborn.

2. The first formal test used to evaluate most newborns is the _____ test.

    Identify the five dimensions assessed with this screening device for newborns.

    a.
    b.
    c.
    d.
    e.

    Explain why this test is given twice within a _____ minute span of time.

    a. The maximum score on this test is _____ and the minimum score is _____.

    b. A score between ___ and ___ indicates that there may be some problems with the newborn.

    c. A score between ___ and ___ indicates a serious risk and a need for immediate action.

    d. A score between ___ and ___ indicates that the newborn does not need immediate assistance.

Becoming a Family

1. The typical amount of time that it takes to adjust to parenthood is from _____ to _____ after the baby's birth.

PRENATAL DEVELOPMENT AND BIRTH

2. Describe a successful transition to parenthood.

3. Identify at least two short-term and two long-term problems that are potentially involved in a sibling's adjustment to a new baby.

   Potential short-term problems

   A.

   B.

   Potential long-term problems

   A.

   B.

⊙ OPTIONS IN GIVING BIRTH: CHOICES AND ALTERNATIVES

Approaches to Labor and Delivery

1. In the United States today, _____ percent of babies are born in a hospital.

PRENATAL DEVELOPMENT AND BIRTH

2. Identify the following four approaches to labor and delivery.

   A. _____ In this approach, women take prenatal classes to learn selective muscle relaxation and controlled breathing.

   B. _____ In this approach, the delivery room is kept quiet and softly lit. The baby is immediately placed on its mother's abdomen to encourage skin-to-skin contact, and the umbilical cord is not cut until it stops pulsing.

   C. _____ This approach incorporates many of the elements above and emphasizes the helpfulness of underwater delivery.

   D. _____ This approach offers immediate infant-family contact, no concern about making it to the hospital on time, and comfort in a familiar environment.

3. Match each of the following statements to the labor and delivery approach(es) with which it is most closely associated.

   A. A warm bath is used to simulate the feel of amniotic fluid.   _____

   B. There is no research that this particular approach is helpful.   _____

   C. Mothers are encouraged to nurse as soon as possible.   _____

   D. Medical equipment and personnel are not readily available.   _____

   E. This method is based on classical conditioning principles.   _____

   F. This approach was the norm in the early 1900s.   _____

   G. A labor coach or companion is present during delivery.   _____

Drugs during Labor and Delivery

1. Fill in the blanks with the correct information.

   A. In the United States, between _____ and _____ percent of all hospital-based deliveries involve some type of pain medication given to the mother.

PRENATAL DEVELOPMENT AND BIRTH

    B. During the middle part of this century, _____ and _____ were commonly used for pain relief, but it was discovered that these drugs crossed the placenta and placed the fetus at risk.

    C. One currently popular technique for administering pain medication is _____.

2. Imagine that Vanessa, your pregnant partner, is debating the pros and cons of using pain medications during her labor and delivery. Vanessa's mother has told her that she was given a general anesthetic during Vanessa's birth and "she turned out all right." Several of Vanessa's friends reported that they were given "epidurals." Briefly describe Vanessa's options and summarize existing research regarding the short-term and long-term effects of pain medications that might help her make a decision.

The Partners Role

Describe a partner's four central tasks during labor and delivery.

    1.

    2.

    3.

    4.

PRENATAL DEVELOPMENT AND BIRTH

When You Have Finished

⊙ Working the Web

1. Start your Internet search at www.obgyn.net/english/ob/labor.htm. This comprehensive Web site for professionals contains information on all aspects of conception, prenatal development, labor, and delivery. The Web site also contains an outstanding library of images of ectopic pregnancies, fetal anomalies, and placental conditions, in addition to intriguing ultrasound images of normal human prenatal development.

2. The following Web sites offer excellent images of embryonic and fetal development:
    www.amnionet.com/contents.htm (ultrasound images)
    www.wprc.org/fetal.html (color photos)
    www.med.unc.edu/embryo_images (scanning electron micrographs)

3. The Teratology Society was founded in 1960 to study the causes of birth defects. Go to www.teratology.org to learn more: How long has teratology been studied? What are some of the ways that humans have explained birth defects throughout history? What kinds of careers exist for people interested in teratology today?

4. Hospital or birthing center? Who will assist? Create your own birth plan at www.kidshealth.org/parent/pregnancy_newborn/pregnancy/birth_plans.html. Then, take a virtual tour of a birth center at www.swmedicalcenter.com/body.cfm?id=56

5. For practical information on the entire experience of pregnancy, go to www.med.umich.edu/obgyn/smartmoms sponsored by the University of Michigan Health System. Here you will read about prenatal tests, common pregnancy discomforts, nutrition, exercise, breastfeeding, labor and delivery, and family relationships. Quizzes throughout will help you integrate the information, as well as review for your child development exam!

PRENATAL DEVELOPMENT AND BIRTH

⊙ PRACTICE TEST #1

Multiple-Choice Questions
For each question, circle the best answer from the choices given.

1. Ovulation is the _____. (p. 84)

a. creation of an egg cell.
b. the maturation process of an egg cell.
c. the release of a matured egg cell.
d. the fertilization of an egg cell.

2. Differentiation is a process that occurs during (p. 85)

a. ovulation.
b. cell division.
c. the penetration of the egg cell by a sperm cell.
d. all of the above.

3. The outer layer of cells of a developing zygote is known as (p. 86)

a. the trophoblast.
b. the blastocyst.
c. the cytoplasm.
d. the germinal layer.

4. The embryonic stage of prenatal development occurs during the _____ weeks of pregnancy. (p. 87)

a. first two
b. 3rd to 8th
c. 9th to 15th
d. 15th to 40th

5. The proximodistal pattern of prenatal development is where (p. 88)

a. areas further from the center of the body develop first.
b. areas closer to the top of the body develop first.
c. areas closer to the center of the body develop first.
d. areas further from the top of the body develop first.

PRENATAL DEVELOPMENT AND BIRTH

6. During the 1960's a new area of research emerged called teratology, which is the study of (p. 90)

a. birth defects.
b. prenatal development.
c. environmental factors that can cause birth defects.
d. genetic factors that can cause birth defects.

7. Experts believe that prenatal exposure to _____ is the leading known cause of mental retardation in the United States.

a. alcohol
b. cocaine
c. lead
d. mercury

8. On a nationwide survey, about 1 out of every 100 women reported _____ during pregnancy. (p. 94)

a. drinking alcohol
b. using cocaine
c. shooting heroin
d. having syphilis

9. Which of the following prenatal problems can be attributed to the more than 450 harmful chemicals found in cigarette smoke? (p. 95)

a. damage to the placenta
b. reduction of blood supply to the uterus
c. reduction in the supply of oxygen available to the fetus
d. all of the above.

10. Cytomegalovirus is a member of the _____ family of viruses. (p. 96)

a. HIV
b. influenza
c. herpes
d. syphilis

PRENATAL DEVELOPMENT AND BIRTH

⊙ PRACTICE TEST #2

Multiple-Choice Questions
For each question, circle the best answer from the choices given.

1. Infection with syphilis causes all of these symptoms in a baby EXCEPT (p. 97)

a. deafness.
b. facial deformities.
c. mental retardation.
d. microcephaly.

2. Why is the risk for developing problems due to teratogens so low for babies in the first two weeks after conception? (p. 98)

a. The baby has not formed enough cells yet to be affected.
b. The mother's body provides antibodies to fight off these teratogens.
c. The placenta has not yet formed.
d. Morning sickness allows all of the teratogens to be vomited out of the body.

3. In most cases, when toxic substances affect sperm cells, the damaged sperm are unable to (p. 99)

a. replicate.
b. propelled out of the testes.
c. survive the long journey to the egg.
d. penetrate the egg cell.

4. Dilation refers to the (p. 101)

a. opening of the ovary to allow the egg cell to pass through.
b. expansion of the uterus to accommodate the growing fetus.
c. enlarging of the fallopian tubes caused by fertilization.
d. opening of the cervix caused by contractions.

5. Afterbirth occurs during the _____ stage of labor and delivery. (p. 101)

a. first
b. second
c. third
d. fourth

PRENATAL DEVELOPMENT AND BIRTH

6. Which of the following is not a birthing complication? (p. 103)

a. malpresentation
b. breech position
c. anoxia
d. teratogens

7. The amount of time needed for the transition to new parenthood depends on the family, but it usually takes about _____ after a baby's birth. (p. 104)

a. 1 – 3 months.
b. 3 – 6 months
c. 6 – 12 months
d. 12 – 24 months

8. Prepared childbirth involves (p. 107)

a. muscle relaxation techniques.
b. using a midwife.
c. avoiding hospital delivery.
d. taking drugs to reduce pain during delivery.

9. Epidural anesthesia (p. 110)

a. is injected directly into the mother's spine.
b. has short-term effects on the newborn's behavior.
c. has the same effect on all babies.
d. blocks sensations from the chest down.

10. Since the advent of prepared childbirth, (p. 111)

a. more women are getting pregnant and having babies.
b. insurance companies are charging more money for epidural anesthesia.
c. more men are opting to take more active roles in the delivery process.
d. less women are using midwives.

PRENATAL DEVELOPMENT AND BIRTH

⊙ COMPREHENSIVE PRACTICE TEST

Multiple-Choice Questions
For each question, circle the best answer from the choices given.

1. Each ovary will nourish _____ ova as they mature and become ready for fertilization. (p. 84)

a. less than one hundred
b. several hundred
c. several thousand
d. several million

2. Of the 500 million or so sperm cells that are ejaculated during intercourse, _____ survive the journey through the woman's uterus to the fallopian tubes. (p. 84)

a. most of them
b. about half
c. a few thousand
d. a few hundred

3. Which of the following activities does NOT take place during the germinal stage? (p. 86)

a. first cell division
b. ectoderm, mesoderm, and endoderm form
c. implantation
d. zygote enters uterus

4. The inner layer of cells of a developing zygote are called (p. 86)

a. trophoblast.
b. blastocyst.
c. embryo.
d. fetus.

5. Another name for miscarriage is _____. (p. 87)

a. trophoblast.
b. blastocyst.
c. spontaneous abortion.
d. induced abortion.

PRENATAL DEVELOPMENT AND BIRTH

6. The placenta is (p. 87)

a. a spongy tissue that provides oxygen to the growing embryo.
b. a bony layer that holds needed nutrients for the embryo.
c. a fluid-filled sac in which the embryo develops.
d. the inner layer of the developing zygote.

7. Which of the following terms best represents the last stage of the developing child? (p. 88)

a. zygote
b. blastula
c. embryo
d. fetus

8. Organogenesis is complete by the _____ week of pregnancy. (p. 88)

a. 3rd
b. 8th
c. 12th
d. 24th

9. The completion of organogenesis signals the end of what stage of prenatal development? (p. 88)

a. germinal
b. fetal
c. embryonic
d. teratogenic

10. Which of the following activities is NOT seen in during weeks 9 through 12 after conception? (p. 89)

a. Arm and leg movements begin to occur.
b. The mother feels the baby kicking and moving.
c. The first reflexes appear.
d. An ultrasound can reveal the sex of the fetus.

PRENATAL DEVELOPMENT AND BIRTH

11. Approximately _____ of birth defects are related to environmental factors that threaten the fetus while it is still developing in the mother's womb. (p. 90)

a. 1/4
b. 1/3
c. 1/2
d. 3/4

12. Which of the following terms refers to babies who are born earlier or smaller than average? (p. 90)

a. premature
b. preterm birth
c. low birth weight
d. small for gestational age

13. What year was fetal alcohol syndrome was first identified?

a. 1957
b. 1968
c. 1974
d. 1983

14. When researchers analyzed the fecal material of newborns to detect prenatal cocaine exposure, they found that (p. 94)

a. privately insured babies had a higher rate of exposure than Medicaid or underinsured babies.
b. privately insured babies had a lower rate of exposure than Medicaid or underinsured babies.
c. no difference was found in exposure between privately insure and Medicaid or underinsured babies.
d. cocaine cannot be detected in the fecal material of newborns.

15. What approximate percentage of all pregnant women smoke cigarettes? (p. 95)

a. 10
b. 25
c. 35
d. 50

PRENATAL DEVELOPMENT AND BIRTH

16. During the early 1990's, approximately 3,000 infants were infected with HIV each year in the United States. More than _____ of those babies mothers abused drugs or had sexual partners who abused drugs. (p. 97)

a. 50%
b. 60%
c. 70%
d. 80%

17. How long does the first stage of labor last on average? (p. 101)

a. 30 minutes to 2 hours
b. 2 hours to 6 hours.
c. 6 hours to 14 hours.
d. 14 hours or longer.

18. What is the purpose of vernix caseosa? (p. 103)

a. to transmit oxygen and nutrients to the baby
b. to protect the baby's skin
c. to shield the baby's eyes from the amniotic fluid
d. to keep the baby warm

19. Which of the following Apgar scores indicates that there are some potential problems with a baby and he or she needs close monitoring? (p. 104)

a. 10
b. 7
c. 4
d. 1

20. _____ is largely based on the work of Grantly Dick-Read. (p. 107)

a. Teratology
b. Prepared childbirth
c. Research on prenatal development
d. Rooming-in

PRENATAL DEVELOPMENT AND BIRTH

Short-Answer Questions
Answer each question in the space provided.

1. In the early weeks of prenatal development, there are two patterns that describe the formation and growth and the embryo. Name and define these two patterns.

2. Define cesarean section. Give an example of an appropriate reason to use this procedure.

3. Hospital births are no longer the only option for pregnant women. Describe at least three alternate birthing options.

PRENATAL DEVELOPMENT AND BIRTH

Crossword Puzzle

Across
2. the gradual opening of the cervix caused by labor contractions
5. stage in which the placenta and other membranes are delivered through the birth canal
8. The _____ test is a brief assessment of the newborn conducted at 1 and 5 minutes after birth.
9. The _____ stage spans from conception to 2 weeks.
10. improper positioning of the fetus in the uterus
11. release of an egg from the ovary

Down
1. _____ development occurs to the organism before its birth.
3. any substance or condition that might disrupt early development and cause birth defects
4. process where bodily organs and systems differentiate within the embryo
6. _____ stage spans from conception to 2 weeks.
7. process where the zygote embeds itself in the lining of the uterus

"Puzzle created with Puzzlemaker at DiscoverySchool.com"

4 PHYSICAL DEVELOPMENT IN INFANTS AND TODDLERS

Before You Read

This chapter offers a detailed description of physical development in infants and toddlers. You'll start by reading about rates of infant mortality and the health risks posed by prematurity. Then, you'll learn about the early physical growth of infants with sections devoted to feeding and nutrition, as well as to the intricate structure and formation of the brain and nervous system. In the remainder of the chapter, you will learn about the sensory capabilities and motor development of young human beings. Research is presented on basic vision, hearing, smell, and taste. In the motor development section, you will discover how infants coordinate movement through early reflexes and how motor development might differ from culture to culture. A final section on toilet training completes the chapter.

Chapter Learning Objectives

After reading this chapter, you should be able to do the following:

- Explain the confusion regarding the term "premature," and identify how the term does and does not relate to the concepts of preterm birth, low birthweight, very low birthweight, and small for gestational age.

- Compare and contrast the risk factors for, and potential effects of, preterm birth and low birthweight.

- Summarize the statistics regarding infant mortality and describe correlated risk factors.

- Identify changes that occur in height and weight during the infant and toddler years.

- Compare and contrast the benefits of breastfeeding and bottlefeeding.

PHYSICAL DEVELOPMENT IN INFANTS AND TODDLERS

- List the major structures in the human brain and describe the basic functions of each.

- Identify the parts of a neuron and summarize how neurons develop.

- Construct a time line detailing the formation and development of the brain, beginning at four weeks after conception and ending at birth.

- Briefly outline the research on infant visual acuity and depth perception.

- Identify three main conclusions regarding infant auditory capabilities.

- Summarize what is known about newborns' reactions to smell and taste.

- Discuss the importance and functional significance of the early reflexes.

- Outline the major milestones of infant motor development.

- Describe how cultural differences exhibited in parental practices influence the development of early motor skills.

- Summarize the emotional, cognitive, and physical milestones that should be achieved before beginning the toilet training process.

PHYSICAL DEVELOPMENT IN INFANTS AND TODDLERS

As You Read

Key terms and concepts are essential to your understanding of the chapter. Your ability to logically discuss and analyze pertinent information is dependent upon your knowledge of these concepts. Terms can be found in boldface throughout the chapter and definitions are listed in a glossary of terms at the end of the chapter. Flashcards may be helpful for memorizing

child-directed speech	low birth weight	programmed cell death
colostrum	myelination	reflexes
fine motor development	neurons	small for gestational age
gross motor development	postural reflexes	synaptogenesis
infant mortalitiy	preterm birth	very low birth weight
locomotor reflexes	primitive reflexes	visual acuity

⊙ INFANTS AT RISK: Prematurity and Infant Mortality

What is Prematurity?

1. Underline the information in parenthesis that will make each statement true.

    A. The average weight for a full-term baby is (9 1/2 / 7 1/2) pounds.

    B. When a baby is born weighing less than (5 1/2 / 3 1/2) pounds, he or she is considered to have a low birth weight.

    C. Infant mortality refers to deaths that occur (during the first two years of life / before the age of one year).

    D. The rate of infant mortality is about 5.7 deaths per 1,000 live births for (Caucasians / African Americans).

    E. Since 1990, the overall trend in the number of women receiving prenatal care is (up / down).

PHYSICAL DEVELOPMENT IN INFANTS AND TODDLERS

2. Discuss the reasons for distinguishing among the classifications low birth weight, very low birth weight, and small for gestational age.

3. What are the main risk factors associated with premature births? Are any of these risk factors controllable? If so, which ones?

4. List five pieces of advice your would give to an expectant couple that could increase their odds of having a healthy, happy baby.

   A.

   B.

   C.

   D.

   E.

PHYSICAL DEVELOPMENT IN INFANTS AND TODDLERS

⊙ GROWTH OF THE BODY AND BRAIN

Physical Growth

Numerically Speaking of Physical Growth
Fill in the blanks with the correct numerical values.

1. The average newborn weighs _____ pounds and is _____ inches in length.

2. By _____ months of age, an infant's birth weight has doubled.

3. Newborns tend to lose a slight amount of weight in the first few days after birth, but usually return to birth levels by about _____ weeks of age.

4. On average, the length of a newborn is about _____ inches.

5. Children will attain about half of their adult height by age _____.

Feeding and Nutrition

1. Discuss the relationship of breast milk to infant health and growth from birth to two weeks of age.

2. In what ways do differences in age and ethnicity affect the number of babies who are breastfed?

PHYSICAL DEVELOPMENT IN INFANTS AND TODDLERS

3. Nearly all health officials agree that human breast milk provides the best form of nutrition for most infants. Describe at least four situations in which breastfeeding would not be encouraged.

   A.

   B.

   C.

   D.

Structure and Formation of the Brain and Nervous System

1. Match each phrase, description, or activity with a term from the list. Each term should be used only once.

   _____ organizes articulation for speech output
   _____ sends messages that control voluntary muscle movement
   _____ information superhighway
   _____ gray matter forming the top portion of the brain
   _____ organization and planning center
   _____ collects sensory input from the body
   _____ processes speech input
   _____ directs posture, body orientation, and complex muscle movements
   _____ responsible for breathing and heart rate

   A. spinal cord
   B. brain stem
   C. cerebellum
   D. cerebral cortex
   E. motor area
   F. somatosensory area
   G. frontal lobe
   H. Wernicke's area
   I. Broca's area

PHYSICAL DEVELOPMENT IN INFANTS AND TODDLERS

2. Brain and Nervous System Timeline from Conception to Birth

Fill in the blanks with the major nervous system developments at each of the given ages. (weeks = wks)

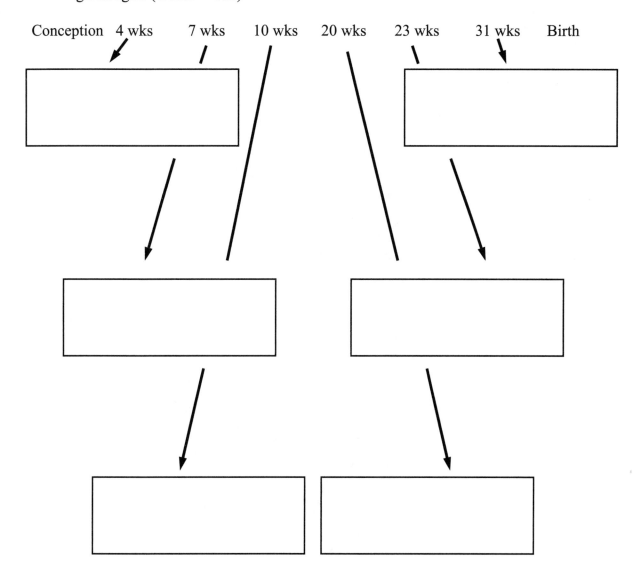

PHYSICAL DEVELOPMENT IN INFANTS AND TODDLERS

3. Label the neural structures indicated by the arrows.

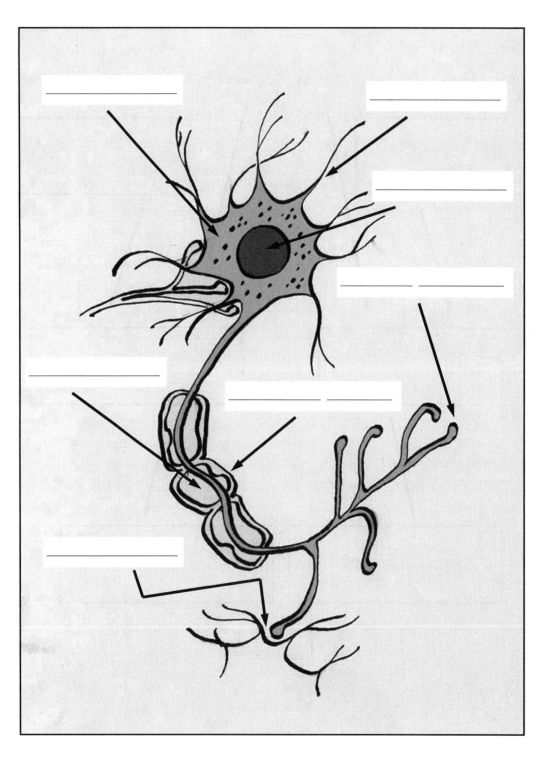

PHYSICAL DEVELOPMENT IN INFANTS AND TODDLERS

4. Discuss synaptogenesis and myelination with respect to neuron formation.

5. What is programmed cell death? Why is it important to the development of the brain and nervous system?

⊙ SENSORY CAPABILITIES

1. Each of the following statements is FALSE. Alter the statement in some way to make it TRUE.

    A. Color vision is mostly mature by the age of 3 months.

    B. The visual cliff is often used to assess color vision.

    C. Infants begin to use only pictoral clues to judge depth at around the age of 3 to 4 months.

    D. The auditory system becomes functional about three days after birth for most infants.

    E. Infants and young children are very sensitive to low frequency sounds.

    F. Infants are incapable of discerning small differences in complicated odors, even when they have repeated, close contact with the smell.

    G. The reaction to salty flavors appears in infants around 1 month of age, earlier than the reaction to sweet or bitter tastes.

2. Match each of the following research techniques with the type of infant perception it was designed to study.

Research Technique

A. visual cliff experiment
B. assessing sucking movements
C. presentation of striped patterns
D. reading *The Cat in the Hat*
E. presentation of gauze pads

Type of Perception

_____ odor discrimination
_____ auditory perception
_____ depth perception
_____ taste preferences
_____ visual acuity

PHYSICAL DEVELOPMENT IN INFANTS AND TODDLERS

3. Describe how the visual cliff experiment is used to study infant depth perception.

4. Define each of the following types of visual cues that humans use to determine depth. Then, rank order each cue in terms of when it appears developmentally.

   ____ Pictorial cues:

   ____ Object motion:

   ____ Binocular disparity:

5. List the three main conclusions researchers have drawn concerning young infants' auditory capabilities.

   A.

   B.

   C.

PHYSICAL DEVELOPMENT IN INFANTS AND TODDLERS

⊙ MOTOR DEVELOPMENT

Reflexes

1. Compare and contrast primitive, postural, and locomotor reflexes.

2. Complete the chart below by adding the stimulus and the reaction for each reflex. For each reflex, indicate its type by placing an X in the correct column.

Reflex	Stimulus	Reaction	Primitive	Postural	Locomotor
A. rooting					
B. sucking					
C. Moro					
D. swimming					
E. Babinski					
F. grasping					
G. parachute					
H. walking					
I. crawling					

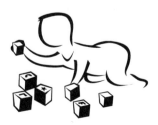

PHYSICAL DEVELOPMENT IN INFANTS AND TODDLERS

3. What is child-directed speech? How does it differ from normal adult speaking patterns?

4. Describe the classic DeCasper and Spence (1986) study of prenatal auditory perception.

5. Summarize the research on newborn and infant reactions to smell. Of the experiments and results discussed in your text, which do you find most interesting and/or surprising?

PHYSICAL DEVELOPMENT IN INFANTS AND TODDLERS

Voluntary Movements

1. Imagine you are the proud parent of a healthy newborn. The months ahead will be filled with many new discoveries for both you and the baby. During this special first year of life, what changes can you expect to see in your infant's gross motor development? What will be the major motor milestones and at which age will each typically appear? What might a serious delay in motor development mean for your child?

2. Each of the following statements is FALSE. Change the sentence to make the statement TRUE.

   A. "Gross motor development" refers to the process of coordinating the movement of the body's small, intricate muscles.

   B. Muscles in an infant's neck are typically strong enough to allow the child to hold its head upright by one week of age.

   C. The ability to crawl is usually attained by about four weeks of age.

   D. When an infant wraps all four fingers and thumb around an object, this is referred to as a "pincer grasp."

   E. A cephalocaudal pattern develops nearer to the body's midline and moves outward.

3. According to Thelen and her colleagues (1989, 2004, 2006), motor development is a complex and interactive process. List three components of their dynamic systems theory.

   A.

   B.

   C.

PHYSICAL DEVELOPMENT IN INFANTS AND TODDLERS

4. Eavesdropping?
Read each snippet of conversation below and assess it for probability in terms of what you know about the progression of motor development. Place a P beside those accomplishments you feel are within range of probability and an I by those you think are more improbable.

"My little Gregory was rolling over by himself when he was two months old and could sit up by himself at three months." _____

"I think Monitia is going to be a famous artist. She was holding a paintbrush with just three fingers and painting when she was ten months old." _____

"Well, when Ivan was only seven months old, he crawled all over the house and could stand by himself holding onto the coffee table." _____

"You can tell Victoria really loves animals. She was reaching out and embracing the cat when she was only five months of age." _____

PHYSICAL DEVELOPMENT IN INFANTS AND TODDLERS

Cultural Differences in Early Experience

Compare and contrast the effects of the typical parenting practices of certain African, Native American, and South American cultures mentioned in your text. In general, how do these practices differ from those with which you are familiar?

Toilet Training

Being the Teacher

You have been recently hired as the education coordinator for a private daycare facility. The daycare center prides itself on the interaction between the staff and the parents they serve. For your first staff/parent presentation, you have been asked to speak on toilet training. How would you explain the process to this particular group in terms of motor development? Which studies would be of the most interest to parents? How might plans to deal with the physical, emotional, and psychological issues surrounding toilet training for the children served by the center?

PHYSICAL DEVELOPMENT IN INFANTS AND TODDLERS

When You Have Finished

⊙ Working the Web

1. Before you read Chapter 4, go to www.zerotothree.org/brainwonders/index.html and take the brief Brain Quiz. Then, after reading Chapter 4, return to this Web site and see how many of the frequently asked questions about brain development you can answer for yourself.

2. This Web site at www.pfizer.com/brain, entitled "Brain: The World Inside Your Head," is an excellent resource for both children and adults. Here you can take a virtual tour of the brain, test your skill at one of the numerous brain games, or browse information for parents, teachers, and caregivers.

3. The Whole Brain Atlas, www.med.harvard.edu/AANLIB/home.htm, is one of the most comprehensive collections of brain images on the Web.

4. Visit the Neuroscience for Kids Web site at faculty.washington.edu/chudler/dev.html, and sign up to receive a copy of the free monthly neuroscience newsletter. This Web site contains accurate information on brain development and is visually appealing and user-friendly for students, teachers, and parents.

5. For excellent information on current research in human sensation and perception, check out "Seeing, Hearing, and Smelling the World" at www.hhmi.org/senses.

6. "Toilet Teaching Your Child" offers advice on when to begin potty training. The Web site discusses issues such as the best time of year to begin training, how long training will last, and types of potties and training pants, as well as common problems and tips. The site can be found at www.kidshealth.org/parent/emotions/behavior/toilet_teaching.html.

PHYSICAL DEVELOPMENT IN INFANTS AND TODDLERS

⊙ PRACTICE TEST #1

Multiple-Choice Questions
For each question, circle the best answer from the choices given.

1. Pierre weighed 5 lbs. at birth, which was 40 weeks gestation. Which of the following classifications best describes his birth weight? (p. 123)

a. preterm birth
b. low birth weight
c. very low birth weight
d. small for gestational age

2. Deaths that occur between birth and one year of age are referred to as (p. 124)

a. spontaneous abortions.
b. stillbirths.
c. infant mortality.
d. infanticide.

3. Experts agree that the steps that would (p. 125)

a. reduce rates of prematurity and low birth weight would reduce the rates of infant mortality.
b. reduce rates of prematurity and low birth weight would increase the rates of infant mortality.
c. increase rates of prematurity and low birth weight would reduce the rates of infant mortality.
d. all of the above.

4. Which of the following is NOT a risk factor for problems during pregnancy? (p. 126)

a. poor nutrition
b. smoking
c. maternal infections
d. adequate prenatal care

5. Colostrum is (p. 128)

a. another name for human breast milk.
b. a dangerous substance that can be excreted in some mother's milk.
c. a thick, yellowish substance secreted during the first few days of breast feeding.
d. a type of special formula given to infants who cannot breastfeed.

PHYSICAL DEVELOPMENT IN INFANTS AND TODDLERS

6. Which of the following structures controls posture, body orientation, and complex muscle movements? (p. 131)

a. the spinal cord
b. the brainstem
c. the cerebellum
d. the cerebral cortex

7. Which lobe is responsible for organizing, planning, and other executive functions? (p. 132)

a. frontal
b. temporal
c. parietal
d. occipital

8. Neurons are specialized cells that are responsible for (p. 132)

a. forming the top layer of the brain.
b. regulating the general alertness throughout the higher levels of the brain.
c. controlling voluntary movements in the peripheral nervous system.
d. controlling communication throughout the nervous system.

9. The end of the axon branches out to form _____. (p. 133)

a. dendrites
b. terminal buttons
c. myelin sheath
d. synaptic vesicles

10. Synaptogenesis is the form of neuron maturation in which (p. 134)

a. dendrites and axons branch out to form connections with neighboring neurons.
b. the fatty insulation, called myelin sheath, forms around the axons.
c. neurons being to die during periods of migration.
d. all of the above forms of neuron maturation take place.

PHYSICAL DEVELOPMENT IN INFANTS AND TODDLERS

⊙ PRACTICE TEST #2

Multiple-Choice Questions
For each question, circle the best answer from the choices given.

1. Which of the following takes place during periods of migration and heavy creation of synapses with neighboring neurons? (p. 135)

a. synaptogenesis
b. myelination
c. programmed cell death
d. neural tube formation

2. What is visual acuity? (p. 136)

a. the ability of an infant to see large objects
b. the ability of an infant to see fine detail
c. the ability of an infant to see color
d. the ability of an infant to perceive depth

3. Binocular disparity is the (p. 137)

a. difference between the images projected on the two eyes.
b. relative size and density of the pattern elements shown to an infant.
c. ability of an infant to see fine detail.
d. ability of an infant to see color.

4. The way that adults talk to children in a singsong pattern is known as _____. (p. 138)

a. child-patterned speech
b. child-directed speech
c. adult-patterned speech
d. adult-directed speech

5. Research has shown that newborns prefer the smell of their mothers over (p. 139)

a. other women.
b. the smell of formula.
c. their favorite toy.
d. none of the above.

PHYSICAL DEVELOPMENT IN INFANTS AND TODDLERS

6. Reflexes are (p. 141)

a. a form of neuron maturation which involves the formation of synapses.
b. the passive, natural sounds that lack intentional meaning.
c. involuntary movements that are elicited by environmental stimuli.
d. the process of coordinating intricate movements with smaller muscles.

7. Gross motor development is the process of coordinating movements with the _____ muscles in the body. (p. 142)

a. large
b. small
c. voluntary
d. involuntary

8. By 3 months of age, infants are able to (p. 143)

a. sit upright without support
b. roll over
c. begin crawling
d. stand up by holding on to something for support

9. Researchers believe that the cross-cultural differences seen in early motor development of infants has something to do with more _____ of babies in certain cultures. (p. 146)

a. emotional encouragement
b. vigorous physical stimulation
c. socialization
d. genetic engineering

10. Most toddlers gain voluntary control and coordination over the muscles that control their bladder and bowel movements by the time that they are _____. (p. 147)

a. 10 to 12 months.
b. 12 to 18 months.
c. 18 to 24 months.
d. 24 to 36 months.

PHYSICAL DEVELOPMENT IN INFANTS AND TODDLERS

⊙ COMPREHENSIVE PRACTICE TEST

Multiple-Choice Questions
For each question, circle the best answer from the choices given.

1. One of the biggest threats by infants in our country is (p. 122)

a. not enough adoptive parents.
b. inadequate medical care.
c. prematurity.
d. pollution and other teratogens.

2. A newborn who was born within two weeks of the expected due date and weighed 8 lbs. 1 oz. would be considered a(n) (p. 123)

a. average weight baby.
b. overweight baby.
c. low birth weight baby.
d. preterm birth.

3. A preterm birth is a birth that occurs (p. 123)

a. before 37 weeks gestation.
b. between 37 – 40 weeks gestation.
c. between 40 – 42 weeks gestation.
d. after 42 weeks gestation.

4. Which of the following countries has the highest rate of infant mortality? (p. 124)

a. Sweden
b. United States
c. Mexico
d. Turkey

5. In 2003, the number of women in America who received prenatal care _____ compared to the number of women in American who received prenatal care in 1990. (p. 126)

a. decreased
b. increased
c. stayed the same
d. There is not enough data to determine the trend.

PHYSICAL DEVELOPMENT IN INFANTS AND TODDLERS

6. During the first few days after birth, infants (p. 127)

a. lose a slight amount of weight.
b. gain a slight amount of weight.
c. stay about the same weight as at birth.
d. cannot be weighed.

7. Babies can be protected from a variety of infections, viruses, and illnesses by (p. 129)

a. feeding them a special formula that contains probiotics.
b. having neonates inoculated with their first vaccines before they leave the hospital.
c. ingesting colostrum in the mother's breast milk.
d. having the mother take antibiotics during the last few days before delivery.

8. Compared to affluent countries, women in poorer countries are (p. 129)

a. more likely to breastfeed.
b. less likely to breastfeed.
c. equally likely to breastfeed.
d. There is not enough data to determine a trend.

9. Which of the following conditions would NOT prohibit a mother from breastfeeding her baby? (p. 130)

a. HIV
b. chickenpox
c. influenza
d. hepatitis B

10. The newborn's head represents _____ of the newborn's total length. (p. 131)

a. 1/2
b. 1/3
c. 1/4
d. 1/8

PHYSICAL DEVELOPMENT IN INFANTS AND TODDLERS

11. The brain stem is responsible for (p. 131)

a. exchanging information between the body and the brain.
b. controlling automatic functions and regulating alertness.
c. controlling posture, body orientation, and complex muscle movements.
d. higher level functioning, such as problem solving, organizing, and planning.

12. Dendrites (p. 132)

a. are specialized neurons that communicate to the muscles.
b. have three main parts.
c. receive information from neighboring neurons.
d. form the myelin sheath that cover the axon.

13. The neural tube begins to form at (p. 133)

a. conception.
b. about 4 weeks gestation.
c. about 20 weeks gestation.
d. about birth.

14. The type of neuron maturation in which the axons are covered in a fatty insulation is known as (p. 134)

a. myelination.
b. organogenesis.
c. synaptogenesis.
d. cell migration.

15. In a visual acuity test, infants are shown a stripe pattern paired with a uniform gray square. If an infant doesn't have sufficient acuity to see the stripes, then he or she would see (p. 136)

a. a black square.
b. a gray square.
c. a white square.
d. a dotted square.

PHYSICAL DEVELOPMENT IN INFANTS AND TODDLERS

16. Most of the evidence collected in the last few decades suggests that the photopigments in the eye that are necessary for normal color vision are present _____. (p. 136)

a. prenatally
b. by birth
c. by three months after birth
d. by six months after birth

17. Depth perception can be determined using which of the following apparatus? (p. 137)

a. visual cliff
b. looking chamber
c. depth monitor
d. dishabituation technique

18. The Moro reflex occurs when (p. 141)

a. the breast or bottle touches their cheek.
b. an object touches an infant's palm.
c. an infant begins to fall.
d. infants are held upright and then tilted face down.

19. Gross motor development follows the (p. 143)

a. cephalocaudal principle.
b. proximodistal principle.
c. both a. and b.
d. neither a. nor b.

20. Which of the following is NOT a developmental milestone? (p. 147)

a. crawling
b. potty training
c. first words
d. first trip to the zoo

PHYSICAL DEVELOPMENT IN INFANTS AND TODDLERS

Short-Answer Questions

Answer each question in the space provided.

1. There is sometimes confusion about the term premature. Define the four most common terms associated with prematurity: preterm birth, low birth weight, very low birth weight, and small for gestational age.

2. Your book defines two forms of neuron maturation. Name and define them.

3. Define gross motor development and fine motor development. Give an example of each.

PHYSICAL DEVELOPMENT IN INFANTS AND TODDLERS

Crossword Puzzle

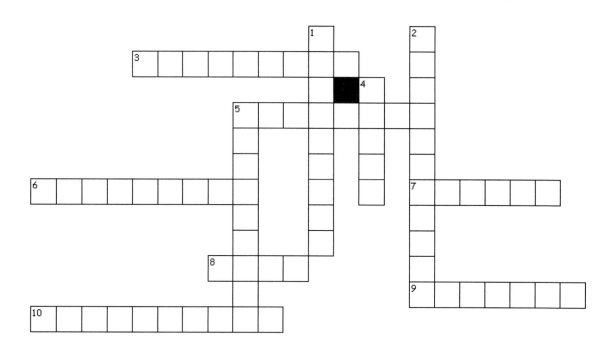

Across
3. _____ reflexes mimic movements such as crawling and stepping.
5. _____ reflexes help with body orientation and balance.
6. a thick, yellowish substance in breast milk containing antibodies
7. Visual _____ refers to the ability to see fine detail.
8. _____ motor development coordinates intricate movements with small muscles
9. specialized cells that process information and allow communication in the nervous system
10. The process by which many neurons die during periods of migration and heavy synaptogenesis is called _____ cell death.

Down
1. Infant _____ refers to deaths that occur between birth and 1 year of age.
2. the growth of fatty insulation around the axon
4. _____ motor development is the process of coordinating movements with large muscles
5. _____ reflexes help the infant find nourishment or protection.

"Puzzle created with Puzzlemaker at DiscoverySchool.com"

5 | COGNITIVE DEVELOPMENT IN INFANTS AND TODDLERS

Before You Read

The chapter begins with the work of Robert Fantz and his advancements in testing visual preferences in newborns, which became known as the preferential looking technique. Other researchers developed the habituation–dishabituation technique to further our understanding of infant preferences. As a key figure in the field of cognitive development, Jean Piaget's views are the subject of the middle portion of the chapter, exploring his early life and how it influenced his subsequent work in psychology. Next, the chapter discusses the concept of "constructivism" and explains why Piaget is considered a constructivist. Next, the first stage of Piaget's theory, sensorimotor thought, is examined. Finally, the chapter focuses on communication and early developments in language production.

Chapter Learning Objectives

After reading this chapter, you should be able to do the following:

- Discuss the importance of Robert Fantz's early research on perception

- Summarize what is known about newborn visual preferences.

- Describe the logic behind the use of the habituation–disabituation technique.

- Define intermodal perception and describe, in detail, a study exploring the topic.

- Describe how Piaget's background in biology and IQ testing is reflected in his theory.

- Explain the constructivist position and discuss why Piaget's theory of cognitive development is often described as a constructivist view.

COGNITIVE DEVELOPMENT IN INFANTS AND TODDLERS

- Discuss how the concepts of adaptation, scheme, organization, assimilation, accommodation, and equilibration form the foundation of Piaget's perspective.

- Name the four stages of Piaget's theory of cognitive development and describe the differences between the thinking that occurs in each of these four stages.

- Define object permanence, trace its development during the first two years of life, and describe how researchers determine if a child has developed this understanding.

- Explain why symbol usage is an important indicator of cognitive development.

- Define language and describe its primary characteristics.

- Compare and contrast the three main theories of language development.

- Describe the LAD and how it affects language development.

- Identify the physical structures that are specialized for language in humans.

- Discuss the roles of social interaction and cognitive ability in language development.

- Describe how child-directed speech (CDS) differs from adult speech and how it helps children acquire language.

- Describe changes in vocalizations that occur during a child's first year of life.

- List major developments in semantics and grammar in early childhood.

COGNITIVE DEVELOPMENT IN INFANTS AND TODDLERS

As You Read

Key terms and concepts are essential to your understanding of the chapter. Your ability to logically discuss and analyze pertinent information is dependent upon your knowledge of these concepts. Terms can be found in boldface throughout the chapter and definitions are listed in a glossary of terms at the end of the chapter. Flashcards may be helpful for memorizing definitions. Begin using the terms as you study, incorporating them into your vocabulary.

accommodation	intermodal perception	preferential-looking technique
adaptation	language	reflective abstraction
assimilation	language acquisition device (LAD)	scheme
constructivist view	learning theory	sensorimotor thought
dishabituation	nativist theory	social interactionist theory
equilibration	object permanence	symbolic
habituation	organization	telegraphic speech
habituation–dishabituation technique	perception	
holophrases	Piaget's cognitive development theory	

⊙ PERCEPTUAL DEVELOPMENT

Robert Fantz and the Early Work in Testing Visual Preferences

1. Explain the logic behind Robert Fantz's (1956) early experiments in perception with chickens and chimpanzees.

2. Describe the *looking chamber* and how it is used in conjunction with the preferential-looking technique.

COGNITIVE DEVELOPMENT IN INFANTS AND TODDLERS

Habituation–Dishabituation Research

1. Compare and contrast the preferential-looking technique with the habituation–dishabituation technique in relation to the development of infant visual acuity.

2. What can the degree of dishabituation in visual trials tell us about intelligence in later life?

Intermodal Perception

1. Define the term "intermodal perception." Cite at least two examples.

2. Summarize research findings measuring the intermodal perception abilities of infants, including the work of Meltzoff and Borton (1979) and Spelke (1979).

COGNITIVE DEVELOPMENT IN INFANTS AND TODDLERS

⊙ EXPLAINING COGNITIVE DEVELOPMENT: PIAGET'S VIEW

Piaget as a Child Prodigy

Describe evidence that illustrates how Piaget's experiences as a child, at the Zurich psychiatric clinic, and at the Binet Laboratory influenced his later work in psychology.

Constructivism and Interaction with the Environment

1. What does it mean when a theory is described as "constructivist"? What kind of belief system is the constructivist position contrasted with in your text? Why is Piaget's theory often described as a "constructivist view"?

2. Match each term with its description, by placing the correct letter in the corresponding blank.

   Terms

   _____ adaptation   _____ accommodation
   _____ organization   _____ cognitive equilibrium
   _____ assimilation   _____ reflective abstraction
   _____ cognitive disequilibrium

   Descriptions

   A. noticing and thinking about the implications of information and experience
   B. dynamic movement between states of cognitive disequilibrium and equilibrium
   C. incorporating new information into an existing scheme
   D. changing a cognitive structure or the surroundings to understand the environment
   E. tendency to integrate individual elements into higher-order structures
   F. imbalance between a new experience and an old scheme
   G. state of cognitive balance

COGNITIVE DEVELOPMENT IN INFANTS AND TODDLERS

Piaget's Stage 1: Sensorimotor Thought (Birth to 2 Years)

Name each of the six sensorimotor substages and give the approximate age range. Then, match each of the following examples with the substage in which it occurs.

Substages of Sensorimotor Thought	Age Range
Substage 1 - _____	_____
Substage 2 - _____	_____
Substage 3 - _____	_____
Substage 4 - _____	_____
Substage 5 - _____	_____
Substage 6 - _____	_____

Examples   Substage

A. Mary grasps her foot for the first time. Afterward,   _____
   she repeats the action several times and laughs each
   time she is successful in grasping her foot.

B. Charles likes the sound of his aunt's keys rattling.   _____
   He pushes them along the counter, then picks them
   up and shakes them again and again.

C. Abby wants to kick the football. She swings her leg   _____
   like they do on TV, and wonders how it would feel
   to make contact with the ball.

D. Jake pushes the toy train off of the table. He then   _____
   pushes it off of the couch, the mantle, and the deck to
   See what will happen.

E. Alex sucks his thumb, and opens and closes his hands.   _____

F. Lulu wants to pet the kitty lying behind the pillow on   _____
   the bed. She quietly moves the pillow and pats the kitty.

COGNITIVE DEVELOPMENT IN INFANTS AND TODDLERS

⊙ LEARNING TO COMMUNICATE

What is language?

1. Define "language" and describe its defining characteristics. Make sure you include examples of semanticity, productivity, and displacement as they relate to language.

2. How does language differ from speech? Why is American Sign Language considered a language?

Learning Theory

1. Identify which of the following names and concepts are directly connected to the learning theory of language development by placing a check mark next to each learning theory concept. Then, discuss how the <u>checked</u> concepts are integrated within the learning theory of language development.

   ___ Skinner   ___ Bandura   ___ Piaget
   ___ operant conditioning   ___ universal grammar   ___ modeling
   ___ biologically programmed   ___ operating principles   ___ imitation
   ___ differential reinforcement   ___ environmental view   ___ shaping

   Discussion:

COGNITIVE DEVELOPMENT IN INFANTS AND TODDLERS

2. In the following example of a mother-child interaction, label <u>modeling</u> (M), <u>imitation</u> (I), <u>extension</u> (E), and <u>reinforcement</u> (R) as they occur.

   MOTHER: Say "mama." Can you say "mama?"   _____

   CHILD: m-m-m-m (while looking at mother).   _____

   MOTHER: m-m-m. Good. That's right! I'm you're mama.   _____, _____

   CHILD: maaaaaaa.   _____

   MOTHER: Mama! That's right. Mama. I'm you're mother. _____, _____

3. Clearly articulate five distinct criticisms of the learning theory of language development.

4. Why does the fact that young children regularly say things they've never heard, such as, "I goed to the store," represent a problem for the learning theory of language development?

COGNITIVE DEVELOPMENT IN INFANTS AND TODDLERS

Nativist Theory

1. Identify which of the following names and concepts are directly connected to the nativist theory of language development by placing a check mark next to each nativist concept. Then, discuss how these concepts are integrated within the nativist view of language development.

   ___ Skinner   ___ Bandura   ___ Chomsky
   ___ LAD   ___ shaping   ___ universal grammar
   ___ biologically programmed   ___ operating principles   ___ imitation
   ___ modeling   ___ "I goed to the store."   ___ reinforcement

   Discussion:

2. How would a proponent of nativist theory respond to the learning theory perspective that language is "a behavior learned just like any other skill"?

3. If language acquisition is biologically programmed, then it should display patterns similar to other biologically-based systems of human development. What should language acquisition in humans "look like" if it is innate or biologically programmed?

COGNITIVE DEVELOPMENT IN INFANTS AND TODDLERS

4. What characteristics of a biologically programmed behavior does language development display?

5. Use the Kanzi research to discuss the nativist position that, "other species lack the biological mechanisms common to all humans." Does the existing primate research support the nativist position? Why or why not?

6. Describe the function of each of the following physical structures and list its location.

Structure	Description	Location
A. Broca's area		
B. Wernicke's area		
C. arcuate fasciculus		
D. angular gyrus		

COGNITIVE DEVELOPMENT IN INFANTS AND TODDLERS

7. Discuss how each of the following lines of research supports the idea of sensitive periods in language development.

   A. Case studies of children deprived of linguistic input:

   B. People's age-related abilities to learn a second language:

   C. Deaf children's age-related abilities to learn ASL:

   D. Case studies of language recovery after brain damage:

8. Clearly articulate at least four distinct criticisms of the nativist theory of language development.

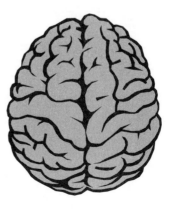

COGNITIVE DEVELOPMENT IN INFANTS AND TODDLERS

Interaction Theories

Briefly describe the following three interaction theories of language development. Then, match each concept or process below with the theory of language development with which it is most closely related by placing the appropriate letter in the space provided.

Interaction Theories

A. cognitive developmental theory

B. connectionist models

C. social interactionist theory

Concept or Process

___ formats
___ object permanence
___ computer simulations
___ recasts
___ CDS

___ cognitive/linguistic correlations
___ units
___ expansions
___ words represent objects
___ changing the strength of connections

COGNITIVE DEVELOPMENT IN INFANTS AND TODDLERS

Infant Communication
1. Complete the following table on the progression of language development by placing the necessary information in both the blanks and blank boxes.

Age	Type of Speech Sound	Examples
Birth	Vegetative sounds: *reflexive, non-intentional sounds*	
2 months	Variation in cries to indicate comfort: _____	Oooooooo, oooooo
	Distinctive cries to signal specific states: *cooing and laughing*	
5 months	_____ _____: *single syllables with one consonant and on vowel sound*	ma
	_____ _____: _____ *vowel* _____ *pairs*	mamama
8 to 12 months	Echolalia: *immediate imitation of words*	
9 to 12 months	Variegated babbling: *multiple, differing syllables;* Jargon babbling: *babbling which includes native language intonation patterns, rhythms, and stresses;* Protowords: *consistent sound patterns used to refer to specific objects and events*	bapadaga
_____ _____	First true words, usually accompanied by gestures, babbling and/or protowords	

COGNITIVE DEVELOPMENT IN INFANTS AND TODDLERS

2. Fill in the following table with the appropriate missing information. Then identify the typical age at which the different word types first appear.

Type of word	Examples	Typical age
Names for *general examples* of a category		
Names for *specific members* of a category		
	go, up, swing, bounce, run, throw, cry	
Words that *describe* objects or events	big, little, mine, yummy, cold	
Words that express *feelings or relationships*		
	what, where, for, is	

3. Create your own example of each of the following language-related concepts:

True babbling:

Telegraphic speech:

Holophrase:

Overregularization:

Protowords:

Overextension:

Underextension:

COGNITIVE DEVELOPMENT IN INFANTS AND TODDLERS

5. Being the Teacher
   You've been asked to present a workshop for parents on ways to enhance their children's language development. Using information from your text as a guide, create an outline including main topics, practical suggestions, and interesting examples that will help aid and encourage parents to improve their skills in working with their children.

6. *Numerically Speaking* of Language Development
   Fill in the blanks with the correct numerical values.

   A. Babies start recognizing differences in speech sounds around _____ of age.

   B. By ____ months, a baby's cries have much more variation than at birth.

   C. Cooing is present by _____ months.

   D. At about _____ months, true babbling begins.

   E. Between ___ and ____ months, infants start to show echolalia.

   F. The use of protowords begins around ____ or ____ months of age.

   G. Somewhere around the age of _____, most children say their first adult word.

   H. Between the ages of ____ and _____ months, toddlers begin to produce two– and three-word sentences.

COGNITIVE DEVELOPMENT IN INFANTS AND TODDLERS

When You Have Finished

⊙ Working the Web

1. For a review of early vision, hearing, and touch capabilities in newborns and infants, visit www.zerotothree.org/brainwonders/care_birth.html. Caregivers can find tips to provide input into the developing brain.

2. For extra practice with Piaget's theory, try answering the critical thinking questions at www.mhhe.com/socscience/devel/kid-c/resources/3-critic/cte-07.htm. Are you confident in your understanding of his theory?

3. To learn more about the fascinating field of linguistics, go to www.zompist.com/langfaq.html. Here you can examine a map of the world's languages, learn why it's hard to lose a foreign accent, and discover if Eskimos really have one hundred words for "snow."

4. The mission of the First Words Program at Florida State University's Department of Communication Disorders (firstwords.fsu.edu/h/hb.html) is to evaluate the communicative development of children between six and twenty-four months of age. In addition, this program provides support and information to parents. Here you can obtain a copy of the Infant-Toddler Checklist, a questionnaire that assesses different developmental characteristics that predict whether a child may have difficulty learning to talk.

5. Teaching infants to use sign language is an intriguing idea. Use your knowledge of language development and your critical thinking skills to evaluate the information contained at the "Sign With Me: Teach Your Child Infant Sign Language" commercial web site (www.signwithme.com/).

COGNITIVE DEVELOPMENT IN INFANTS AND TODDLERS

⊙ PRACTICE TEST #1

Multiple-Choice Questions
For each question, circle the best answer from the choices given.

1. Which of the following is NOT an example of an area of research in cognitive development? (p. 154)

a. perception
b. memory
c. problem solving
d. weight gain

2. Which of the following theorists claimed that the newborn's mind was a "blank slate"? (p. 154)

a. John Locke
b. Sigmund Freud
c. William James
d. Robert Fantz

3. The apparatus known as a looking chamber was essential in the research of (p. 155)

a. Jean Piaget.
b. Robert Fantz.
c. Sigmund Freud.
d. William James.

4. Which of the following techniques were created to answer the question: "What if infants can see the difference between two stimuli but find both stimuli to be equally interesting?" (p. 157)

a. equal stimulation technique
b. preferential looking technique
c. habituation-dishabituation technique
d. constructivist technique

5. What is intermodal perception? (p. 158)

a. the tendency to integrate separate elements into increasingly complex higher-order structures
b. the recovery in response when a familiar stimulus is replaced by one that is new
c. the tendency of infants to reduce their response to stimuli that are presented repeatedly
d. the process of combining or integrating information across sensory modalities

COGNITIVE DEVELOPMENT IN INFANTS AND TODDLERS

6. The most influential theorist in the study of cognitive development was (p. 161)

a. Jean Piaget.
b. Robert Fantz.
c. Sigmund Freud.
d. William James.

7. Jean Piaget thought that children were _____ in their thinking. (p. 162)

a. active
b. passive
c. inconsistent
d. irregular

8. The constructivist view states that people construct their own knowledge and understanding of the world by (p. 162)

a. explaining the reasons for their answers rather than simply giving an answer.
b. using what they already know and understand to interpret new experiences.
c. organizing patterns of physical or mental actions.
d. changing a cognitive structure of the environment in order to understand it.

9. Sensorimotor thought is based on (p. 166)

a. intuitive logic.
b. concrete, tangible materials and experience.
c. hypothetico-deductive reasoning.
d. sensory input and motor actions.

10. Symbolic thought is the ability to form (p. 167)

a. an understanding of mathematical operations.
b. mental representations that stand for objects or events in the world.
c. schemes about inborn reflexes.
d. schemes about behaviors that are discovered accidentally.

COGNITIVE DEVELOPMENT IN INFANTS AND TODDLERS

⊙ PRACTICE TEST #2

Multiple-Choice Questions
For each question, circle the best answer from the choices given.

1. What is object permanence? (p. 169)

a. the fact that objects, events, and people continue to exist even when they are out of a child's direct line of sensory input or motor action
b. the fact that objects, events, and people do not continue to exist even when they are out of a child's direct line of sensory input or motor action
c. both a. and b.
d. neither a. nor b.

2. Semanticity is a key feature of (p. 172)

a. the sensorimotor stage.
b. habituation-dishabituation technique.
c. object permanence.
d. language.

3. Learning theory is based upon the _____ theories of learning. (p. 172)

a. psychoanalytic
b. biological
c. behaviorist
d. cognitive

4. A brain mechanism in humans that is specialized for obtaining and processing language is the (p. 173)

a. Language Acquiring Device.
b. Language Acquisition Device.
c. Language Access Device.
d Language Attainment Device.

5. The productivity of language refers to (p. 173)

a. the degree of novelty of children's language utterances.
b. the passive, natural sounds that lack intentional meaning.
c. the production of vowel-like sounds.
d. the imitation and modeling of parents' language.

COGNITIVE DEVELOPMENT IN INFANTS AND TODDLERS

6. Which of the following theorists proposed the nativist theory of language? (p. 173)

a. Jean Piaget.
b. B. F. Skinner.
c. Albert Bandura.
d. Noam Chomsky.

7. How does the angular gyrus assist in the processing of language? (p. 175)

a. muscle movements to write
b. muscle movements to speak
c. spoken language
d. written language

8. Cognitive developmental theory is a theory of language proposed by (p. 177)

a. Jean Piaget.
b. B. F. Skinner.
c. Albert Bandura.
d. Noam Chomsky.

9. The immediate imitation of others' sounds or words is called (p. 180)

a. vegetative sounds.
b. cooing.
c. echolalia.
d. true babbling.

10. Fast mapping is (p. 181)

a. the mapping of language across the neural structures responsible for processing language.
b. where children acquire at least a partial understanding of a word after only a single exposure.
c. the expansion of a word's meaning to include more objects that it should.
d. the consistent patterns of sounds that refer to specific people, objects, or events.

COGNITIVE DEVELOPMENT IN INFANTS AND TODDLERS

⊙ COMPREHENSIVE PRACTICE TEST

Multiple-Choice Questions
For each question, circle the best answer from the choices given.

1. Sensation is the (p. 154)

a. group of mental processes, such as perceiving, thinking, remembering, solving problems, and communicating with language.
b. physical process of detecting information about a stimulus in the environment.
c. cognitive process of organizing, coordinating, and interpreting sensory information.
d. complex skill sets of understanding the permanence of objects and the grammatical rules of language.

2. Perception is the cognitive process of (p. 154)

a. group of mental processes, such as perceiving, thinking, remembering, solving problems, and communicating with language.
b. physical process of detecting information about a stimulus in the environment.
c. cognitive process of organizing, coordinating, and interpreting sensory information.
d. complex skill sets of understanding the permanence of objects and the grammatical rules of language.

3. William James believed that the mental experience of the infant was (p. 154)

a. a blank slate.
b. one great blooming, buzzing confusion.
c. an organized entity that can use sensory information in a meaningful way.
d. an active, rather than passive, process.

4. On which of the following stimuli did newborns spend the LEAST amount of time focused? (p. 155)

a. face
b. bull's eye
c. newsprint
d. dark red circle

COGNITIVE DEVELOPMENT IN INFANTS AND TODDLERS

5. Research on infants' visual perception has shown that infants prefer which of the following stimuli the MOST? (p. 156)

a. patterns that resemble the human face
b. bull's eyes or other geometric shapes
c. newsprint or other writing
d. dark red circles or other single color shapes

6. The tendency of infants to reduce their response to stimuli that are presented repeatedly is known as _____. (p. 157)

a. preference
b. habituation
c. dishabituation
d. intermodal perception

7. Dishabituation is (p. 157)

a. the tendency of infants to reduce their response to stimuli that are presented repeatedly.
b. the amount of time that infants spend looking at a presented stimulus.
c. when an infant increases their response because a familiar stimulus has been replaced by a novel one.
d. when an infant decreases their response because a familiar stimulus has been replaced by a novel one.

8. If a child is able to see a kitten, hear the kitten meow, and feel the kitten's fur as she pets him, this type of sensory input is best explain by which of the following theories? (p. 158)

a. habituation
b. dishabituation
c. preferential looking
d. intermodal perception

9. Which of the following theorists held a separatist view of intermodal perception? (p. 158)

a. John Locke
b. Jean Piaget
c. T.G.R. Bower
d. Eleanor Gibson

COGNITIVE DEVELOPMENT IN INFANTS AND TODDLERS

10. Which of the following theorists held a constructivist view of intermodal perception? (p. 158)

a. John Locke
b. Jean Piaget
c. T.G.R. Bower
d. Eleanor Gibson

11. The _____ was used by Jean Piaget in his efforts to understand children's thinking. (p. 162)

a. clinical method
b. looking chamber
c. preferential-looking technique
d. habituation-dishabituation technique

12. A scheme is (p. 163)

a. the tendency to integrate separate elements into increasingly complex higher-order structures.
b. an organized pattern of physical or mental action.
c. the recovery in response when a familiar stimulus is replaced by one that is new
d. the process of combining or integrating information across sensory modalities

13. The tendency to integrate separate elements into increasingly complex higher-order structures is called _____. (p. 163)

a. a scheme
b. organization
c. adaptation
d. reflective abstraction

14. Assimilation is (p. 164)

a. the process of bringing new objects or information into a scheme that already exists.
b. the process of modifying old schemes or creating new ones to better fit assimilated information.
c. the tendency to make modifications in order to survive and succeed in the environment.
d. the tendency to integrate separate elements into increasingly complex higher-order structures.

COGNITIVE DEVELOPMENT IN INFANTS AND TODDLERS

15. Accommodation is (p. 165)

a. the process of bringing new objects or information into a scheme that already exists.
b. the process of modifying old schemes or creating new ones to better fit assimilated information.
c. the tendency to make modifications in order to survive and succeed in the environment.
d. the tendency to integrate separate elements into increasingly complex higher-order structures.

16. Noticing and thinking about the implications of information and experiences is known as _____. (p. 165)

a. assimilation
b. accommodation
c. equilibration
d. reflective abstraction

17. Adults are able to study an object and form a mental code that represents what they know about this object. They are even able to access this mental code later when the object is no longer available. These abilities are due to the fact that adults are capable of _____. (p. 167)

a. sensorimotor thought
b. symbolic thought
c. semanticity
d. equilibration

18. The idea that language can communicate about a vast range of things instead of being limited to immediate circumstances is known as _____. (p. 172)

a. semanticity
b. productivity
c. displacement
d. shaping

19. The theory that language is an innate human capability is called the (p. 173)

a. social interactionist theory.
b. cognitive developmental theory.
c. learning theory.
d. nativist theory.

COGNITIVE DEVELOPMENT IN INFANTS AND TODDLERS

20. The theory that says that language development is the result of a complex interaction between the child's biological predispositions and social interactions is called the (p. 178)

a. social interactionist theory.
b. cognitive developmental theory.
c. learning theory.
d. nativist theory.

Short-Answer Questions
Answer each question in the space provided.

1. Describe the two techniques outlined in your text for how experiments can be conducted to test infant visual perception. Be sure to include why researchers use the two different techniques.

2. Explain the difference between the constructivist view and the separatist view of intermodal perception.

3. Outline the three key features that distinguish human language.

COGNITIVE DEVELOPMENT IN INFANTS AND TODDLERS

CROSSWORD PUZZLE

Across
1. single words used to express an entire idea or sentence
3. the reduction of response to repeatedly presented stimuli
7. the process of bringing new objects or information into an existing scheme
9. an organized pattern of physical or mental action
10. _____ speech includes only words essential for basic meaning

Down
2. modifying previous schemes or creating new ones in order to fit new information
4. the cognitive process of organizing, coordinating, and interpreting sensory information
5. _____ thought is based on sensory input and physical actions.
6. a system of symbols allowing communication about things distant in time or space
8. _____ perception is the process of combining or integrating information across sensory systems.

"Puzzle created with Puzzlemaker at DiscoverySchool.com"

6 SOCIOEMOTIONAL DEVELOPMENT IN INFANTS AND TODDLERS

Before You Read

This chapter introduces you to the interrelated topics of attachment, temperament, and emotional development. Here you will learn how, and on what basis, early attachment relationships between infants and their primary caregivers are formed. You'll become more familiar with Bowlby's theory of attachment and Harlow's experimental research on attachment in rhesus monkeys. These two developmentalists lay the groundwork for contemporary theory and research on human attachment. You'll see that the quality of attachment bonds that develop during the first year of life set the foundation for later emotional development, and you'll learn about a number of techniques, including Mary Ainsworth's Strange Situation, that are used to assess individuals' attachment styles at different ages. You'll also learn that children's temperaments play a vital role in the development of attachment because children's basic styles of interacting with their environments influence the qualities of their ongoing social interactions and their own emotional experiences. The sections on emotion cover infants' early responses to other people's emotions and the emergence of basic emotions.

Chapter Learning Objectives

After reading this chapter, you should be able to do the following:

- Define attachment and discuss how it is measured today.

- Explain why Bowlby's ethological theory and Harlow's classic primate experiments are considered the scientific roots of modern attachment research.

- Delineate Bowlby's four states of attachment.

- Distinguish stranger anxiety and separation anxiety and explain how they signify attachment.

SOCIOEMOTIONAL DEVELOPMENT IN INFANTS AND TODDLERS

- Outline the steps of the strange situation, explain how it is used to measure infant attachment and describe the different kinds of attachment identified using this procedure.

- Distinguish the characteristics of healthy and less healthy attachment relationships.

- Describe the infant characteristics related to different attachment forms.

- Explain how cultural differences may affect parenting and attachment behavior.

- Discuss the impact of fathers and daycare on attachment.

- Explain how emotional bonds established early in life influence later development.

- Define temperament and describe the behavioral dimensions used as indicators of temperament.

- List and describe the three main temperamental styles that researchers have identified.

- Explain how temperaments form, including the influences of both nature and nurture.

- Explain the usefulness of Rothbart's (1981) temperament questionnaires.

- Describe Kagan's research on shyness.

- Summarize how infants typically interact with one another.

- Outline the basic differences between sensorimotor play and symbolic play.

SOCIOEMOTIONAL DEVELOPMENT IN INFANTS AND TODDLERS

As You Read

Key terms and concepts are essential to your understanding of the chapter. Your ability to logically discuss and analyze pertinent information is dependent upon your knowledge of these concepts. Terms can be found in boldface throughout the chapter and definitions are listed in a glossary of terms at the end of the chapter. Flashcards may be helpful for memorizing definitions. Begin using the terms as you study, incorporating them into your vocabulary.

attachment	insecure—avoidant attachment	separation anxiety
Attachment Q-Sort (AQS)	insecure—disorganized (disoriented) attachment	slow-to-warm-up temperament
contact comfort	insecure—resistant attachment	social referencing
coordinated imitation	mutual gaze	Strange Situation
difficult temperament	secure attachment	stranger anxiety
easy temperament	self-conscious emotions	symbolic play
emotion contagion	sensitive responsiveness	temperament
goodness of fit	sensorimotor play	

⊙ ATTACHMENT

The Story of Attachment Research

1. How do researchers generally define attachment?

2. Why do researchers distinguish between attachment and the layperson's definition of love?

SOCIOEMOTIONAL DEVELOPMENT IN INFANTS AND TODDLERS

3. Take a moment and reread the section in Chapter 1 of your text regarding ethological theory. Discuss how Charles Darwin's idea of natural selection and Konrad Lorenz's concept of imprinting are relevant to John Bowlby's theory of attachment.

4. Describe at least five ways in which infants and children may evoke adults' attachment behaviors.

5. According to Bowlby, an infant's _____ is a powerful elicitor of nurturing behavior in adults.

6. Explain what Bowlby meant when he stated that an attachment figure provides a secure base for the infant.

SOCIOEMOTIONAL DEVELOPMENT IN INFANTS AND TODDLERS

7. Outline Bowlby's four stages of attachment, including a brief description of each stage and its associated age range.

	Stage Name	Brief Description	Age Range
Stage 1			
Stage 2			
Stage 3			
Stage 4			

8. Match the appropriate stage number above with each example written below.

Example	Stage

A. Aunt Louise wants to hold Beatrice, but Beatrice has other ideas. She immediately holds out her arms for her father to take her from Aunt Louise. _____

B. Patrick is content to be held by anybody who has a free moment. He smiles and gazes steadily as adults pass him from one pair of arms to another. _____

C. Juan cries mournfully and inconsolably whenever his mother leaves the room. _____

D. Beth, Tracy's mother, buys groceries every Wednesday with Tracy clinging to her leg. _____

E. Angelique wants her uncle to play in the sandbox with her, but understands he must finish mowing the lawn first. _____

F. Whenever Willie's dad enters the room, Willie grins, laughs, and opens and closes his fists while raising his arms. _____

G. Doreen walks over to investigate the new toys, then runs back to her brother for a hug before approaching the toys again. She looks back continually to see if her brother is watching. _____

SOCIOEMOTIONAL DEVELOPMENT IN INFANTS AND TODDLERS

9. Clearly describe the research procedure that Harry Harlow used to examine attachment in rhesus monkeys. Include a description of Harlow's fear stimulus.

10. Explain why Harlow's research findings were so theoretically compelling at the time. In other words, explain how Harlow's work altered our understanding of the foundation of attachment behavior as postulated by behaviorism and psychoanalytic theory.

Mary Ainsworth and the Strange Situation

1. Imagine that you are the main research assistant working on a study using the Strange Situation. Your job is to make sure the procedure is used correctly.
   Using the outline provided below, describe the actions that occur in each episode of the Strange Situation. What instructions would you give parents? How might their children react?

Episode	Parent's Actions	Possible Infant Reactions
A.		
B.		
C.		
D.		
E.		
F.		
G.		
H.		

SOCIOEMOTIONAL DEVELOPMENT IN INFANTS AND TODDLERS

2. What aspect of the Strange Situation is similar to Harlow's introduction of a fear stimulus?

3. Distinguish between stranger anxiety and separation anxiety. Identify the episodes of the Strange Situation in which each is most likely to occur.

4. Explain why separation anxiety and stranger anxiety are considered positive signs of attachment.

5. What is the most reliable indicator of secure attachment?

6. At several points in Chapter 6, the authors describe various limitations of the Strange Situation procedure that limit its ability to help us better understand human attachment. See if you can identify at least TWO limitations of this procedure. Good for you if you can identify even more!

   A.

   B.

SOCIOEMOTIONAL DEVELOPMENT IN INFANTS AND TODDLERS

7. *Numerically Speaking* of Attachment
   Fill in the blanks with the correct numerical values.

   A. Using the strange situation procedure, approximately _____ percent of infants in the U.S. show signs of secure attachment.

   B. Ainsworth identified _____ patterns of insecure attachment.

   C. Approximately _____ percent of infants studied in the United States display insecure-avoidant attachment and _____ percent show insecure-resistant attachment.

   D. In one study conducted in Sweden, _____ percent of infants whose mothers were diagnosed with schizophrenia displayed multiple indicators of insecure attachment.

   E. At the conclusion of an intervention study with at-risk families, _____ percent of infants in the non-intervention group displayed insecure attachment characteristics, whereas only _____ percent of infants in the home visitation program (i.e., the intervention group) displayed similar insecure attachments.

   F. Cross-cultural comparisons indicate that infants in Great Britain (___ percent) and Sweden (___ percent) tend to be "most securely attached," whereas infants in Chile (___ percent) and Germany (___ percent) tend be "least securely attached."

   G. In comparing _____ infants in _____ studies, researchers have found that the percentages of secure versus insecure attachments was _____ for fathers and _____ for mothers.

8. What infant behaviors are used to identify an insecure–avoidant attachment?

9. Explain the developmental debate regarding interpretation of the infant behaviors you just described.

SOCIOEMOTIONAL DEVELOPMENT IN INFANTS AND TODDLERS

10. What infant behaviors are used to identify an insecure–resistant attachment?

11. Explain why the insecure–resistant attachment category is sometimes labeled "insecure–ambivalent."

12. Name and describe the attachment category that other researchers have added to Ainsworth's original classification scheme.

Parent, Infant, and Cultural Factors in Attachment

1. Each of the following statements is FALSE. Make some change to a part or parts of the statement to make it TRUE.

    A. All of Ainsworth's research was done using the Strange Situation procedure in the lab.

    Change(s):

    B. Caregivers must hold their babies frequently and talk to them a lot to insure the development of a secure attachment.

    Change(s):

SOCIOEMOTIONAL DEVELOPMENT IN INFANTS AND TODDLERS

1. (continued)

    C. Healthy attachments are facilitated when mothers anticipate their infants' needs even before the infants communicate them.

       Change(s):

    D. When parenting is intrusive, overstimulating, or hostile, insecure–resistant attachments are likely to develop.

       Change(s):

    E. Infants who have been frightened by their parents are likely to develop an insecure–avoidant attachment.

       Change(s):

    F. Research indicates that the number of stressors with which a family is dealing does not influence the quality of attachment.

       Change(s):

    G. Interventions programs have not proven successful in influencing quality of attachment bonds.

       Change(s):

    H. Basic personality or temperament is an exceptionally strong predictor of attachment quality.

       Change(s):

    I. Cause-and-effect relations regarding the relative influences of caregiver and infant behaviors on attachment are easy to identify.

       Change(s):

    J. The Strange Situation procedure was originally developed with lower-SES and at-risk families.

       Change(s):

SOCIOEMOTIONAL DEVELOPMENT IN INFANTS AND TODDLERS

2. Being the Teacher: Daycare and Attachment

Imagine that you are teaching an early childhood class and you want your students to be familiar with research concerning the effects of daycare on infant attachment. To prepare for an active debate among your students, YOU need to know all the facts. Outline below research findings that indicate positive effects, negative effects, or negligible effects of daycare on infant attachment.

Positive effects	Negative effects	No discernible effects

Early Attachment and Long-Term Outcomes

1. As your text discusses, Alan Sroufe and Michael Lamb are both interested in understanding how early attachment is related to subsequent behavioral outcomes. Briefly describe Sroufe's research method and summarize his results.

2. Explain why researchers discuss the long-term correlates of early attachment rather than the causal effects of early attachment.

3. Explain how Sroufe and Lamb differ in their underlying assumptions about the ways early attachment influences subsequent behavior.

SOCIOEMOTIONAL DEVELOPMENT IN INFANTS AND TODDLERS

Other Measures of Attachment

1. Describe the Attachment Q-Sort (AQS) method.

2. Compare the AQS with Ainsworth's Strange Situation.

3. What is the main limitation of the AQS?

4. After completing the above assignment, you should easily be able to answer the following questions.

    A. Which assessment uses direct observation of a child to evaluate attachment?

    B. Which device can be used to assess children between 12 months and 5 years of age?

    C. Which assessment measures level of security, dependency, sociability, and social desirability in a child?

    D. Which device does NOT rely on direct observation of children?

    E. Which assessment asks parents, teachers, and other adults to evaluate a child they know?

    F. Which assessment consists of eight strictly scripted episodes?

    G. Which device includes the use of 90 cards containing behavioral descriptions?

SOCIOEMOTIONAL DEVELOPMENT IN INFANTS AND TODDLERS

⊙ TEMPERAMENT

Types of Temperaments

1. Read the section labeled "How Do Different Temperaments Form?" in Chapter 6. What percent of the variation in temperament is due to genetic factors?

2. Now, review Jerome Kagan's assertion in Chapter 2 that some aspects of culture actually may reflect genetic influences. What did he mean?

3. Finally, take a deep breath and explain how these ideas come together in Thomas and Chess's interactionist model.

SOCIOEMOTIONAL DEVELOPMENT IN INFANTS AND TODDLERS

4. The most widely accepted system for classifying temperaments, developed by _____ and _____, identifies the following distinct dimensions of temperament:

   A.   F.

   B.   G.

   C.   H.

   D.   I.

   E.

5. Using these nine distinct dimensions, the researchers identified the following three clusters of temperament characteristics:

Cluster	Description	Percent of population
The _____ child		
The _____ child		
The _____ child		

6. Think about your own behavior during early childhood (or rely on your caregivers' reports). Do you think you fall easily into one of these constellations? If so, which one?

7. Give examples of the behavior that would place you in that category. If you don't think you fit neatly into one of these categories (and 35 percent of children do not!), describe the individual temperament dimensions on which you think you would score highest. Can you give your own unique cluster a name?

SOCIOEMOTIONAL DEVELOPMENT IN INFANTS AND TODDLERS

8. If there is an infant in your life, take the opportunity to test out Thomas and Chess's temperament model for yourself. Can you identify specific dimensions on which the infant would score low, medium, or high? From there, can you identify a particular cluster that seems to fit best?

9. Remember the early childhood class you are teaching? Now you want to explain the concept of "goodness of fit."

10. Next, give clear examples of the following situations.

    A. A good fit between caregiver(s) and child:

    B. A poor fit between caregiver(s) and child:

    C. A match between caregiver(s) and child:

    D. A complementary fit between caregiver(s) and child:

11. Circle T for TRUE or F for FALSE in these two statements regarding consistency in temperament over time.

    A. T F Measurements of individuals' temperaments are highly consistent over time.

    B. T F Because it is genetically based, temperament is unaffected by environmental conditions.

SOCIOEMOTIONAL DEVELOPMENT IN INFANTS AND TODDLERS

Other Approaches to Temperament

1. Briefly discuss the two temperament questionnaires developed by Mary Rothbart.

    A.

    B.

2. What is a primary advantage in using a questionnaire rather than an interview?

3. Using Table 6.5 in your text, describe the degree of consistency between data gathered using Rothbart's questionnaires and data gathered using Thomas and Chess's method.

4. Describe Kagan's longitudinal research on shyness. Include in your description a summary of the changes Kagan observed among his young participants from 16 weeks of age to 2 years, to 4 years, and to adolescence.

5. Explain what Kagan means when he states that shy children have a genetic predisposition to shyness. What evidence does he use to support this statement?

SOCIOEMOTIONAL DEVELOPMENT IN INFANTS AND TODDLERS

⊙ EMOTION

Infant Responses to Emotions

1. Place an X beside each of the following statements that is an accurate reflection of a newborn's emotional life.

    ___ Newborns have the capacity to be emotionally influenced by other individuals.

    ___ Newborns cannot distinguish between different sources of crying and respond to all sources similarly.

    ___ Newborns can intentionally produce certain facial expressions.

    ___ Newborns can imitate specific facial expressions modeled by adults.

    ___ Newborns respond differently to happy faces than to faces showing no emotion.

    ___ Newborns can distinguish among anger, sadness, and fear.

    ___ Newborns rely more on their interpretation of other people's vocal expressions of emotion than on other people's facial expressions.

2. Research indicates that infants as young as 4 months of age can correctly interpret the emotions underlying other people's facial expressions of joy, anger, surprise, and sadness. How have researchers obtained evidence of these early infant abilities? Specifically, describe the visual cliff procedure used by Sorce, Emde, Campos, and Klinnert (1985).

SOCIOEMOTIONAL DEVELOPMENT IN INFANTS AND TODDLERS

Basic Emotions

Identify the typical age at which each of the following emotional skills develops.

	Typical Age	Emotional Ability or Skill
A.	_____	display negative emotions to discomfort
B.	_____	imitate other people's facial expression
C.	_____	respond differently to different facial expressions of emotion
D.	_____	respond differently to different vocal expressions of emotion
E.	_____	display evidence of envy and guilt
F.	_____	smile in response to pleasurable physical stimulation
G.	_____	display happiness in interacting with caregivers
H.	_____	show fear of strangers

⊙ SOCIAL RELATIONS AND PLAY

1. Give an example and typical age ranges for each of these types of play.

Type of Play	Example	Typical Age Range
A. Sensorimotor		
B. Symbolic		

SOCIOEMOTIONAL DEVELOPMENT IN INFANTS AND TODDLERS

2. After reading the material in your text regarding children's early play behavior, try to think of activities or games that would promote children's social or cognitive development at each of the following ages. Then, briefly explain why you think the activity or game would be effective.

Age Group	Activity or Game	Explanation
0 – 3 months		
3 – 6 months		
6 – 9 months		
9 – 12 months		
12 – 18 months		
18 – 24 months		
2 to 3 years		

SOCIOEMOTIONAL DEVELOPMENT IN INFANTS AND TODDLERS

When You Have Finished

◉ Working the Web

1. Attachment Parenting International (www.attachmentparenting.org/) describes itself as an organization based in the fields of child development and child psychology. After carefully reading Chapter 6, visit this Web site and critically evaluate the extent to which the information being conveyed is consistent with research described in your text. Is API an accurate and useful application of attachment theory or is this "pop psychology"?

2. Don't miss this one!! The International Attachment Network (www.attachmentnetwork.org) has a mission "promoting knowledge and understanding of attachment theory." You can find answers to the following questions:

    Are attachment and bonding the same thing?
    What is the ethological theory of attachment?
    Is skin-to-skin contact essential for bonding to take place?
    What is attachment parenting?

3. Reactive Attachment Disorder (RAD) is a relatively new disorder of childhood first described in the *Diagnostic and Statistical Manual* (DSM-III) in 1980. As you can see from a quick Internet search, there is an enormous amount of information regarding this disorder. How do you know what is accurate? You might start by reading the DSM criteria at www.behavenet.com/capsules/disorders/reactatt.htm. After you've read this material, explain why RAD is considered a disorder of attachment.

4. Will a robot ever be able to pass the Strange Situation test? Go to www.csl.sony.fr/General/Publications/BibliographyItem.php?reference=kaplan%3A01f and download the Adobe Acrobat file to read an article about an experimental procedure designed to "measure the attachment of a robot to its master." This intriguing paper purports to "build bridges between robotics, psychology, and ethology." Does thinking about the attachment process from this perspective alter your thinking about human attachment and social bonds?

5. Visit www.ai.mit.edu/projects/sociable/emotions.html to see how research on human emotional development is being applied to the field of artificial intelligence (AI). You'll meet and interact with Kismet, a robot who displays different emotions and responds to social interaction in very human ways. Can you see how knowledge of human emotional and social development was used in Kismet's creation?

SOCIOEMOTIONAL DEVELOPMENT IN INFANTS AND TODDLERS

6. For an interesting handout on "Temperament Types and Traits," visit www.headstartinfo.org/pdf/infant-toddler_transitions/Handout5.pdf. Do you think you would have been classified as a "flexible," "feisty," or "fearful" child? If possible, have someone who knew you as a child read through the handout. Would they agree with your assessment?

7. How might you create an outdoor play space for infants and toddlers? What considerations would you give to types of play and social interaction? Go to www.earlylearning.ubc.ca/CHILD/research_child_outdoorplay.htm for ideas.

SOCIOEMOTIONAL DEVELOPMENT IN INFANTS AND TODDLERS

⊙ PRACTICE TEST #1

Multiple Choice Questions
For each question, circle the best answer from the choices given.

1. An enduring emotional tie that forms between an infant and another person is called (p. 190)

    a. sensitive responsiveness.
    b. attachment.
    c. temperament.
    d. self conscious emotions.

2. Which developmental theorist(s) believed attachment comes from traits and behaviors which evolved to increase the infant's chances of survival? (p. 190)

    a. Thomas and Chess
    b. Kagan
    c. Bowlby
    d. Rothbart

3. Sarah, who is 13 months old, has a soft blanket she holds when she goes to bed. Sarah also takes it to day care for nap time. According to Harlow, the blanket provides her with (p. 191)

    a. contact comfort.
    b. safe base attachment.
    c. sensitive responsiveness.
    d. all of the above

4. What is measured by Ainsworth's Strange Situation? (p. 193)

    a. temperament
    b. self conscious emotions
    c. orientation with discrimination
    d. Attachment
    e.

5. Erica is a new mother. When her newborn son cries, she goes to check on him. Erica talks to him is a soothing voice, checks his diaper and rearranges his blanket. Erica is displaying (p. 196)

    a. indulgent parenting.
    b. surrogate parenting.
    c. sensitive responsiveness.
    d. insecure attachment.

SOCIOEMOTIONAL DEVELOPMENT IN INFANTS AND TODDLERS

6. Which of the following statements is FALSE? (p. 199)

a. Infants who are securely attached to their mothers tend to have insecure attachments to their fathers.
b. The type of attachment shown by an infant tends to be consistent between the infant's parents.
c. Infants are as likely to form secure attachments with their fathers as with their mothers.
d. Both b and c are false.

7. Besides the Strange Situation, another measure of infant attachment is the (p. 202)

a. Harlow Attachment Scale.
b. Thomas and Chess Test.
c. Kagan Attachment Measure.
d. Attachment Q Sort.

8. All of the following are dimensions of temperament developed by Alexander Thomas and Stella Chess EXCEPT (p. 204)

a. adaptability
b. goodness of fit
c. distractibility
d. attention span

9. Rasheed is 11 months old. His mother describes him as a good baby. Rasheed is usually happy and is consistent with when he eats and sleeps. What type of temperament would Rasheed be classified as having? (p. 205)

a. easy
b. slow to warm up
c. secure
d. difficult

10. What did Kagan find in his research on shyness in children? (p. 207 - 208)

a. As they grow up, shy children usually enjoy a great deal of sensory stimulation.
b. Infants who were calm when presented with new stimuli became shy children.
c. Children with low thresholds for arousal tend to react more intensely to unfamiliar stimuli.
d. Shy children show lower heart rates than other children.

SOCIOEMOTIONAL DEVELOPMENT IN INFANTS AND TODDLERS

⊙ PRACTICE TEST #2

Multiple Choice Questions
For each question, circle the best answer from the choices given.

1. The tendency of an infant to copy the emotional state of another is called (p. 209)

a. sensitive responsiveness.
b. self conscious emotion.
c. coordinated imitation.
d. emotional contagion.

2. One year old Brian is starting to walk by himself. He falls as he is walking to the door. Brian immediately looks to his mother, who smiles at him. Brian picks himself up without crying. Brian is demonstrating (p. 210)

a. social referencing.
b. a difficult temperament.
c. goodness of fit.
d. an insecure attachment.

3. Which of the following is a self conscious emotion? (p. 211)

a. surprise
b. anger
c. shame
d. joy

4. Sammy and Joseph are both 5 months old. When their mothers place them near each other they are likely to engage in (p. 212)

a. coordinated imitation.
b. mutual gaze.
c. symbolic play.
d. all of the above.

5. Infants repeating actions using their own bodies is (p. 213)

a. coordinated imitation.
b. social referencing.
c. the first noticeable signs of play.
d. an indication of an easy temperament.

SOCIOEMOTIONAL DEVELOPMENT IN INFANTS AND TODDLERS

6. Four month old Roberto is in his crib. He reaches for a stuffed animal and tries to put it in his mouth. He laughs and tries again. Roberto is displaying (p. 213)

a. sensorimotor play.
b. symbolic play.
c. coordinated imitation.
d. social referencing.

7. Caitlin and Lauren are both 2 years old. Caitlin puts a teddy bear on her head and runs around the room. Lauren takes another stuffed animal, puts it on her head and runs behind Caitlin. The two girls look at each other and laugh. These toddlers are engaged in (p. 215)

a. symbolic play.
b. coordinated imitation.
c. self conscious emotions.
d. contact comfort.

8. Which of the following is the main reason toddlers choose a child as a playmate? (p. 215)

a. The child is available to play.
b. The child has interesting toys.
c. The child is nearby.
d. All of the above are important reasons.

9. What is the most common cause for conflicts between toddlers? (p. 215)

a. different temperament types
b. struggles over toys
c. a lack of goodness of fit
d. one child does not have sensitive responsiveness

10. Nathan sits on a chair and pretends to fish, using a mop as his fishing pole. Nathan is demonstrating (p. 216)

a. sensorimotor play.
b. coordinated imitation.
c. social referencing.
d. symbolic play.

SOCIOEMOTIONAL DEVELOPMENT IN INFANTS AND TODDLERS

⊙ COMPREHENSIVE PRACTICE TEST

Multiple Choice Questions
For each question, circle the best answer from the choices given.

1. Developmental researchers refer to the love between an infant and its caregiver as (p. 190)

   a. sensitive responsiveness.
   b. attachment.
   c. temperament.
   d. emotional contagion.

2. Kevin is 6 weeks old. When he is hungry, he cries. Whether his mother, father, grandmother or babysitter comes in to feed him, he responds happily. According to Bowlby, what stage of attachment is he in? (p. 191)

   a. orientation without discrimination
   b. orientation with discrimination
   c. safe-base attachment
   d. goal-corrected partnership

3. Between 6 months and 2 years old, most children display (p. 194)

   a. symbolic play.
   b. preoperational thinking.
   c. stranger anxiety.
   d. two or three different temperament types.

4. In the Strange Situation, the mother leaves and her infant cries, and seeks contact with the mother upon her return. This describes what type of attachment? (p. 194)

   a. Insecure-Avoidant
   b. Insecure-Resistant
   c. Insecure-Disorganized
   d. Secure

5. Parenting that is abusive, or parents who have suffered childhood traumas, are more likely to have children with which type of attachment? (p. 197)

   a. insecure-disorganized
   b. insecure-avoidant
   c. insecure-resistant
   d. none of the above

SOCIOEMOTIONAL DEVELOPMENT IN INFANTS AND TODDLERS

6. Infants with which type of attachment tend to cry less, greet their mothers more positively and initiate more physical contact with their mothers? (p. 197)

a. insecure-disorganized
b. insecure-avoidant
c. insecure-resistant
d. secure

7. Which of the following statements is TRUE? (p. 199 – 200)

a. Day care has a negative effect on attachment in infants.
b. Day care in itself does not have a negative effect on attachment.
c. The amount of time infants spend in day care influences their attachment.
d. Attachment is decreased in infants who begin day care before they are 6 months old.

8. Preschool aged children who had been securely attached as infants were compared to insecurely attached children. The securely attached preschoolers were observed to be (p. 201)

a. happier.
b. more popular with their peers.
c. more empathetic.
d. all of the above.

9. An important limitation of the Attachment Q-Sort is it (p. 202)

a. is limited to infants between 6 and 12 months old.
b. is designed for children who can answer the questions.
c. does not involve a direct observation of the child.
d. requires ratings from both a parent and a day care provider.

10. A child's typical pattern of reacting to the environment is his/her (p. 204)

a. temperament
b. attachment type
c. goodness of fit
d. threshold of responsiveness

SOCIOEMOTIONAL DEVELOPMENT IN INFANTS AND TODDLERS

11. Suki is almost a year old. She is usually in a good mood and adapts well to changes. Her mother can always predict when Suki will want to be fed and will fall asleep for her nap. Most likely, Suki's temperament is (p. 205)

a. secure
b. easy
c. slow to warm up
d. difficult

12. Thomas and Chess called the match between a child's temperament and his/her environment (p. 206)

a. attachment type.
b. sensitive responsiveness.
c. goodness of fit.
d. coordinated imitation.

13. From Kagan's work, he hypothesized that one of the main causes of shyness in young children is (p. 208)

a. early trauma.
b. role modeling by parents.
c. damage to the hippocampus.
d. genetic.

14. The tendency of emotional cues displayed by one person to cause similar emotions in another person is called (p. 299)

a. emotional contagion
b. self-conscious emotion
c. coordinated imitation
d. sensitive responsiveness

15. While Nina's mother is answering the door, Nina climbs onto the kitchen counter and accidentally knocks over a glass, which breaks. Which **self-conscious** emotion is Nina likely to experience? (p. 211)

a. sadness
b. anger
c. guilt
d. surprise

SOCIOEMOTIONAL DEVELOPMENT IN INFANTS AND TODDLERS

16. Compared to infants with little exposure to peers, infants who have more exposure tend to (p. 213)

a. be more aggressive with their peers.
b. show more frequency in their social interactions.
c. display shyness.
d. have less social skills with peers.

17. Infants engage in a type of play that involves using their senses and developing their movement capabilities. This type of play is called (p. 213)

a. sociodramatic.
b. symbolic.
c. temperamental.
d. sensorimotor.

18. Two toddlers, Jasmine and Jenna, are playing in a wading pool. Jasmine fills a pail with water and dumps it on her own head. Jenna takes another pail and does the same thing. The two girls watch each other and laugh. They are engaged in (p. 215)

a. coordinated imitation.
b. symbolic play.
c. associative play.
d. cooperative play.

19. Ivan and Aaron are both 2 ½. They are playing together at day care when they begin fighting. What is the MOST LIKELY cause of their conflict? (p. 215)

a. Ivan does not want Aaron imitating him.
b. They are struggling over a toy.
c. Aaron wants to engage in sensorimotor play.
d. They do not have goodness of fit.

20. At what age does early symbolic play first appear? (p. 216)

a. 6 months
b. 9 months
c. 12 – 14 months
d. 18 – 24 months

SOCIOEMOTIONAL DEVELOPMENT IN INFANTS AND TODDLERS

Short-Answer Questions
Answer each question in the space provided.

How did Ainsworth's research build on Bowlby's theory? How did her observations of stranger and separation anxiety support the ethological theory?

Your niece is now 2 years old. She has a slow to warm up temperament. Describe her behavior using at least 4 of the dimensions of temperament outlined by Thomas and Chess.

Describe how toddlers interact with their peers. Include the types of activities toddlers enjoy and how their symbolic play develops.

SOCIOEMOTIONAL DEVELOPMENT IN INFANTS AND TODDLERS

Crossword Puzzle

Across
1. _____ play involves the use of make-believe and pretending to embellish objects or actions.
4. Intent eye contact between two people is referred to as _____ gaze.
5. _____ responsiveness is a quality of infant care in which caregivers respond quickly and warmly to a baby's signals.
7. an emotional tie to someone that endures across space and time
8. _____ anxiety is experienced by infants when parted from their primary caregivers.

Down
1. In uncertain situations, _____ referencing is the tendency of infants and children to look for emotional cues from caregivers.
2. Emotion _____ is the tendency of emotional cues displayed by one person to generate similar states in others.
3. a child's behavioral style
6. _____ anxiety is the wariness or fear of unfamiliar adults.
8. A structured laboratory procedure used to observe attachment behavior in infants is called the _____ Situation.

"Puzzle created with Puzzlemaker at DiscoverySchool.com"

7 PHYSICAL DEVELOPMENT IN EARLY CHILDHOOD

Before You Read

From the age of three to the age of six, we see many changes in physical development. Growth during this period is not as rapid as in infancy or in the adolescent stage to come. Yet, eating habits and diet in early childhood can affect growth in later years. In this chapter, you will discover the main trends in brain development for this age range, including the proliferation of glial cells, continued synaptic pruning, and the processes of experience-expectant and experience-dependent development. Additionally, you will learn about the progress of both gross- and fine-motor development, the trends in physical activity patterns, and the main safety issues seen in early childhood. Finally, the chapter concludes with a discussion of child maltreatment sources and effects.

Chapter Learning Objectives

After reading this chapter, you should be able to do the following:

- Describe the changes in height that children experience between the toddler years and early childhood.

- Identify the changes in body proportion seen between toddlers and young children.

- Discuss the gender differences in physical development during early childhood.

- Outline the four components of a healthy diet.

- Define malnutrition and discuss both its short- and long-term effects.

PHYSICAL DEVELOPMENT IN EARLY CHILDHOOD

- List the major changes in the growth and development of the brain during the early childhood years.

- List the two types of brain development described by Greenough and Black (1999) and discuss how experience influences the developing brain.

- Identify the larger developmental patterns in the brain during early childhood, especially in the occipital, temporal, and frontal lobes.

- Outline the advances in gross-motor development and the increases in fine-motor development during this period.

- Note the pertinent research about physical activity and exercise during early childhood.

- Describe the major effects of cerebral palsy.

- List the major causes of death in children ages one to four.

- Discuss six things parents can do to better protect children during early childhood.

- Note the four main elements of child maltreatment.

- Summarize information regarding the prevalence of child abuse in the United States, including information on individuals who are most likely to be abused or commit abuse.

- Compare and contrast the effects of physical abuse with those of neglect.

PHYSICAL DEVELOPMENT IN EARLY CHILDHOOD

As You Read

Key terms and concepts are essential to your understanding of the chapter. Your ability to logically discuss and analyze pertinent information is dependent upon your knowledge of these concepts. Terms can be found in boldface throughout the chapter and definitions are listed in a glossary of terms at the end of the chapter. Flashcards may be helpful for memorizing definitions. Begin using the terms as you study, incorporating them into your vocabulary.

cerebral palsy (CP)	Individuals with Disabilities Education Act (IDEA)	neglect
child maltreatment	infantile amnesia	palmar grasp
compulsive compliance	*kwashiorkor*	physical abuse
experience-dependent development	locomotor skills	psychological abuse
experience-expectant development	malnutrition	sexual abuse
glial cells	mature tripod grasp	synaptic pruning

⊙ GROWTH OF THE BODY AND BRAIN

Physical Growth

Read each of the following statements carefully, then underline the word(s) in parentheses that will make the statement correct.

1. On average, children will have gained (50/70) percent of their adult height by six years of age.

2. Compared to overall growth in infancy, children between the ages of three and six grow (slower/faster).

3. During early childhood, youngsters gain about (5 ½/8 ½) pounds per year.

4. Boys and girls are similar in size and shape at this age, however (boys/girls) have slightly more muscle mass and thicker bones.

5. Height increases approximately (2 to 3/4 to 5) inches per year during early childhood.

6. By the age of six, children have gained (⅓/⅔) of their adult weight.

PHYSICAL DEVELOPMENT IN EARLY CHILDHOOD

Nutrition

1. Match each of the following nutrition-related terms with the appropriate descriptors. Each term may be used more than once.

    A. proteins

    B. carbohydrates

    C. fats

    D. minerals and vitamins

    _____ provide our bodies with amino acids, the building blocks of growth

    _____ help maintain normal body growth and functions

    _____ an important source of fuel for the body

    _____ supply energy for muscle activity and the generation of body heat

    _____ contribute to the formation of body insulation, giving protection from environmental temperature fluctuations

    _____ are necessary to support new growth in the body

2. Define malnutrition.

3. Discuss the short- and long-term effects of malnutrition.

4. Compare and contrast the rate of malnutrition in the United States and in developing countries.

PHYSICAL DEVELOPMENT IN EARLY CHILDHOOD

Growth and Development of the Brain

1. Define and describe glial cells. What functions do they serve in the nervous system?

2. Compare and contrast synaptic pruning and programmed cell death.

3. Listed below are a group of experiences and activities. Decide whether each is an experience-expectant development or an experience-dependent development, then place an X in the correct space.

Experience/Activity	experience-expectant	experience-dependent
A. attachment to a caregiver	_____	_____
B. communication by speech	_____	_____
C. vocabulary of a particular language	_____	_____
D. riding a unicycle	_____	_____
E. waving goodbye	_____	_____
F. hand-eye coordination	_____	_____
G. mastering long division	_____	_____
H. recognition of the human face	_____	_____

PHYSICAL DEVELOPMENT IN EARLY CHILDHOOD

4. Label the areas of the brain identified in the diagram below. Then, using the statements below, match the development to the area of the brain in which it occurs.

A. _____ lobe

B. _____ lobe

C. _____ lobe

D. _____ lobe

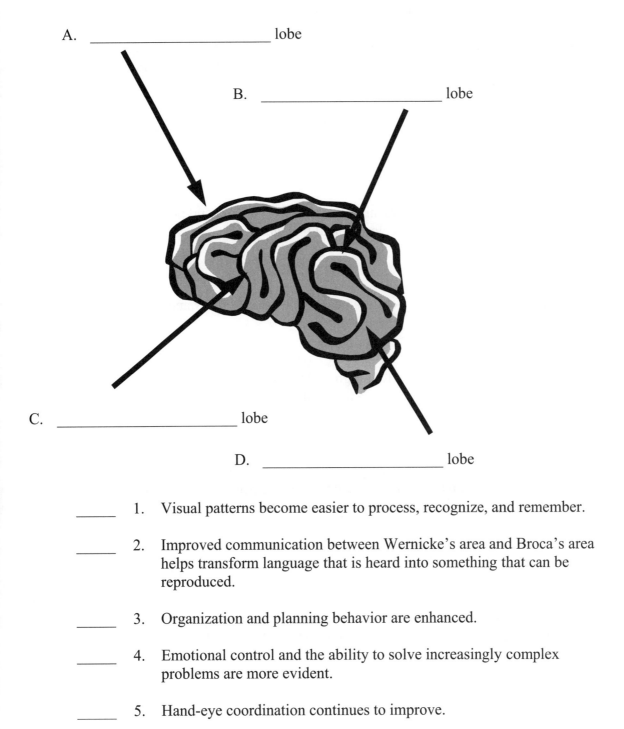

_____ 1. Visual patterns become easier to process, recognize, and remember.

_____ 2. Improved communication between Wernicke's area and Broca's area helps transform language that is heard into something that can be reproduced.

_____ 3. Organization and planning behavior are enhanced.

_____ 4. Emotional control and the ability to solve increasingly complex problems are more evident.

_____ 5. Hand-eye coordination continues to improve.

PHYSICAL DEVELOPMENT IN EARLY CHILDHOOD

⊙ MOTOR DEVELOPMENT AND PHYSICAL ACTIVITY

Gross-Motor and Fine-Motor Development

1. Fill in the blanks to make each of the following statements regarding gross-motor development correct. Circle GM or FM to indicate whether the statement refers to gross-motor or fine-motor skills.

    A. Around the age of _____, children are able to use their leg muscles to peddle a tricycle.

    GM   or   FM

    B. Working easy buttons, washing their hands and face, and pouring a drink from a pitcher are skills that develop around the age of _____.

    GM   or   FM

    C. By the age of _____, children can walk for a short distance on a balance beam.

    GM   or   FM

    D. In order to jump about a foot high and hop 8 to 10 times on one foot, a child must be approximately _____ years of age.

    GM   or   FM

    E. The _____ _____ _____, in which a child places the base of their hand on the writing surface, holds the pencil with the index finger and thumb, and moves the wrist along with the fingers, emerges at about the age of _____.

    GM   or   FM

2. How are experience-expectant and experience-dependent patterns of brain development related to gross-motor and fine-motor development?

PHYSICAL DEVELOPMENT IN EARLY CHILDHOOD

Physical Activity and Exercise

1. Discuss the recommended levels of physical activity suggested by the National Association for Sport and Physical Education. How many children achieve these goals?

2. What gender differences exist in physical activity and exercise during early childhood?

Cerebral Palsy

1. Define cerebral palsy and describe the generalized symptoms.

2. Fill in the blanks below to complete a brief summary of the causes of cerebral palsy.

   Cerebral palsy is a serious disorder, but it is important to remember it is not a disease. It was first medically described during the decade of the _____s. About _____ new cases are diagnosed each year in the United States. In approximately _____ percent of these cases the brain damage occurs during prenatal development and may not be noticed until several months after birth. _____ and/or severe pressure on the baby's head during the birth process are responsible for about _____ percent of the cases. In the remaining 10 percent of the cases, the damage occurs during the first few years of life, typically due to _____, _____, or_____.

PHYSICAL DEVELOPMENT IN EARLY CHILDHOOD

⊙ HEALTH AND SAFETY ISSUES

Childhood Deaths and Safety Issues

Being the Teacher
You have been appointed the chairperson for this month's parent and teacher program, "Safety at Home." Using the text and other sources as your guide, prepare a flyer for use during your presentation and for quick reference when taken home by the parent.

Child Maltreatment: Abuse and Neglect

1. Define child maltreatment.

2. Now, using the table below, identify the four main types of child maltreatment. For each type, identify the most likely victim and the most likely abuser.

Type of Maltreatment	Most Likely Victim	Most Likely Perpetrator
A.		
B.		
C.		
D.		

3. Each of the following statements is FALSE. Make some change to a part or parts of the statement to make it TRUE.

   A. In a national survey, 14 percent of parents reported that they use objects to hit or spank their children.

   Change(s):

   B. Most abuse falls within one of the above categories of maltreatment with little or no overlap.

   Change(s):

PHYSICAL DEVELOPMENT IN EARLY CHILDHOOD

3. Continued

   C. In the United States, only those individuals who are licensed to work with children must report any suspected case of child maltreatment to child protection authorities or police.

   Change(s):

   D. Of the approximately 906,000 cases of child maltreatment in 2003, physical abuse is by far the most frequently reported type of maltreatment.

   Change(s):

   E. Overall maltreatment rates are highest for those in the early childhood years from ages three to six.

   Change(s):

   F. In cases of physical abuse, boys are more likely than girls to be abused in all age ranges.

   Change(s):

   G. In 2003, the rates of child maltreatment were highest in the Asian community, closely followed by the Hispanic ethic group.

   Change(s):

   H. Fathers are twice as likely to commit acts of physical abuse and neglect as mothers.

   Change(s):

   I. Of the 1,500 fatalities caused by child abuse or neglect in 2003, three-quarters of the deaths were caused by extended family members or strangers.

   Change(s):

PHYSICAL DEVELOPMENT IN EARLY CHILDHOOD

Effects of Abuse and Neglect

1. Compare and contrast the effects of physical abuse and neglect on children's outcomes by indicating whether or not each of the following problems has been identified with each specific form of abuse.

	Physical Abuse	Neglect
Insecure attachments		
Aggression and hostility		
Risk for suicide		
Depression		
Compulsive compliance		
Language delays		
Poor academic performance		
Lower IQ		
Poor impulse control		
Drug abuse		
Social withdrawal		

2. *Numerically Speaking* of Abuse and Neglect
   Fill in the blanks with the correct numerical values.

   A. According to various studies, between ____ and ____ percent of abused infants show insecure attachments with their caregivers.

   B. Of those children physically abused or neglected, about ____ percent grow up to abuse or neglect their own children.

   C. Children who experience physical abuse are sometimes compulsively compliant, trying hard not to anger the abuser. This pattern is most noticeable in children aged ____ to ____.

   D. Physically abused children score an average of ____ points lower on IQ tests and about ____ years below their grade level on standardized verbal and mathematical tests.

PHYSICAL DEVELOPMENT IN EARLY CHILDHOOD

After You Have Finished

⊙ Working the Web

1. This Science Net links web site, at www.sciencenetlinks.com/lessons.cfm?BenchmarkID=6&DOCID=346, gives an example of a lesson plan and activities for teaching students about "the stages of human growth and development that take place during infancy and early childhood." Use your text and this information to improve upon a lesson plan you could deliver to students of a particular age group.

2. You might want to join Zero to Three (www.zerotothree.org), a group devoted to supporting "the healthy development and well-being of infants, toddlers and their families." Enter "On the Move" in the search box and read "On the Move: The Power of Movement in Your Child's First Three Years," by download through Adobe Acrobat. There is also a section of frequently asked questions and interesting activities.

3. For a good overview of fine- and gross-motor development in children, take a look at Tufts Open CourseWare "A Look at Motor Development in Children" (ocw.tufts.edu/Content/35/lecturenotes/375738). The section on the common gross motor skills of early childhood offers an interesting look at what to expect developmentally in walking, running, kicking, and jumping skills.

4. Check out the web site at www.public.asu.edu/~shannonr/Lab1.htm and look at two interesting lab assignments for assessing the development of fine- and gross-motor control. You'll find helpful observation check lists for grasping development, and for running, jumping, galloping, and skipping.

5. Use information from your text and from the internet to create a frequently asked questions (FAQ) sheet for adults and children on the topic of cerebral palsy. Use the following web sites for assistance:
    www.ucp.org
    www.ninds.nih.gov/disorders/cerebral_palsy/cerebral_palsy.htm
    www.about-cerebral-palsy.org

6. An excellent place to start learning more about childhood safety issues is at the U.S. Consumer Product Safety Commission (www.cpsc.gov/about/about.html). Click on the "Especially for Kids" section and meet Kidd Safety, learn about safety on scooters and bicycles, and play challenging safety games.

PHYSICAL DEVELOPMENT IN EARLY CHILDHOOD

⊙ PRACTICE TEST #1

Multiple Choice Questions
For each question, circle the best answer from the choices given.

1. What is the average increase in height, per year, during early childhood? (p. 226)

   a. 1 inch or less
   b. 2 – 3 inches
   c. 4 – 5 inches
   d. 6 – 7 inches

2. How do children's body proportions change in early childhood? (p. 227)

   a. Their heads become smaller relative to the rest of their bodies.
   b. Their chest and legs become longer.
   c. Their stomachs are flatter and they are trimmer.
   d. all of the above

3. Which of the following regions has the largest percentage of children under 5 who are malnourished? (p. 229)

   a. South Asia
   b. West Africa
   c. East Africa
   d. Central America

4. Kwashiorkor is (p. 230)

   a. an inability to remember things and events that occurred before age 3 or 4.
   b. a disorder caused by damage to the area of the brain which controls movement.
   c. a disease caused by lack of protein in the diet.
   d. a leading cause of death in Europe.

5. The specialized cells in the nervous system that support nerve cells are called (p. 230)

   a. glial cells.
   b. temporal lobe cells.
   c. experience-dependent cells.
   d. cephalocaudal cells.

PHYSICAL DEVELOPMENT IN EARLY CHILDHOOD

6. The process in which unused synapses are lost is called   (p. 230)

a. proximodistal development.
b. kwashiorkor.
c. synaptogenesis.
d. synaptic pruning.

7. The development of universal skills in which excess synapses form and then are pruned according to a child's individual experience is called (p. 231)

a. experience-dependent development.
b. experience-expectant development.
c. glial cell production.
d. synaptogenesis.

8. Yuri is a young child in Russia. Learning new words in Russian, his native language, requires which type of development? (p. 232)

a. occipital lobe
b. cephalocaudal
c. experience-dependent
d. experience-expectant

9. What type of learning is associated with growth in the temporal lobes of the brain in early childhood? (p. 233)

a. language
b. fine motor
c. locomotor
d. visual

10. Which lobes of the brain are responsible for organizing and planning behavior?   (p. 233)

a. temporal lobes
b. occipital lobes
c. parietal lobes
d. frontal lobes

PHYSICAL DEVELOPMENT IN EARLY CHILDHOOD

⊙ PRACTICE TEST #2

Multiple Choice Questions
For each question, circle the best answer from the choices given.

1. Skills used to move around, such as walking, running and climbing are called (p. 235)

    a. palmar grasp skills.
    b. fine motor skills.
    c. locomotor skills.
    d. none of the abov.e

2. Which of the following is an example of a fine motor skill? (p. 236)

    a. pedaling a tricycle
    b. tying shoelaces
    c. hitting a ball with a bat
    d. jumping off a step

3. In a study of physical activity in children aged 3 to 5, what percentage of their activity was rated as moderate to vigorous? (p. 238)

    a. 20%
    b. 40%
    c. 60%
    d. 90%

4. Cerebral palsy is a serious disorder of (p. 239)

    a. cognitive development.
    b. emotional development.
    c. language development.
    d. motor development.

5. Seventy percent of cases of cerebral palsy are caused by (p. 239)

    a. brain damage during prenatal development.
    b. lack of oxygen to the brain during birth.
    c. brain damage caused by head injuries before age 2.
    d. negligence by doctors.

PHYSICAL DEVELOPMENT IN EARLY CHILDHOOD

6. In the U.S., the rate of death is highest for (p. 242)

a. infants under age 1.
b. toddlers between 1 and 3 years old.
c. young children between 4 and 7 years old.
d. school aged children between 5 and 14 years old.

7. Which of the following statements about physical abuse is TRUE? (p. 243)

a. Spanking children, in the U.S., is considered physical abuse.
b. In a national survey, 50% of parents said they had physically abused their children.
c. Most cases are unintentional and result from punishment that got out of hand.
d. Physical abuse is the most common type of child maltreatment.

8. Ashley is 6 years old. She doesn't attend school regularly and wanders around her neighborhood alone. Sometimes she goes to her next door neighbor's home to ask for a sandwich. Which type of maltreatment is Ashley experiencing? (p. 244)

a. psychological abuse
b. neglect
c. physical abuse
d. none of the above

9. What do children who are physically abused learn from their parents? (p. 246)

a. aggression
b. fear
c. to use violence to solve conflicts
d. all of the above

10. Some physically abused children show a behavior pattern of trying to please adults and not being disobedient or oppositional. This is called (p. 247)

a. infantile amnesia.
b. compulsive compliance.
c. obedience compliance.
d normal.

PHYSICAL DEVELOPMENT IN EARLY CHILDHOOD

⊙ COMPREHENSIVE PRACTICE TEST

Multiple Choice Questions
For each question, circle the best answer from the choices given.

1. Gabriela is 6 years old. If she is average for her age, what percentage of her adult height is she? (p. 226)

a. 40%
b. 60%
c. 70%
d. 90%

2. Which of the following statements about physical growth in the early childhood years is FALSE? (p. 226 – 227)

a. Most children gain a great deal of "baby fat" during early childhood.
b. Children are not growing as fast as they did during infancy.
c. Gender differences in physical growth are minimal during this period of development.
d. Children's bones become thicker and they gain muscle mass.

3. Stunted growth and lower intelligence are side effects of (p.229)

a. obesity.
b. malnutrition.
c. synaptogenesis.
d. synaptic pruning.

4. In the U.S., how many children under age 17 are believed to not have adequate supplies of food? (p. 229)

a. 10 – 12 million
b. 8 million
c. 6 million
d. 3 – 4 million

5. When are most nerve cells in the brain formed? (p. 230)

a. midway during pregnancy
b. near the end of pregnancy
c. between birth and 3 months old
d. from 1 to 2 years old

PHYSICAL DEVELOPMENT IN EARLY CHILDHOOD

6. Providing nourishment to brain cells, removing waste products and forming the myelin sheath are functions of (p. 230)

a. the occipital lobe.
b. pruning cells.
c. glial cells.
d. synaptogenesis.

7. Which of the following statements is TRUE? (p. 231)

a. Genetics does not affect synaptogenesis.
b. There do not appear to be any critical periods for synapse production and pruning.
c. Pruning synapses results in lowered intelligence.
d. Recent research shows that new neurons continue to form throughout life.

8. Ineffective synaptic pruning has been linked to what disorder? (p. 232)

a. infantile amnesia
b. Fragile X syndrome
c. kwashiorkor
d. cerebral palsy

9. This area of the brain reaches its peak of synaptic density around age 4 months and has adult levels of synaptic density by age 10. (p. 233)

a. the frontal lobes
b. the temporal lobes
c. the occipital lobes
d. the hippocampus

10. Immaturity in the hippocampus and other areas of the brain related to memory are believed to be responsible for (p. 233)

a. infantile amnesia.
b. cerebral palsy.
c. Fragile X syndrome.
d all of the above.

PHYSICAL DEVELOPMENT IN EARLY CHILDHOOD

11. Which of the following is an example of a gross motor skill? (p. 235)

a. buttoning a coat
b. turning the pages in a book
c. drawing
d. dribbling a basketball

12. Control over the small muscles in the hands and fingers is what kind of skill? (p. 236)

a. locomotor
b. fine motor
c. gross motor
d. palmar grasp

13. Which of the following statements about exercise in early childhood is TRUE? (p. 238)

a. Children get most of their physical activity from physical education classes.
b. Almost all of children's moderate to vigorous physical activity occurs for periods of 20 minutes or more.
c. Children were found to be more active on weekdays than weekends.
d. Health officials recommend that children have a minimum of 90 minutes per day of vigorous physical activity.

14. Symptoms of cerebral palsy usually include (p. 239)

a. uncontrolled body movements.
b. weak muscles.
c. poor coordination.
d. all of the above.

15. The federal law requiring services to all children with disabilities is the (p. 239)

a. IDEA.
b. CP Act.
c. FDA.
d. mainstreaming law.

PHYSICAL DEVELOPMENT IN EARLY CHILDHOOD

16. In the U.S., the largest numbers of childhood deaths occur at what age? (p. 242)

a. under 1 year old
b. 1 to 4 years old
c. 5 to 10 years old
d. 11 to 14 years old

17. What type of abuse is present, to some degree, in almost every form of child maltreatment? (p. 244)

a. physical
b. sexual
c. psychological
d. neglect

18. Who is most likely to be the perpetrator of child maltreatment in the U.S.? (p. 245)

a. the father
b. the mother
c. siblings
d. someone outside of the family

19. Which of the following statements is FALSE? (p. 246 – 247)

a. Different types of maltreatment usually overlap.
b. Childhood abuse can have a permanent effect on the brain.
c. Children who have been abused usually become abusive parents.
d. Abuse is never the fault of the child.

20. Ethan is 7 years old. He has experienced physical abuse at home. What effects is he likely to suffer as a result? (p. 246 - 247)

a. aggression
b. lack of empathy
c. poor school performance
d all of the above

PHYSICAL DEVELOPMENT IN EARLY CHILDHOOD

Short-Answer Questions
Answer each question in the space provided.

1. How are experience-expectant development and experience-dependent development different in young children? Be sure to include in your answer the role of the synapses and the child's environment.

2. What has research found about the effects of neglect on children? How are these effects similar to or different from the effects of other types of maltreatment?

PHYSICAL DEVELOPMENT IN EARLY CHILDHOOD

Crossword Puzzle

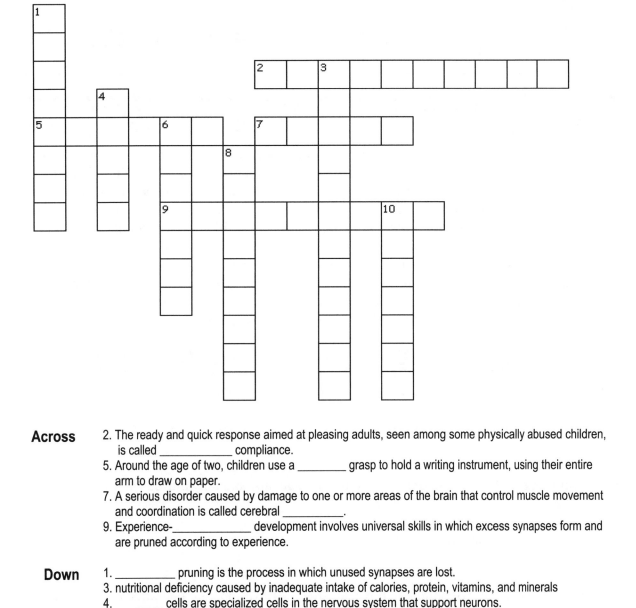

Across
2. The ready and quick response aimed at pleasing adults, seen among some physically abused children, is called _____ compliance.
5. Around the age of two, children use a _____ grasp to hold a writing instrument, using their entire arm to draw on paper.
7. A serious disorder caused by damage to one or more areas of the brain that control muscle movement and coordination is called cerebral _____.
9. Experience-_____ development involves universal skills in which excess synapses form and are pruned according to experience.

Down
1. _____ pruning is the process in which unused synapses are lost.
3. nutritional deficiency caused by inadequate intake of calories, protein, vitamins, and minerals
4. _____ cells are specialized cells in the nervous system that support neurons.
6. The inability to remember events occurring before the age of three or four is called infantile _____.
8. Experience-_____ development involves specific skills in which new synapses form to code the experience.
10. the failure to provide for a child's basic physical, educational, or psychological needs

Puzzle created with Puzzlemaker at DiscoverySchool.com

8 | COGNITIVE DEVELOPMENT IN EARLY CHILDHOOD

Before You Read

In this chapter, you will continue to learn about cognitive development, beginning with the second stage of Jean Piaget's work: preoperational thought. In this stage, thought is intuitive and egocentrism, animism, and artificialism are prominent features. Several of Piaget's classic investigations are discussed. The sociocultural view of Vygotsky is introduced and explored, as are the basics of the information-processing approach. You will also learn about the major language accomplishments of early childhood, including increases in vocabulary, the gradual incorporation of grammar rules, and the social rules of discourse that allow us to effectively communicate with others. Bilingualism and its benefits and effects on children is addressed later in the chapter. Finally, your authors look at the effectiveness of early education programs and whether it helps or hinders a child's development to delay kindergarten attendance.

Chapter Learning Objectives

After reading this chapter, you should be able to do the following:

- Describe the basis for Piaget's second stage, preoperational thought.

- Summarize childrens' use of symbols in language, art, and play during early childhood.

- Define intuitive thought.

- Define the concepts of animism, artificialism, conservation, and operations, within Piaget's theory.

- Discuss Vygotsky's ideas regarding the roles of speech and language in cognitive development.

COGNITIVE DEVELOPMENT IN EARLY CHILDHOOD

- Describe how the concepts of private speech, internalization, and mediation form the foundation of Vygotsky's theory.

- Explain how the zone of proximal development and scaffolding are related.

- Describe Vygotsky's influence on newer sociocultural views of cognitive development.

- Briefly describe the information-processing approach and identify its basic assumption regarding human thinking.

- Define and discuss changes in processing capacity and processing efficiency.

- Summarize changes in children's abilities to attend.

- Define metacognition and distinguish it from a theory of mind.

- Describe a typical child's language skills at 2 years of age and 5 years of age.

- Define bilingualism and describe how it develops.

- Distinguish Project Head Start, the Abecedarian Project, and the High/Scope Perry Preschool program in terms of focus and goals.

- Explain how kindergarten readiness is assessed.

COGNITIVE DEVELOPMENT IN EARLY CHILDHOOD

As You Read

Key terms and concepts are essential to your understanding of the chapter. Your ability to logically discuss and analyze pertinent information is dependent upon your knowledge of these concepts. Terms can be found in boldface throughout the chapter and definitions are listed in a glossary of terms at the end of the chapter. Flashcards may be helpful for memorizing definitions. Begin using the terms as you study, incorporating them into your vocabulary.

Abecedarian Project	High/Scope Perry Preschool Program	processing capacity
animism	internalization	processing efficiency
artificialism	intuitive thought	Project Head Start
attention	mediation	scaffolding
automaticity	metacognition	social rules of discourse
bilingual	operations	social speech
collaborative learning	overregularization	theory of mind
conservation	preoperational thought	zone of proximal development (ZPD)
egocentrism	private speech	

⊙ PIAGET'S STAGE 2: Preoperational Thought

Flourishing Mental Representations

1. Representational thought is also referred to as "symbolic thought." Why did Piaget consider representational thought critical to child development? Give two forms of evidence used to establish that an infant has achieved representational thought.

COGNITIVE DEVELOPMENT IN EARLY CHILDHOOD

2. The _____ stage of cognitive development, from 2 to 7 years, is characterized by an enormous increase in representational thought in several domains. Describe typical evidence of the development of symbolic or representational thought during this period in the following areas:

   Children's Language -

   Children's Artwork -

   Children's Play -

Emergence of Intuitive Thought

Evidence of intuitive thought can be observed in three characteristics of thinking that are common during the preoperational period. List each below and give two examples of this type of thought.

   A.

   Examples: 1.
             2.

   B.

   Examples: 1.
             2.

   C.

   Examples: 1.
             2.

COGNITIVE DEVELOPMENT IN EARLY CHILDHOOD

Conservation Problems

1. Children's answers to Piaget's conservation problems have given us the most famous examples of preoperational thought. Define conservation as related to cognition and describe the liquid conservation problem.

2. Identify three important limitations of preoperational thought and discuss the major aspects of each.

    A.

    B.

    C.

COGNITIVE DEVELOPMENT IN EARLY CHILDHOOD

Piaget's Legacy

Using the understanding you gained in Chapter 5 and all you have learned in Chapter 8, imagine you could communicate with Jean Piaget. Draft a letter in which you describe for him (1) the current criticisms of his theory, (2) recent research that supports of refutes his theoretical model, and (3) how his work has influenced the fields of psychology and education.

COGNITIVE DEVELOPMENT IN EARLY CHILDHOOD

⊙ VYGOTSKY'S SOCIOCULTURAL VIEW OF COGNITIVE DEVELOPMENT

1. Identify which of the following concepts are directly connected to Lev Vygotsky's theory by placing a check mark next to each Vygotskian concept. Then, discuss how the <u>checked</u> concepts are integrated within Vygotsky's sociocultural view of cognitive development.

   ___ Private speech   ___ Situated cognition   ___ Social speech
   ___ Internalization   ___ Assimilation   ___ Mediation
   ___ Guided participation   ___ ZPD   ___ Scaffolding
   ___ Collaborative learning   ___ Logical thinking   ___ Abstract reasoning

   Discussion:

2. Match each phrase, word or sentence on the left with the identifying concept on the right by placing a letter in the blank provided. Use each concept once.

   ___ Speech that we hear from others   A. scaffolding
   ___ Speech that children say aloud to themselves   B. ZPD
   ___ Introducing new concepts to a child   C. social speech
   ___ Providing help as children are learning   D. mediation
   ___ Difference between independent ability and potential   E. internalization
   ___ Working together to help one another learn   F. private speech
   ___ Taking external speech and making it internal and mental   G. collaborative learning

COGNITIVE DEVELOPMENT IN EARLY CHILDHOOD

⊙ INFORMATION PROCESSING

What is the Information Processing Approach?

1. As your text indicates, information-processing approaches often use the computer as a metaphor for the way humans think. In the table below, insert key words that would accurately complete each human–computer comparison. If there is no clear analogous human component or process, simply write "not applicable."

Computer	Human thought
CPU	
RAM	
Software	
Storage	
Monitor/Speakers	

2. Your text authors are careful to explain that information-processing psychologists do not claim that human thought and computer processing are equivalent. Identify at least three ways in which computers and humans "think" differently.

   A.

   B.

   C.

3. Identify one of the most important assumptions of the information-processing view and explain why this assumption is important in understanding the approach.

COGNITIVE DEVELOPMENT IN EARLY CHILDHOOD

The Development of Basic Cognitive Processes

Match each of the following information-processing terms with its appropriate descriptor.

   A. Automaticity
   B. Attention
   C. Processing capacity
   D. Processing efficiency
   E. Operating space
   F. Storage space

   _____ a place for storing and remembering information that is being worked on
   _____ amount of information an individual can think about at one time
   _____ ability to focus on a specific stimulus without being distracted
   _____ ability to perform an activity with little or no conscious thought or effort
   _____ place where the actual manipulation of information occurs
   _____ speed and accuracy with which an individual can process information

Metacognition and the Child's Developing Theory of Mind

1. Select a topic in this chapter that you think you're going to have the most difficulty learning for your exam. How do you intend to study this particular material? What will you need to know about the cognitive tasks involved? Which cognitive strategies and knowledge about people will aid you in your studying? Notice that you are thinking about your own thinking! What is this processed called?

2. Define "theory of mind."

3. Describe a typical 3-year-old's theory of mind.

COGNITIVE DEVELOPMENT IN EARLY CHILDHOOD

4. Explain how Maynard the cat, red milk, and fake rocks, have been used to examine children's theories of mind.

5. In what ways might language be an important component in developing a theory of mind?

⊙ LANGUAGE DEVELOPMENT

An Expanding Vocabulary

1. Briefly discuss the changes that occur to a child's vocabulary between the ages of two and six years of age.

2. If you overheard someone say "Cisco is at the library *abbendecking* next week's term paper on a CD," what conclusions might you reach about the italicized term, using syntactical bootstrapping?

COGNITIVE DEVELOPMENT IN EARLY CHILDHOOD

Learning Grammar

1. Define overregularization and give two examples.

2. Being the Teacher
   You've been asked to present a workshop for parents on ways to enhance their children's language development. Using Table 8.1 in your text as a guide, create an outline including main topics, practical suggestions, and interesting examples that will aid and encourage parents in improving their skills in working with their children.

COGNITIVE DEVELOPMENT IN EARLY CHILDHOOD

Learning the Social Rules of Discourse

1. Define social rules of discourse and list two examples.

2. How might cultural differences affect rules for social discourse?

Bilingual Children

1. Match each term with the correct description.

    _____ learning a second language wile maintaining a first language

    _____ loss of fluency in the first language as a result of acquiring a second language

    _____ learning two languages at the same time, beginning in infancy

    _____ acquiring one language first, then learning a second

    A. sequential bilingualism

    B. additive bilingualism

    C. simultaneous bilingualism

    D. subtractive bilingualism

COGNITIVE DEVELOPMENT IN EARLY CHILDHOOD

2. What impact does the age of a person learning a second language play?

3. Are there cognitive advantages in being bilingual?

⊙ EARLY CHILDHOOD EDUCATION AND KINDERGARTEN READINESS

Early Childhood Education

1. Describe the primary purpose of each of the following early childhood education programs.

   Project Head Start   Abecedarian Project   High/Scope Perry Preschool

2. Now, describe the known effects of each of these early childhood programs.

   Project Head Start   Abecedarian Project   High/Scope Perry Preschool

COGNITIVE DEVELOPMENT IN EARLY CHILDHOOD

3. Identify six factors that may account for differences in benefits among the three early childhood education programs described above.

   A.

   B.

   C.

   D.

   E.

   F.

4. Discuss how early intervention programs may produce long-term positive effects on children's lives.

Kindergarten Readiness

1. Identify similarities and differences among the factors that teachers and parents believe are important school readiness indicators.

   | Teachers Only | Parents Only | Teachers and Parents |

COGNITIVE DEVELOPMENT IN EARLY CHILDHOOD

2. List the five school readiness characteristics usually assessed.

   A.

   B.

   C.

   D.

   E.

COGNITIVE DEVELOPMENT IN EARLY CHILDHOOD

When You Have Finished

⊙ Working the Web

1. For brief descriptions and teaching ideas on the application of Piagetian principles, visit chiron.valdosta.edu/whuitt/col/cogsys/piagtuse.html. This material is formatted as a handout on Cognitive Development Applications for use with toddlers, children in early childhood, and adolescents.

2. A good resource for information of the life and work of Lev Vygotsky can be found at www.kolar.org/vygotsky/. The Web site contains a collection of links to other relevant sites of interest to those exploring Vygotsky's theories.

3. Read the article, "What Research Says About Technology and Child Development," at www.nwrel.org/request/june01/child.html. In what ways do the authors think technology affects socioemotional, physical, language, and cognitive development?

4. Visit Early Childhood Education at What Works Clearinghouse (www.whatworks.ed.gov). The primary focus of the early childhood education (ECE) sector is on cognition, literacy and language. What is this organization currently investigating in ECE and how does it do this?

5. If your interest is in the line of special education in early childhood, a fine source of information exists at www.ericec.org, the Council for Exceptional Children. Here, you'll find links to discussion groups, special projects, and law related to exceptional children.

6. *Early Childhood Research & Practice*, "a bilingual Internet journal on the development, care, and education of young children," is sponsored by the Early Childhood and Parenting Collaborative at the University of Illinois at Urbana-Champaign. The peer-reviewed online journal is available at ecrp.uiuc.edu.

COGNITIVE DEVELOPMENT IN EARLY CHILDHOOD

⊙ PRACTICE TEST #1

Multiple Choice Questions
For each question, circle the best answer from the choices given.

1. According to Piaget, when children are able to think about objects and events that are not physically present, they have attained what cognitive level? (p. 256)

   a. sensorimotor
   b. preoperational
   c. concrete operational
   d. formal operational

2. Which of the following uses a symbol system, according to Piaget's theory? (p. 257)

   a. language
   b. art
   c. pretend play
   d. all of the above

3. Svetlyna, who is 4, is talking on the telephone to her father who is at work. She says, "Look at the picture I drew!", while holding the drawing up to the phone. In Piaget's theory, Svetlyna's actions would be considered to demonstrate (p. 258)

   a. egocentrism.
   b. animism.
   c. artificialism.
   d. symbolic thinking.

4. Conservation, in Piaget's theory, means (p. 259)

   a. that the child cannot understand another person's perspective.
   b. children believe inanimate objects can think and have feelings.
   c. realizing the basic properties of an object remain the same even if the appearance changes.
   d. that a child cannot reverse mental operations.

5. How did Piaget's theory influence the field of education? (p. 260)

   a. Educators realized that they could cause children to skip stages of development if they exposed the children to certain types of learning experiences.
   b. Educators focused more on lectures and worksheets for children to learn better.
   c. School boards dropped Physical Education and music classes.
   d. Curricula became more interactive and "hands-on".

COGNITIVE DEVELOPMENT IN EARLY CHILDHOOD

6. Which theorist developed a sociocultural theory of cognitive development? (p. 262)

a. Jean Piaget
b. Lev Vygotsky
c. Socrates
d. Erik Erikson

7. Three year old Christopher talks to himself while building with his blocks. According to Vygotsky's theory, Christopher's vocalizations are (p. 263)

a. private speech.
b. social speech.
c. collaborative learning.
d. abnormal.

8. You are teaching your young cousin to ride a bike. As you run down the street holding the bike, you remind her to steer and to pedal. The teaching process you are using, according to Vygotsky's theory is called (p. 264)

a. collaborative learning.
b. private speech.
c. mediation.
d. automaticity.

9. The top boundary of the ZPD consists of (p. 264 – 265)

a. conservation tasks.
b. internalized mediation.
c. tasks the child can solve independently.
d. tasks that the child cannot solve, no matter how much help is received.

10. When a parent helps a young child build a tower of blocks by putting the top blocks on very carefully, the parent is engaging in (p. 265 - 266)

a. egocentric thinking.
b. scaffolding.
c. processing efficiency.
d. code switching.

COGNITIVE DEVELOPMENT IN EARLY CHILDHOOD

⊙ PRACTICE TEST #2

Multiple Choice Questions
For each question, circle the best answer from the choices given.

1. The belief that humans are limited in their capacity to process information is an important assumption of which theory? (p. 269)

   a. information processing
   b. Piaget's theory
   c. Vygotsky's Sociocultural view
   d. Theory of mind

2. Tatyana is being tested by a cognitive researcher. The researcher says a list of words and asks Tatyana to repeat them back in the same order. The researcher is measuring Tatyana's (p. 269)

   a. cognitive scaffolding.
   b. processing efficiency.
   c. processing capacity.
   d. metacognition.

3. Which of the following statements about metacognition is TRUE? (p. 271)

   a. Metacognition is the ability to focus on a particular stimulus without becoming distracted.
   b. Metacognitive skills are not good during early childhood, but improve rapidly after age 5.
   c. Metacognition is the speed and efficiency with which a person can process information.
   d. All of the above are true.

4. The theory of mind is (p. 272)

   a. part of Vygotsky's sociocultural theory.
   b. the ability to carry out a mental process with little or no conscious effort.
   c. the understanding a child has about his or her own thought processes.
   d. an integrated understanding of what the mind is, how it works and why it works that way.

5. What is the average vocabulary for a 6 year old child? (p. 274)

   a. 2,000 words
   b. 5,000 words
   c. 10, 000 words
   d. 15,000 words

COGNITIVE DEVELOPMENT IN EARLY CHILDHOOD

6. Four year old Michael said "We goed to the pet store and buyed two baby mouses." His statement is an example of (p. 275)

a. syntactical bootstrapping.
b. overregularization.
c. code switching.
d. a child who is bilingual.

7. Learning that in a conversation one person talks and then the other is (p. 275)

a. part of the social rules of discourse.
b. called fast mapping of language.
c. one of the types of code switching.
d. a category of language dysfluency.

8. Jungae is the daughter of Korean immigrants. She learned English in preschool while continuing to speak Korean at home with her family. What type of bilingualism does Jungae have? (p. 277)

a. code switching bilingualism
b. subtractive bilingualislm
c. simultaneous bilingualism
d. additive bilingualism

9. The early childhood education program that was designed to assess the impact of full-time, high quality intervention beginning in infancy, and that served mostly poor African American children is the (p. 281)

a. Children's Television Workshop.
b. Abecedarian Project.
c. Redshirt Project.
d. High/Scope Perry Preschool Program.

10. When children are old enough to start kindergarten but are identified as not yet ready, they may be held back a year. This is known as (p. 284)

a. scaffolding.
b. code switching.
c. redshirting.
d. none of the above.

COGNITIVE DEVELOPMENT IN EARLY CHILDHOOD

⊙ COMPREHENSIVE PRACTICE TEST

Multiple Choice Questions
For each question, circle the best answer from the choices given.

1. Children from 2 to 7 years old are most likely in which stage of Piaget's theory? (p. 256)

   a. sensorimotor
   b. preoperations
   c. concrete operations
   d. formal operations

2. Shaneika, age 2 1/2, calls her blanket a "bankie." According to Piaget, her invented words demonstrate (p. 257)

   a. Shaneika has reversible thinking.
   b. she has not yet entered the preoperational stage.
   c. language as a symbol system.
   d. animism.

3. Antonio is afraid of the vacuum cleaner. He believes that while it lives in the closet it is planning to sneak up on him and suck him into the bag. Antonio believes that the vacuum is jealous of him because he has toys and it doesn't. According to Piaget's theory, Antonio's beliefs are an example of (p. 258)

   a. animism.
   b. symbolic thinking.
   c. conservation.
   d. centration.

4. Jordan's teacher makes two identically sized balls of clay. While Jordan watches, the teacher shapes one ball into a "hot dog." When asked which has more clay, Jordan answers "the hot dog, because it's longer." Jordan's answer demonstrates which concept from Piaget's theory? (p. 259)

   a. lack of conservation
   b. centration
   c. lack of reversibility
   d. all of the above

COGNITIVE DEVELOPMENT IN EARLY CHILDHOOD

5. Choose the statement about Piaget's legacy that is TRUE. (p 260)

a. Educators now use less debates and conflicting opinions when teaching children.
b. Before Piaget's theory, educators saw children as active learners.
c. Piaget's stages have influenced school guidelines for when to introduce different topics in the curriculum.
d. Piaget's theory is not used often nowadays in education.

6. Which of the following was NOT a factor in Vygotsky's background that affected his sociocultural theory? (p. 263)

a. believing in Marxism
b. having the opportunity to study with Freud in Vienna
c. being Jewish
d. having a teacher who used the Socratic method

7. When children take their external private speech and transform it into purely mental language, what process has occurred? (p. 264)

a. internalization
b. mediation
c. scaffolding
d. automaticity

8. When a skilled teacher mediates a new skill with a child, the teacher (p. 264)

a. selects a few strategies at a time to focus on.
b. introduces concepts and knowledge.
c. should tailor the teaching to the child's level.
d. all of the above.

9. Kelechi can put together simple puzzles by himself. These types of puzzles are where in his zone of proximal development? (p. 265)

a. at the top
b. in the middle
c. at the bottom
d. in cannot be determined from the information given

COGNITIVE DEVELOPMENT IN EARLY CHILDHOOD

10. Mr. Eisenberg's science class is working in the lab. He has given each member of the lab groups a one step in the procedure. Each group must work together to do the lab in the correct sequence. Mr. Eisenberg is using what technique with his class? (p. 266)

a. scaffolding
b. mediation
c. ZPD
d. collaborative learning

11. In the information processing approach, the computer's working memory, or RAM, is compared to (p. 268)

a. short-term memory in humans.
b. long-term memory in humans.
c. a CD ROM.
d. executive processes.

12. Hiroko is 14 months old and is becoming proficient at walking on her own. Although she has a good vocabulary for her age, she doesn't talk while she is walking. This is an example of how she has not yet gained (p. 270)

a. sensorimotor development.
b. automaticity for walking.
c. scaffolding of language.
d. code switching.

13. Attention is defined in the in the information processing approach as the (p. 271)

a. speed and accuracy with which a person can process information.
b. ability to focus without becoming distracted.
c. amount of information a person can remember at one time.
d. basic cognitive scaffold.

14. Janae is given the following scenario: a doll shows another doll her dog and then puts the dog in a basket. After the second doll leaves, the first doll transfers the dog into a box. The second doll believes the dog is still in the basket. This test is used to assess Janae's (p. 272)

a. Zone of Proximal Development.
b. scaffolding.
c. theory of mind.
d. syntactical bootstrapping.

COGNITIVE DEVELOPMENT IN EARLY CHILDHOOD

15. Dustin's older brother tells him "The Apatosaurus was a large creature like the Tyrannosaurus Rex that lived in prehistoric times. There are none alive today." Dustin figures out that Apatosaurus is a dinosaur. This language learning process is called (p. 274)

a. syntactical bootstrapping.
b. fast mapping.
c. code switching.
d. automaticity.

16. When children incorrectly apply the language rules for producing tenses and plurals to irregular words, they are showing (p. 275)

a. the social rules of discourse.
b. the negative effects of bilingualism.
c. code switching.
d. overregularization.

17. Adults try to teach children not to interrupt when someone is speaking. This is an example of (p. 275 – 276)

a. social rules of discourse.
b. compulsive compliance.
c. overregularization.
d. scaffolding.

18. The type of bilingualism that occurs when a child learns two languages at the same time is (p. 277)

a. fast mapping.
b. additive bilingualism.
c. sequential bilingualism.
d. simultaneous bilingualism.

19. The initial purpose of Head Start was to (p. 281)

a. assess the impact of high quality intervention for young African American children.
b. provide early intervention for children with disabilities.
c. improve academic achievement and opportunity for disadvantaged children from 3 to 5 years old.
d. increase reading among 4 year olds.

COGNITIVE DEVELOPMENT IN EARLY CHILDHOOD

20. Research has shown that all of the following factors affect a child's readiness for kindergarten EXCEPT (p. 283 - 284)

a. age of the child.
b. the child's personality type.
c. the mothers' educational level.
d. the family's income level.

Short-Answer Questions
Answer each question in the space provided.

1. Compare and contrast Piaget's and Vygotsky's theories of cognitive development. On what main points do they differ?

2. Describe the computer model comparison to the mind that is used in the information processing approach. Be sure to give the computer parts that correspond to sensory memory, short-term and long-term memories and executive processes.

3. Explain the different forms of bilingualism. How does learning two languages affect a young child?

COGNITIVE DEVELOPMENT IN EARLY CHILDHOOD

Crossword Puzzle

Across
1. the process a more skilled person uses to introduce concepts and cognitive structures to less skilled children
3. _____ speech is speech that children say aloud to themselves, then later internalize
5. the idea that inanimate objects have conscious life and feelings
7. a child's inability to take another person's perspective
10. support given to a child developing a new mental function or performing a new task

Down
2. logical processes that can be reversed
4. _____ efficiency is the speed and accuracy with which a person can process information.
6. fluent in two languages
8. the understanding or knowledge that people have about their own thought processes
9. the ability to carry out a process with little or no conscious effort

Puzzle created with Puzzlemaker at DiscoverySchool.com

9 SOCIAL AND EMOTIONAL DEVELOPMENT IN EARLY CHILDHOOD

Before You Read

This chapter continues to delve into the topic of social and emotional development about which you began learning in Chapter 6, moving from infancy and toddler ages into early childhood. The chapter begins by focusing on how we learn to ask and answer the question, "Who am I?" You will become familiar with what children in early childhood understand about gender and moral issues. Parenting styles and a discussion of discipline form the middle of the chapter. Research investigating play and friendship during this period is covered, as well as research exploring cultural differences in play. Finally, the impacts of nonparental child care and those of "quality" child care and education are examined.

Chapter Learning Objectives

After reading this chapter, you should be able to do the following:

- Briefly outline Williams James's conception of self.

- Describe the self-knowledge that children have during childhood.

- Define self-regulation, describe how children develop this ability, and summarize factors that influence self-regulation.

- Distinguish between the meanings of gender identity, gender stability, and gender constancy.

- List the major trends in gender development between the ages of two and seven years of age.

SOCIAL AND EMOTIONAL DEVELOPMENT IN EARLY CHILDHOOD

- Summarize research on the development of gender differences in cognitive skills, emotions, and social behavior.

- Describe the six stages and three levels of Kohlberg's moral reasoning.

- Describe how parental warmth and parental control influence children's outcomes.

- Discuss the contributions and limitations of Baumrind's research on parenting styles.

- Distinguish discipline from punishment and explain why spanking is ineffective as a method of discipline.

- Outline a positive program of discipline that is consistent with the AAP guidelines.

- Discuss the prominent theories used to explain why girls and boys avoid playing with members of the opposite sex and the effects this gender segregation has on development.

- Summarize Parten's classic theory and research on the social levels of play.

- Describe the functions of sociodramatic play for young children.

- Summarize research on cultural differences in play.

- Summarize the effects of non-parental childcare on children's attachment to parents, peer relations, and cognitive competence.

- Discuss the components of quality childcare and explain how the quality of childcare influences children's developmental outcomes.

SOCIAL AND EMOTIONAL DEVELOPMENT IN EARLY CHILDHOOD

As You Read

Key terms and concepts are essential to your understanding of the chapter. Your ability to logically discuss and analyze pertinent information is dependent upon your knowledge of these concepts. Terms can be found in boldface throughout the chapter and definitions are listed in a glossary of terms at the end of the chapter. Flashcards may be helpful for memorizing definitions. Begin using the terms as you study, incorporating them into your vocabulary.

authoritarian parents	me-self	positive emotion bias
authoritative parents	moral reasoning	preconventional level
conscience	morality	process quality
convention	nonparental child care	punishment
discipline	parental control	rejecting/neglecting parents
gender constancy	parental warmth	self
gender cultures	permissive parents	self-regulation
gender segregation	perspective taking	sociodramatic play
I-self	play	structural quality

⊙ THE SOCIAL AND EMOTIONAL SELF

The Self

1. What is the "self"?

2. Identify and define the two basic aspects of the self as described by William James.

   A.

   B.

SOCIAL AND EMOTIONAL DEVELOPMENT IN EARLY CHILDHOOD

Self-Regulation

1. Define self-regulation.

2. Describe four abilities that are necessary for self-regulation. Give an example of each.

    A.

    B.

    C.

    D.

3. Discuss at least three positive outcomes associated with the ability to self-regulate.

4. Identify biological and environmental factors that influence children's ability to self-regulate.

    <u>Biological Factors</u>   <u>Environmental Factors</u>

SOCIAL AND EMOTIONAL DEVELOPMENT IN EARLY CHILDHOOD

Developing Ideas About Gender

1. For each of the following trends in gender development, choose the letter of the approximate age range in which the ability emerges.

   _____ show an understanding of gender stability

   _____ understand the category labels "boy" and "girl"

   _____ show stereotyped differences in personality-social characteristics

   _____ exhibit a strong negative reaction to cross-gender behavior

   _____ display a high rigidity in gender beliefs and behavior

   _____ show a knowledge of gender stereotypes regarding objects and activities

   A. 2 to 3 years

   B. 3 to 5 years

   C. 6 to 7 years

2. Define and differentiate between gender identity, gender stability, and gender constancy. During which ages does each stage of gender understanding tend to occur?

SOCIAL AND EMOTIONAL DEVELOPMENT IN EARLY CHILDHOOD

Moral Development

1. Match each phrase or description with a term from the list below.

   _____ ideas we have about right and wrong

   _____ rules or practices, mutually agreed upon, that guide behaviors, choices, and decisions

   _____ the ability to understand the psychological views, motives, and needs of others

   _____ ways in which we think about what is right and what is wrong

   _____ knowing the difference between right and wrong, then acting on that knowledge

         A.   perspective taking   D.   morality

         B.   convention   E.   moral reasoning

         C.   conscience

2. Identify Kohlberg's six stages of moral reasoning. For each stage, include a brief description of the typical behavior or thinking process.

Stage	Example of Reasoning
A.	
B.	
C.	
D.	
E.	
F.	

SOCIAL AND EMOTIONAL DEVELOPMENT IN EARLY CHILDHOOD

⊙ PARENTING

Dimensions of Parenting

Identify and define the two main dimensions of parenting that influence children's outcomes. Give examples of parental behaviors that are "high" and "low" on each of these dimensions.

    A.

    B.

Parenting Styles

1. Below are two separate 2 x 2 matrices. First, label the matrices using the concepts of parental warmth and control. Then, fill in the first matrix with information regarding Baumrind's four parenting styles. In the second matrix, you are to enter information regarding how each of the four parenting styles is related to specific outcomes for children.

PARENTING STYLES

SOCIAL AND EMOTIONAL DEVELOPMENT IN EARLY CHILDHOOD

1. (Continued)

CHILDREN'S OUTCOMES

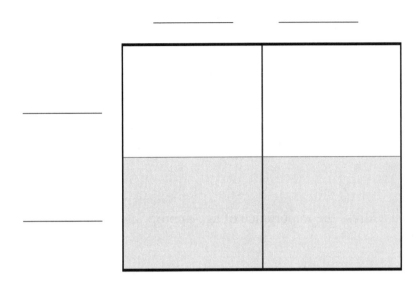

2. In her later research Baumrind added three parenting styles and two parenting dimensions. Below, list the four dimensions and seven styles of parenting.

Dimensions	Styles
A.	A.
B.	B.
C.	C.
D.	D.
	E.
	F.
	G.

225

SOCIAL AND EMOTIONAL DEVELOPMENT IN EARLY CHILDHOOD

Discipline

Being the Teacher
Imagine that you have been asked to give a presentation to new parents on the importance of using discipline rather than punishment with their children.

How would you distinguish discipline from punishment?

How would you explain the potential negative effects of punishment?

How would you address the importance of age-appropriate disciplinary strategies?

Make sure that you include the five guidelines for effective discipline in your talk.

    A.

    B.

    C.

    D.

    E.

SOCIAL AND EMOTIONAL DEVELOPMENT IN EARLY CHILDHOOD

⊙ FRIENDS AND PLAY

Gender Segregation

1. Explain the assertion that gender segregation is a cultural universal.

2. Identify four prominent explanations for gender segregation.

    A.

    B.

    C.

    D.

Play

1. Identify the elements of play as defined by developmental psychologists.

SOCIAL AND EMOTIONAL DEVELOPMENT IN EARLY CHILDHOOD

2. Identify Parten's six levels of children's play behavior and the typical age ranges during which each type of play occurs.

Level of Play	Age Range	Level of Play	Age Range
A.		D.	
B.		E.	
C.		F.	

3. Now, match each of the following descriptions and examples to the level of play with which it is most closely associated.

   ____ A child sits and plays by himself while other kids are playing around him.

   ____ Dot, Carla, and Patty are "playing house," and each takes on a specific role to get ready for "dinner."

   ____ Two or more children play together, but in a relatively uncoordinated and independent manner.

   ____ Paloma and Chico are both making sandpaintings, but they are not interacting.

   ____ Trish and Pete are washing dishes in separate play sinks, but they talk and splash each other as they clean their own dishes.

   ____ Tom and Joe are both playing in the kitchen area, but they are not interacting in any way and they are not engaged in the same activities.

   ____ Mahalia watches and talks to children playing with the vacuum cleaner.

   ____ Sam sits by herself in the playroom, while other children are playing together.

   ____ Two or more children are playing alone but with similar toys.

   ____ A child may play with his own body, follow a teacher, or just sit alone.

   ____ Two or more children are working toward a common goal, acting out adult situations, or playing a formal game.

SOCIAL AND EMOTIONAL DEVELOPMENT IN EARLY CHILDHOOD

4. Give an example of each of the following types of play. Then, identify the typical age range for each.

Type of Play	Example	Typical Age Range
A. Sensorimotor		
B. Symbolic		
C. Sociodramatic		

5. Identify and give an example of the five functions that children's sociodramatic play can serve.

Function of Play	Example of Function
A.	
B.	
C.	
D.	
E.	

5. Describe at least two cultural universals (similarities) and two cultural differences in children's play behavior.

Cultural universals	Cultural differences
A.	A.
B.	B.

SOCIAL AND EMOTIONAL DEVELOPMENT IN EARLY CHILDHOOD

⊙ NONPARENTAL CHILD CARE

1. As the authors of your text note, the effects of non-parental childcare on children's outcomes are complex and not always clear-cut. To help you summarize the important concerns regarding the effects of nonparental childcare, try completing the following table.

Outcome	Effects of Nonparental Childcare	Quality Important	Other Relevant Factors
Attachment			
Social skills			
Behavior Problems			
Cognitive Competence			

2. In regard to child care, compare and contrast structural quality and process quality.

3. If you had a friend or relative seeking quality child care, what questions would you urge them to ask of a prospective care-giver or facility manager?

SOCIAL AND EMOTIONAL DEVELOPMENT IN EARLY CHILDHOOD

When You Have Finished

⊙ WORKING THE WEB

1. Go to the National Association for the Education of Young Children (NAEYC) web site (www.naeyc.org). Search for "self-regulation" and read the article, "Self-Regulation: A Cornerstone of Early Childhood Development." Afterward, conduct a literature search for "self-regulation" on your favorite search engine.

2. Go to www.casel.org, The Collaborative for Academic, Social, and Emotional Learning, a web site of the University of Illinois at Chicago, and download a form for assessing children's social and emotional learning (SEL). At the collaborative you may also find instructional activities and measures for assessing school climate.

3. For general teaching and learning strategies, including those of special needs children, go to www.newhorizons.org, a non-profit international network of educators. Of special interest is the newsletter, "News from the Neurosciences", where you'll find an excellent group of articles on brain research and its implications for teaching and learning,

4. At www.futureofchildren.org, search the web site for documents on parenting and parenting styles. Published by The Woodrow Wilson School of Public and International Affairs at Princeton University and The Brookings Institution, *The Future of the Children* seeks to "promote effective policies and programs for children by providing policymakers, service providers, and the media with timely, objective information." Look especially for the following documents:
    Does Parenting Matter?
    Research on the Effects of Family Structure on Children
    Why Do Single-Parent Families Put Children at Risk?

5. "Are You Having Behavior Challenges?," asks the Positive Discipline Association (PDA), found at posdis.org. PDA "promotes and encourages the development of life skills and respectful relationships in families, schools, businesses and community systems." At this web site you can:
    *download an in-depth article on positive discipline.
    *learn what a CPDA is and how to become one.
    *look for research supporting the positive discipline approach.
    *read advice for parents on dealing with discipline issues.

6. Want to learn more about cultural differences in play during middle childhood? Visit the Early Childhood Research and Practice at the University of Illinois, Urbana-Champagne at ecrp.uiuc.edu and conduct a literature search using related information from your text.

SOCIAL AND EMOTIONAL DEVELOPMENT IN EARLY CHILDHOOD

⊙ PRACTICE TEST #1

Multiple Choice Questions

For each question, circle the best answer from the choices given.

1. Asia is 3 ½ years old. She describes herself as a "girl with black hair and eyes. I live in the white house with trees in front and I can run fast." This is a description of Asia's (p. 290 – 291)

   a. internalized self.
   b. egocentric self.
   c. I-self.
   d. me-self.

2. When a child has the ability to control his or her own behavior, emotions or thoughts and change them to meet situational demands, the child is said to have achieved (p. 291)

   a. self-regulation.
   b. stage 3 of moral development.
   c. perspective taking.
   d. a positive emotional bias.

3. Which of the following statements is TRUE? (p. 293)

   a. Children are more accurate in recognizing other people's negative emotions than positive emotions.
   b. Children don't spontaneously talk about their feelings until age 5.
   c. Children have a tendency to report positive emotions more than negative emotions in themselves.
   d. There are significant gender differences in emotional expression during early childhood.

4. The tendency for children to associate with playmates of the same sex is gender (p. 295)

   a. stability.
   b. segregation.
   c. compliance.
   d. constancy.

5. All of the following are stages in Kohlberg's theory of gender understanding EXCEPT (p. 295)

   a. gender segregation.
   b. gender identity.
   c. gender constancy.
   d. gender stability.

SOCIAL AND EMOTIONAL DEVELOPMENT IN EARLY CHILDHOOD

6. Knowing the difference between right and wrong and acting on that knowledge is (p. 296)

a. moral reasoning.
b. perspective taking.
c. morality.
d. the preconventional level.

7. The two most important dimensions of parenting that have been found in research are (p. 298 – 299)

a. discipline and punishment.
b. indulgence and neglect.
c. authoritarian and permissive.
d. warmth and control.

8. Mr. and Mrs. Campbell exert firm control over their children, but are rejecting and unresponsive to the children's emotional needs. Their parenting style is (p. 300)

a. authoritative.
b. authoritarian.
c. permissive.
d. neglecting.

9. In his research, Straus found what percentage of parents reported using a belt, paddle, or other object to spank their children? (p. 302)

a. 1 out of 2
b. 2 out of 3
c. 1 out of 4
d. 1 out of 10

10. Wiim is 4 years old. Her mother uses time-out for misbehavior. If she follows experts' advice, how many minutes should Wiim's mother give her in time out? (p. 306)

a. 4 minutes
b. 5 minutes
c. 8 minutes
d. 10 minutes

SOCIAL AND EMOTIONAL DEVELOPMENT IN EARLY CHILDHOOD

⊙ PRACTICE TEST #2

Multiple Choice Questions
For each question, circle the best answer from the choices given.

1. From the toddler years to the school aged years, how does the amount of time spent with peers change? (p. 308)

a. The amount of time doubles.
b. The amount of time triples.
c. The amount of time increases 100%.
d. The amount of time with peers remains unchanged.

2. When you go to observe a kindergarten class at recess, you notice that the girls play in small groups together and the boys play together, usually in large groups. You are observing (p. 309)

a. gender segregation.
b. parallel play.
c. play compatibility.
d. all of the above.

3. A pleasurable activity that is engaged in voluntarily, is intrinsically motivated and contains non-literal elements is (p. 311)

a. moral reasoning.
b. gender segregation.
c. play.
d. development of the self.

4. Which of the following is NOT one of Parten's categories of play? (p. 311 - 313)

a. Solitary
b. Parallel
c. Associative
d. Sociodramatic

5. Play that involves acting out different social roles or characters is called (p. 313)

a. sociodramatic.
b. cooperative.
c. associative.
d. parallel.

SOCIAL AND EMOTIONAL DEVELOPMENT IN EARLY CHILDHOOD

6. The symbolic thinking that children are developing in early childhood is reflected in their (p. 314)

a. response to discipline.
b. reaction to day care.
c. play.
d. gender cultures.

7. In a study of play in German, Swedish, Indonesian and American children, which group showed the most friendliness, were the most helpful, and used the most peaceful problem solving? (p. 315)

a. German
b. Indonesian
c. American
d. Swedish

8. In the past several decades, how has child care arrangements changed for preschool children? (p. 316 – 317)

a. The percentage in day care centers has increased dramatically.
b. The percentage of children cared for by a relative has decreased.
c. The number of children cared for at home by a parent has decreased.
d. All of the above have occurred.

9. Children who come from what type of background show the greatest benefits from high quality day care? (p. 317)

a. disadvantaged
b. middle-class
c. bilingual
d. authoritative parenting

10. The quality of the actual experiences that children have in day care is (p. 318)

a. structural quality.
b. process quality.
c. determined by the training of the child care staff.
d. linked to the education credentials of the staff.

SOCIAL AND EMOTIONAL DEVELOPMENT IN EARLY CHILDHOOD
⊙ COMPREHENSIVE PRACTICE TEST

Multiple Choice Questions
For each question, circle the best answer from the choices given.

1. The component of self that is aware of one's existence as a separate, unique individual is (p. 290)

   a. the I-self.
   b. the me-self.
   c. the differentiated self.
   d. none of the above.

2. Hannah is 6 years old. In many situations she is able to control her behavior and emotions and even change them as the situation requires. Hannah is developing (p. 291)

   a. scaffolding.
   b. moral reasoning.
   c. self-regulation.
   d. mediation.

3. Which of the following helps a child to understand individual differences in emotion? (p. 293)

   a. gender identity
   b. theory of mind
   c. positive emotion bias
   d. the me-self

4. All of the following are true of gender development in children aged 2 to 3 EXCEPT (p. 294)

   a. Children understand the categories of "boy" and "girl".
   b. Children show knowledge of gender stereotypes.
   c. Children prefer same sex playmates.
   d. Children understand that gender stays the same even if a person's appearance changes.

5. The ways in which people think about right and wrong is called (p. 296)

   a. morality.
   b. moral reasoning.
   c. perspective taking.
   d. universal ethical principles.

SOCIAL AND EMOTIONAL DEVELOPMENT IN EARLY CHILDHOOD

6. Kohlberg's theory of moral reasoning states that (p. 296)

a. all children move through the stages in the same order.
b. people from all cultures experience the same stages of development.
c. the pace of moral reasoning development varies with each individual.
d. all of the above.

7. In studying parenting styles, researchers make a distinction between physical control and (p. 299)

a. psychological control.
b. positive discipline.
c. compulsive compliance.
d. punishment.

8. Mr. and Mrs. Kim are very warm and loving with their three sons. However, they are usually very lenient about misbehavior and the boys are becoming the neighborhood bullies. What is the best categorization of the Kim's parenting style? (p. 300)

a. authoritative
b. authoritarian
c. permissive
d. neglecting

9. Your textbook authors say that in disciplining children, parents should NOT (p. 302)

a. hit or grab their children.
b. spank.
c. yell harshly.
d. Parents should not do any of the above.

10. An important limitation of the research on physical punishment is that it is (p.304)

a. unreliable.
b. correlational.
c. focused entirely on mothers' behavior.
d. mostly about boys.

SOCIAL AND EMOTIONAL DEVELOPMENT IN EARLY CHILDHOOD

11. When Mr. and Mrs. Eshera take their young children on long car trips they always bring games and books to keep the children entertained. Which kind of strategy of positive discipline are they using? (p. 305)

a. setting limits
b. using time-outs
c. managing the situation
d. using explanations and reasoning

12. Gender segregation occurs when (p. 309)

a. children prefer to associate with same sex peers.
b. teachers put girls and boys in separate lines for recess.
c. parents send their daughters to ballet lessons and sons to sports camp.
d. girls and boys are put on separate teams.

13. Steven, who is 6, refuses to play with girls. He says that "girls are boring and don't like to play video games." This is an example of a typical (p. 310)

a. gender culture.
b. cognitive schema.
c. play incompatibility.
d. gender constancy.

14. Which of the following is NOT a benefit of play? (p. 311)

a. development of motor skills
b. improved social interactions
c. cognitive development
d. all of the above are benefits

15. In Parten's studies of children's play, she found 3 to 5 year olds to split their playtime evenly among which types? (p. 313)

a. onlooker and solitary
b. associative and cooperative
c. parallel, associative and cooperative
d. onlooker, solitary and parallel

SOCIAL AND EMOTIONAL DEVELOPMENT IN EARLY CHILDHOOD

16. Jeremy has a toy tool set. He loves to pretend he is building things like his father, who is a carpenter. Jeremy's play serves what function? (p. 314)

a. imitation of adults
b. expression of needs
c. outlet for forbidden impulses
d. role reversal

17. In studies of children's play across many cultures, all of the following have been found EXCEPT (p. 314 - 315)

a. Culture has a great influence on how much children play.
b. The main themes in children's play are influenced by culture.
c. Children learn skills that are important in their culture.
d. No differences have been found in children's levels of cooperation and aggression during play.

18. High quality day care has been associated with (p. 316)

a. positive social outcomes.
b. negative effects on cognitive development.
c. more aggression and lower social competence.
d. more anxiety and dependence on adults.

19. What are the most important components of quality day care? (p. 317)

a. structural quality
b. process quality
c. both a and b
d. none of the above

20. Which of the following statements about child care in the U.S. is TRUE? (p. 318 - 319)

a. There are federal standards for structural qualities in child care centers.
b. The majority of child care centers are not of high quality.
c. Licensing of child care centers is based on process qualities.
d. Most child care centers meet the standards of the National Association for the Education of Young Children.

SOCIAL AND EMOTIONAL DEVELOPMENT IN EARLY CHILDHOOD

Short-Answer Questions

Answer each question in the space provided.

1. What is the "self"? Explain the two main aspects of the self. How does the self develop in early childhood?

2. Describe the four styles of parenting postulated by Baumrind. What are the outcomes for children associated with each style?

3. What is "quality" child care? What has research found to be the effects of day care in early childhood?

SOCIAL AND EMOTIONAL DEVELOPMENT IN EARLY CHILDHOOD

⊙ CROSSWORD PUZZLE

Across
9. techniques used to teach children appropriate behavior
11. knowing the difference between right and wrong, then acting on that knowledge
12. _____ parents are warm but have little control over their children.
13. _____ warmth is the degree to which parents are accepting, responsive, and compassionate with their children.

Down
2. _____ child care is provided for a child by someone other than the child's parents.
3. Gender _____ is the tendency of children to associate with others of their same sex.
4. _____ parents are warm and exert firm control.
6. ideas about right and wrong
8. techniques used to eliminate or reduce undesirable behavior
10. Gender _____ refers to the understanding that gender remains the same despite superficial changes in appearance or behavior.

Puzzle created with Puzzlemaker at DiscoverySchool.com

10 PHYSICAL DEVELOPMENT IN MIDDLE CHILDHOOD

Before You Read

The topics covered in this chapter all focus on physical development in middle childhood. You'll learn about the typical patterns of physical growth during this period, as well as such problems as overweight. This chapter deals with the topics of motor development and physical activity and the gender differences associated with each. Also covered are the pros and cons of participation in organized sports and common threats to safety during middle childhood. One of the more universal threats is that of child sexual abuse. You'll learn about the risk factors and effects associated with this danger. Later in the chapter, the authors address the developmental psychopathology perspective and its relationship to physical development during this stage of childhood. Finally, you'll read about ADHD, some of the more common communication and learning disorders, and Autism Spectrum Disorders before ending with guidelines for children with exceptional needs.

Chapter Objectives

After reading this chapter, you should be able to do the following:

- Outline the average growth patterns for boys and for girls during middle childhood.

- Define overweight and its relationship to the body mass index.

- Summarize the various risk factors identified in being overweight.

- List the major genetic and environmental factors that contribute to being overweight.

- Explain how the brain grows and matures during middle childhood.

- Note the highlights in motor development for children ages seven to eleven.

PHYSICAL DEVELOPMENT IN MIDDLE CHILDHOOD

- Summarize the benefits of regular exercise.

- Describe the main causes for lack of exercise in middle childhood.

- Summarize the physical, emotional, and social benefits of organized sports.

- Discuss the concerns over involvement in organized sports.

- Outline the most common threats to the health and safety of children aged seven to eleven.

- Describe several precautions adults and other care-givers can take to reduce hazards to children's safety.

- Explain the main risk factors for child abuse.

- Summarize the most common effects of child abuse.

- Define and describe the developmental psychopathology perspective.

- Discuss attention deficit/hyperactivity disorder, including information on what researchers believe to be the cause.

- Identify the most common types of communication and learning disorders.

- Give an overview of autism and its varied symptoms.

PHYSICAL DEVELOPMENT IN MIDDLE CHILDHOOD

As You Read

Key terms and concepts are essential to your understanding of the chapter. Your ability to logically discuss and analyze pertinent information is dependent upon your knowledge of these concepts. Terms can be found in boldface throughout the chapter and definitions are listed in a glossary of terms at the end of the chapter. Flashcards may be helpful for memorizing definitions. Begin using the terms as you study, incorporating them into your vocabulary.

attention deficit/hyperactivity disorder (ADHD)	cortisol	overweight
autism spectrum disorders (ASDs)	developmental psychopathology perspective	prevalence rates
body mass index (BMI)	individualized education plan (IEP)	risk of overweight
children with exceptional needs	learning disorders	rough-and-tumple play
communication disorders	least restrictive environment	sensitization
comorbidity	organized sports	child sexual abuse

⊙ GROWTH OF THE BODY AND BRAIN

Physical Growth

Fill in the missing information in the chart.

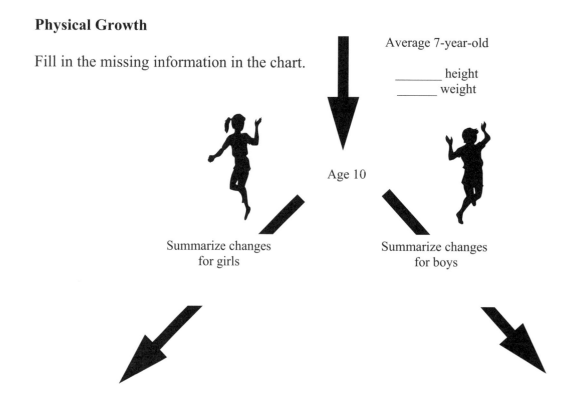

Average 7-year-old

_____ height
_____ weight

Age 10

Summarize changes for girls

Summarize changes for boys

244

PHYSICAL DEVELOPMENT IN MIDDLE CHILDHOOD

Childhood Overweight

1. *Numerically Speaking* of Overweight

    A. Overweight is defined as having a body mass index at or above the _____ th percentile for the child's age and sex.

    B. From the 1960s to 2002, the percentage of U.S. children who were overweight grew from _____ to _____ percent.

    C. Among adults, _____ percent were overweight during the 1999-2002 test period.

    D. Among ethnic minorities, _____ percent of Mexican-American boys and _____ percent of African-American girls are overweight.

    E. One survey showed that _____ percent of U.S. children watch _____ or more hours of television per day.

    F. Approximately _____ percent of children in lower-income families have TV sets in their bedrooms.

    G. About _____ percent of overweight 4-year-olds and _____ percent of overweight adolescents will be obese in adulthood.

2. List at least four potential health problems linked to being overweight.

3. What are the environmental and genetic factors that lead to being overweight?

    Environmental factors   Genetic factors

PHYSICAL DEVELOPMENT IN MIDDLE CHILDHOOD

4. According to the American Academy of Pediactrics (2003), which five actions taken by parents and caregivers could help solve the problem of overweight children.

   A.

   B.

   C.

   D.

   E.

Growth and Maturation of the Brain

1. Fill in the missing information in the chart.

Area of the Brain	Basic Functions	Pruning and Maturation Rank (early, middle, late)
occipital lobe		early
sensory cortex		
motor cortex		
	integrate information, control language	middle
	abstract reasoning, complex problem solving	late

2. Describe the research focused on the effects of trauma and negative experiences on brain maturation.

PHYSICAL DEVELOPMENT IN MIDDLE CHILDHOOD

⊙ MOTOR DEVELOPMENT AND PHYSICAL ACTIVITY

Motor Development

Identify the major changes seen during middle childhood in each of the following categories. Give examples when possible. Note any differences between boys and girls.

Strength and Flexibility

Movement

Coordination of Skills

PHYSICAL DEVELOPMENT IN MIDDLE CHILDHOOD

Physical Activity and Exercise

1. List the health benefits of regular exercise.

   Physical   Emotional

2. What are the main obstacles in getting sufficient exercise?

3. Discuss any differences in the types of physical activities preferred by each gender in middle childhood.

Organized Sports

1. Participation in organized sports has a number of potential benefits. List each under its respective column.

   Physical   Social   Emotional/Cognitive

PHYSICAL DEVELOPMENT IN MIDDLE CHILDHOOD

2. As the parent of a second-grader and a fourth-grader you are very concerned about the health and well-being of your children. Yesterday, your kids brought home a notice from the school they attend stating that due to system-wide funding cuts they will be unable to continue offering physical education courses or any organized sports. Draft a letter to the school superintendent stating your position on the matter. Include any pertinent research from your text to support your view.

PHYSICAL DEVELOPMENT IN MIDDLE CHILDHOOD

⊙ HEALTH AND SAFETY ISSUES

Childhood Injuries and Safety Issues

Being the Teacher
Prepare a 30-minute presentation for a third grade class on "Safety at Home and Away." What props might you use to make your talk more visually appealing? What three things would you want the children to remember the most? How would you change the presentation if you were speaking to a group of parents gathered for a conference on safety issues.

PHYSICAL DEVELOPMENT IN MIDDLE CHILDHOOD

Child Sexual Abuse

1. How do each of these factors influence the risk for child sexual abuse?

    A. Poor family environment

    B. Marital disruptions

    C. Individual differences

2. Place an X in the blank if sexual abuse has been connected to each of the following.

    _____ chronic stress   _____ teenage pregnancy and prostitution

    _____ psoriasis   _____ diabetes

    _____ smaller corpus callosum   _____ eating disorders

    _____ compromised immune system   _____ lower levels of income as an adult

    _____ dementia   _____ drug and alcohol abuse

    _____ depression   _____ low self-esteem

    _____ increased sexual behavior   _____ cerebral palsy

PHYSICAL DEVELOPMENT IN MIDDLE CHILDHOOD

⊙ CHILDREN WITH EXCEPTIONAL NEEDS

What is Developmental Psychopathology?

1. How would you explain the developmental psychopathology perspective?

2. List at least four factors developmental psychopathologists believe influence both normal and abnormal paths of development.

    A.

    B.

    C.

    D.

3. What are prevalence rates? Why are prevalence rates considered the experts' best estimates?

4. Define comorbidity. Give at least two examples of a comorbidity situation.

    A.

    B.

Attention Deficit/Hyperactivity Disorder

1. Describe the two phases identified with ADHD.

    A.

    B.

PHYSICAL DEVELOPMENT IN MIDDLE CHILDHOOD

2. List the four types of ADHD recognized by clinicians.

   A.

   B.

   C.

   D.

3. Each of the following "facts" about ADHD is FALSE. Change some part or parts of each statement to make it TRUE.

   A. Parents and teachers typically identify as many as three-quarters of all children as "hyperactive."

   Change(s):

   B. Of the group of children labeled as "hyperactive" by parents and teachers, only about 10 percent meet the clinical criteria for some type of ADHD.

   Change(s):

   C. The cause of ADHD is a malfunction in the frontal lobe of the brain.

   Change(s):

   D. Researchers estimate that the heritability of ADHD is approximately .20.

   Change(s):

   E. Of the children being treated with stimulant medications, about 90 percent show improvements in concentration, motor control, and the ability to stay on task.

   Change(s):

   F. There are no known behavior management programs that can be helpful to children with ADHD.

   Change(s):

PHYSICAL DEVELOPMENT IN MIDDLE CHILDHOOD

Communication and Learning Disorders

Read each phrase below. Place a CD in the blank if the phrase pertains only to communication disorders, an LD for learning disorders, or a B if the phrase refers to both.

_____ significant difficulty producing speech sounds

_____ "hidden" problems of childhood

_____ difficulty understanding what other people say

_____ struggles to understand mathematics

_____ experiences trouble with either reading or writing

_____ tend to have average to above-average intelligence

_____ difficulty using spoken language to communicate

_____ receive half of all special education services provided by schools

_____ strong genetic factor, related to abnormalities in brain function

_____ often corrects itself or the child learns a way to compensate for the difficulty

Autism Spectrum Disorders

Read each of the following statements carefully, then underline the word(s) in parentheses that will make the statement correct.

A. Autism Spectrum Disorders (ASDs) are a group of serious (developmental/ behavioral) disorders characterized by impairments in (social interaction and communication/articulation and production of language sounds).

B. A (spectrum/sensorimotor) disorder can take forms that range from mild to severe.

C. Of every 1000 children in the U.S., approximately (1 to 6/7 to 10) have an autism spectrum disorder.

PHYSICAL DEVELOPMENT IN MIDDLE CHILDHOOD

Educating Children with Exceptional Needs

1. Describe the use of an IEP. How is it related to a least restrictive environment?

2. Summarize the ideas of the Individuals with Disabilities Education Act (IDEA). How has the passage of IDEA affected schools?

PHYSICAL DEVELOPMENT IN MIDDLE CHILDHOOD

When You Have Finished

⊙ WORKING THE WEB

1. In the United States, the most frequent nutritional problem is overweight. To learn more about the prevalence and identification of childhood overweight go to the American Obesity Association web site at www.obesity.org/subs/childhood. Learn the body mass index BMI percentiles used for identifying "overweight" and "obese" children. What percentage of U.S. parents believe physical education or recess should not be reduced or replaced with academic classes? Check out the AOA survey of parents and the excellent links to various sources of information.

2. Curious about your child's body mass index (BMI)? Go to the National Center for Health Statistics at www.cdc.gov/growthcharts/ to find information on how to calculate a body mass index and to obtain downloadable copies of clinical growth charts in both English and Spanish.

3. The American Speech-Language-Hearing Association at www.asha.org has vital information on a wide variety of communication related issues, including speech and language development, disorders and diseases, and finding a speech-language pathologist. You will also find pertinent links to language and literacy, as well as bilingualism.

4. Bright Futures at Georgetown University (www.brightfutures.org), a "national health promotion initiative," is an excellent source of information on promoting and improving "the health, education, and well-being of infants, children, adolescents, families, and communities." Download or read online from the publication "Bright Futures in Practice: Physical Activity," which includes topics such as asthma and activity, injury, nutrition, and coaching.

5. What is developmental dyspraxia? Read about developmental coordination disorder at the following web sites to find out more about the disorder, treatment options, and the prognoses.
www.autistics.org/access/information/motor/dyspraxia.html
library.advanced.org/11799/data/dyspraxia.html
www.dyspraxiafoundation.org.uk
www.ninds.nih.gov/disorders/dyspraxia/dyspraxia.htm

6. Are you interested in studying developmental psychopathology? Learn more about this field by investigating the graduate program at the University of Wisconsin, Madison web site (psych.wisc.edu./gradstudies/devpsypath.html).

PHYSICAL DEVELOPMENT IN MIDDLE CHILDHOOD

⊙ PRACTICE TEST #1

Multiple Choice Questions
For each question, circle the best answer from the choices given.

1. At what age does the gender difference in physical growth occur? (p. 328)

a. 6 years old
b. 8 years old
c. 10 years old
d. 12 years old

2. A child having a body mass index (BMI) at or above the 95th percentile is considered (p.329)

a. obese.
b. at risk of overweight.
c. overweight.
d. none of the above.

3. For which of the following does being overweight in childhood increase the risk? (p. 330)

a. heart disease
b. diabetes
c. asthma
d. all of the above

4. By what age does the child's brain reach 90% of its adult size? (p. 331)

a. 6
b. 8
c. 12
d. 16

5. The last area of the brain to mature is the (p. 331)

a. occipital lobe
b. prefrontal cortex
c. hippocampus
d. parietal lobe

PHYSICAL DEVELOPMENT IN MIDDLE CHILDHOOD

6. Kandace and Kevin are 8 year old fraternal twins. If they are normal for their age, (p. 333)

a. Kandace will be taller than Kevin.
b. Kevin has more physical flexibility than Kandace.
c. Kevin will be stronger than Kandace.
d. Kandace has better balance than Kevin.

7. Which of the following groups reported significantly less free time physical activity than the other groups? (p. 334)

a. girls
b. boys
c. Caucasian children
d. Asian-American children

8. As children move through middle childhood to adolescence, how does their physical activity level change? (p. 335)

a. They get more exercise.
b. 90% or adolescents do not participate in any physical activity.
c. Girls become more physically active than boys.
d. They get progressively less exercise.

9. Which of the following statements about organized sports in middle childhood is TRUE? (p. 337)

a. Girls outnumber boys in participation in sports outside school.
b. Injuries due to sports have increased in recent years.
c. Participation in sports has been found to be linked to higher academic achievement and lower delinquency rates.
d. In organized youth sports, soccer has the highest rate of injuries.

10. What percentage of children's sports program are organized, coached and led by adults? (p. 338)

a. 50%
b. 70%
c. 85%
d. 99%

PHYSICAL DEVELOPMENT IN MIDDLE CHILDHOOD

⊙ PRACTICE TEST #2

Multiple Choice Questions
For each question, circle the best answer from the choices given.

1. Which of the following is the most common cause of childhood injuries treated in a hospital emergency room? (p. 339)

    a. falls
    b. cuts
    c. car accidents
    d. all of the above

2. Which of the following is NOT a risk factor for childhood sexual abuse? (p. 343)

    a. domestic violence
    b. early puberty
    c. delayed puberty
    d. separated or divorced parents

3. Georgia was sexually abused as a child by her step-father. Which psychological disorder is she MOST LIKELY to have? (p. 345)

    a. depression
    b. attention deficit hyperactivity disorder
    c. a communication disorder
    d. multiple personality disorder

4. What percentage of children in the U.S. suffers from mental illness or another serious developmental, emotional or behavioral problem? (p. 347)

    a. 10%
    b. 1 out of 5 children
    c. 50%
    d. 4 out of 5 children

5. The percentage or number of individuals with a particular problem or condition is called the (p. 348)

    a. IDEA.
    b. comorbidity.
    c. prevalence rate.
    d. IEP.

PHYSICAL DEVELOPMENT IN MIDDLE CHILDHOOD

6. What are the most common symptoms of ADHD in children? (p. 349)

a. hyperactivity, inattentiveness and difficulty concentrating
b. distractibility and hyperactivity
c. problems concentrating and low IQ scores
d. inattentiveness and delayed speech development

7. Although ADHD seems to be a common diagnosis in children nowadays, what percentage of children actually meet the clinical criteria for this disorder? (p. 349)

a. 2%
b. 4 to 6 %
c. 10 to 12%
d. 25%

8. Conditions involving difficulties with specific academic skills such as reading, math or writing are called (p. 351)

a. achievement disorders.
b. mental retardation spectrum.
c. mixed receptive-expressive language disorders.
d. learning disorders.

9. Nick is 10 years old. He has very little language skills and prefers to play alone. Nicky does not make eye contact when people talk to him, likes to spend hours lining up his Matchbox cars and is upset by changes in his routine. His mostly likely diagnosis is (p. 353)

a. autism spectrum disorder.
b. dyslexia.
c. ADHD.
d. mixed receptive-expressive language disorder.

10. Federal law requires that children receiving special educational services be placed with non-disabled peers whenever possible. This is called the (p. 355)

a. individualized educational plan.
b. least restrictive environment.
c. Learning Disabilities Act.
d. developmental psychopathology rule.

PHYSICAL DEVELOPMENT IN MIDDLE CHILDHOOD

⊙ COMPREHENSIVE PRACTICE TEST

Multiple Choice Questions
For each question, circle the best answer from the choices given.

1. Padraic is an average 7 year old. How tall would he be? (p. 238)

a. 3 ½ feet tall
b. 4 feet tall
c. 4 ½ feet tall
d. 5 feet tall

2. A national survey found what percentage of American children watch more than 4 hours of TV per day? (p. 329)

a. 10%
b. 20%
c. 26%
d. 35%

3. Which of the following statements about overweight children is FALSE? (p. 330)

a. Children today have more positive role models for health and fitness than in the past.
b. A mix of genetic and environmental factors contribute to children being overweight.
c. Children from poor families have a higher risk of being overweight.
d. When both parents are overweight, a child's risk of being overweight increases 10 times.

4. In certain areas the brain actually shrinks after age (p. 331)

a. 10.
b. 16.
c. 21.
d. 50.

5. Which type of skills become more controlled and coordinated in middle childhood? (p. 333)

a. fine motor
b. gross motor
c. moral reasoning
d. both a and b

PHYSICAL DEVELOPMENT IN MIDDLE CHILDHOOD

6. Which of the following is NOT a reason children don't get more exercise? (p. 335)

a. Children spend increased time watching TV and playing computer games.
b. Children cannot walk or bicycle safely to school.
c. Rough and tumble play decreases in middle childhood.
d. Transportation problems and the high cost of sports limits access.

7. Maleka takes dance lessons at her local community center. This is an example of (p. 336 - 337)

a. sociodramatic play.
b. organized sports.
c. a sedentary lifestyle.
d. gender segregation.

8. What percentage of accidental childhood deaths in the U.S. occur in or around the home? (p. 340)

a. 10%
b. 25%
c. 35%
d. 40%

9. Approximately how many children are treated each year in hospital emergency rooms for bicycle injuries? (p. 340)

a. 10,000
b. 100.000
c. 250,000
d. 500,000

10. What is the ratio of boys in the U.S. who suffer some form of sexual abuse before they grow up? (p.343)

a. 1 in 5
b. 1 in 9
c. 2 in 10
d. 2 out of 3

PHYSICAL DEVELOPMENT IN MIDDLE CHILDHOOD

11. Chronic stress, such as that caused by ongoing sexual abuse, can cause high levels of (p. 344)

a. cortisol.
b. myelination.
c. synaptic pruning.
d. estrogen production.

12. Marty has mild mental retardation and problems with aggressive behavior. He would be considered a child (p. 347)

a. with a learning disability.
b. without comorbidity.
c. suffering from developmental psychopathology.
d. with exceptional needs.

13. Maria has ADHD and a communication disorder. This is an example of (p. 348)

a. comorbidity.
b. prevalence rate.
c. autism spectrum disorder.
d. all of the above.

14. Oscar has difficulty concentrating, gets distracted easily, is very active and does things without thinking first. The MOST LIKELY diagnosis for him is (p. 349)

a. learning disorder.
b. phonological disorder.
c. attention deficit hyperactivity disorder, predominantly hyperactive-impulsive.
d. attention deficit hyperactivity disorder, predominantly inattentive.

15. The heritability of ADHD is estimated to be as high as (p. 349)

a. 25.
b. 39.
c. 55.
d. 80.

PHYSICAL DEVELOPMENT IN MIDDLE CHILDHOOD

16. Thomas is 5 years old, but has problems with correctly articulating speech sounds. For example, he says "wed" for "red". He would be diagnosed as having (p. 352)

a. stuttering disorder.
b. phonological disorder.
c. mixed receptive-expressive language disorder.
d. none of the above.

17. Research has shown expressive language disorders related to (p. 352)

a. autism spectrum disorders.
b. ADHD.
c. recurrent ear infections.
d. overactivity in the left brain.

18. A small percentage of children with autism spectrum disorders show splinter skills. All of the following are examples of splinter skills EXCEPT (p. 353)

a. writing poetry.
b. memory for music.
c. calculating dates.
d. speed in building puzzles.

19. Which of the following behaviors would NOT be typical for a child with autism spectrum disorder? (p. 354)

a. language and speech problems
b. seems to be in own world
c. has an unusual need for a certain order of activities
d. likes to play with other children

20. The IEP is (p. 355)

a. the educational placement of children with exceptional needs in mainstreamed classrooms.
b. a written plan that describes the services needed and instructional goals for children with disabilities.
c. a form of therapy for autism spectrum disorders.
d. a sub-type of ADHD.

PHYSICAL DEVELOPMENT IN MIDDLE CHILDHOOD

Short-Answer Questions

Answer each question in the space provided.

1. Describe three factors related to the increased problem of children being overweight. What recommendations has the American Academy of Pediatrics made to combat childhood obesity?

2. What are communication disorders and learning disorders? Compare and contrast these disorders.

3. Explain why autism has been changed as a diagnosis to autism spectrum disorders (ASD). What is the prevalence rate for ASDs in the U.S.? What causes ASDs?

PHYSICAL DEVELOPMENT IN MIDDLE CHILDHOOD

⊙ CROSSWORD PUZZLE

Across
5. more than one psychological disorder at the same time
9. _____ rates refer to the percentages of individuals who show particular problems or conditions.
10. written plan describing services and instructional goals for special needs children

Down
1. Children with _____ needs require help beyond that of their peers.
2. development of a tendency to overreact strongly and quickly even when the situation is relatively mild
3. a disorder characterized by impairments in social interaction and communication
4. a hormone released in response to stress
6. body mass index at or above the 95th percentile for age and gender
7. _____ sports are coached and/or supervised by adults.
8. Child _____ abuse includes fondling, intercourse, or other sexual acts with a child.

Created by Puzzlemaker at DiscoverySchool.com

11 COGNITIVE DEVELOPMENT IN MIDDLE CHILDHOOD

Before You Read

Many new cognitive developments occur in middle childhood. Children enter Piaget's third stage of development, concrete operational thought (7 to 11 years of age). The development of logic enables a child to understand class inclusion and transitive inference. As you read, you will learn more about memory, and how information is stored and accessed. A new model of the information-processing perspective is introduced and the limitations of this approach are examined. The continued development of language is addressed, including the use of passive voice and making inferences. An overview of mathematical skills describes strategies children use to count and to solve word problems. The chapter closes with an examination of the phases through which children move in the development of reading and writing skills.

Chapter Learning Objectives

After reading this chapter, you should be able to do the following:

- Compare and contrast intuitive and logical thought, giving examples of each.

- Explain Piaget's third stage of cognitive development.

- Define the terms "class inclusion," "seriation," "and transitive inference."

- Compare and contrast the stores model and the network model of memory.

- Describe the characteristics of working and long-term memory and identify how each type of memory develops.

COGNITIVE DEVELOPMENT IN MIDDLE CHILDHOOD

- Define and give examples of semantic memory, episodic memory, and scripts.

- Explain why memory is described as reconstructive and give examples of when it may and may not matter.

- Define autobiographical memory and explain why researchers are interested in this phenomenon.

- Distinguish between a knowledge base and strategies and explain how each affects cognitive development.

- Identify three specific memory strategies and describe the development of each.

- Compare and contrast production systems and connectionist models of cognitive development.

- Describe the main idea of fuzzy trace theory.

- Discuss the contributions and limitations of information-processing approaches.

- Explain metalinguistic awareness and its importance to language development.

- Describe the connectionist model of language development.

- Outline the highlights in the development of mathematical, reading, and writing skills during middle childhood.

COGNITIVE DEVELOPMENT IN MIDDLE CHILDHOOD

As You Read

Key terms and concepts are essential to your understanding of the chapter. Your ability to logically discuss and analyze pertinent information is dependent upon your knowledge of these concepts. Terms can be found in boldface throughout the chapter and definitions are listed in a glossary of terms at the end of the chapter. Flashcards may be helpful for memorizing definitions. Begin using the terms as you study, incorporating them into your vocabulary.

access	inventive spelling	reconstructive memory
autobiographical memories	knowledge base	retrieval
chunking	knowledge telling	scripts
computational models	long-term memory	storage
concrete operational thought	metalinguistic awareness	stores model (of memory)
connectionist models	network models (of memory)	strategies
counting strategies	personal narratives	strategy choice model
encoding	phonemic awareness	subitizing
fuzzy trace theory	production systems	working memory

⊙ PIAGET'S STAGE 3: CONCRETE OPERATIONAL THOUGHT

What is Concrete Operational Thinking?

1. What do the terms "decentered," "dynamic transformations," "reversibility," and "operations" mean in concrete operational thought?

2. What is the one major limitation of this stage of thought?

COGNITIVE DEVELOPMENT IN MIDDLE CHILDHOOD

Class Inclusion, Seriation, and Transitive Inference Skills

You have now learned about the first three stages of Piaget's theory of cognitive development. Identify these three stages and their age ranges. Then, in the blanks provided beside each concept, check the developmental stage(s) in which it occurs. When a box appears at the end of a row, define the term.

        <u>Age Range</u>
Stage 1: _____
Stage 2: _____
Stage 3: _____

Concept	Stage		
	1	2	3
accommodation			
adaptation			
animism			
assimilation			
centration			
class inclusion			
conservation			
decentration			
egocentrism			
equilibration			
intuitive thought			
knowing through sensory input			
object permanence			
organization			
operations			
reflective abstraction			
scheme			
seriation			
symbolic play			
transitive inference			
representational thought			

COGNITIVE DEVELOPMENT IN MIDDLE CHILDHOOD

⊙ INFORMATION PROCESSING: MEMORY DEVELOPMENT

Match each of the following memory-related terms with the appropriate descriptors. Each type of memory will appear twice in the statements below.

A. metamemory
B. episodic memory
C. semantic memory
D. long-term memory

E. reconstructive memory
F. autobiographical memory
G. working memory
H. chunking

_____ most common type of children's earliest memories
_____ memories that are of great personal relevance and importance
_____ knowledge about the processes and contents of one's own memory
_____ type of memory that was the main focus of long-term memory research
_____ process of retrieving some stored memories and making inferences about the rest
_____ memory for events that occur in one's everyday life
_____ memory of knowledge related to words and concepts
_____ conceptualization of memory as inferential and non-literal
_____ the nonactivated part of an integrated memory network
_____ type of memory that is similar to STS in the stores model
_____ memory that is currently active and available for use
_____ memory of knowledge that is permanent
_____ memories that help children develop a sense of their own identity
_____ memory that includes information you are consciously aware of at any moment
_____ includes information on memory tasks and strategies and person variables
_____ recoding individual elements in memory into larger information group

Two Models of Memory: Stores and Networks

Describe the main differences between the stores model of memory and the network models of memory.

COGNITIVE DEVELOPMENT IN MIDDLE CHILDHOOD

Working Memory

1. Describe the two important characteristics of working memory.

    A.

    B.

2. In what ways does working memory affect cognitive tasks?

Long-term Memory

1. Identify and describe two fundamental characteristics of long-term memory.

    A.

    B.

2. Compare and contrast access and retrieval.

3. How are episodic memory and scripts related? Can you think of a unique script you had as a child?

COGNITIVE DEVELOPMENT IN MIDDLE CHILDHOOD

4. As your textbook indicates, scripts are mental representations of the manner in which things typically occur in certain situations or during specific events. After reading the material regarding how children's scripts change with age, pick a situation or event and create a script containing content likely to be described by children at each of the following ages. Better yet, go out and ask some children about the event you chose!

Event or situation: _____

    1-year-old's script:

    2-year-old's script:

    7-year-old's script:

COGNITIVE DEVELOPMENT IN MIDDLE CHILDHOOD

Other Characteristics of Memory Development

1. Reconstructive Memory Activity
    This activity is more long-term than usual and will take you about a week to complete. You will need three separate sheets of paper on which to write. Below, you will find a brief paragraph. Please read this paragraph slowly once. Then, continue studying this chapter for thirty minutes. After waiting thirty minutes, take out one of your sheets of paper, write "Memories after 30 minutes" on it, and then write down as much as you can remember about the paragraph. DON'T LOOK BACK! Wait two days and repeat the process. This time write "Memories after 2 days" on the top of your second sheet of paper. Don't read your first written version or the original paragraph. Finally, wait five more days, and use your third piece of paper to write down your memories of the paragraph. Now, compare your three versions of the paragraph with the original. What kinds of information did you remember? What information did you forget after 30 minutes? After 2 days? After 7 days? Do you see any evidence that you added material not in the original? Do you see any evidence that you altered any details? In what ways might your own cultural background influence your reconstructed memories?

(Adapted from Bartlett, 1932)

Amalias and Pyrgos are 14-year-old monozygotic twins from Coos Bay, Oregon. Since learning they were conceived during a visit to the Peloponnese region of Greece, the boys have become fascinated with the country and its culture. Their mom, Delores is going to make diples (Greek honey twists) and kourambiethes (Greek crescent cookies) for the twins to take to a school party. Ms. Wickes, their social studies teacher, has asked the students to bring a dessert from their favorite country. Delores has all of the ingredients she needs for the concoctions except ouzo, the anise-flavored liqueur. She and the twins are planning to walk over to Hazeltine's Market to buy the liqueur before baking this evening.

COGNITIVE DEVELOPMENT IN MIDDLE CHILDHOOD

2. Autobiographical Memory Activity

   A. Get a friend to help you with this memory project. First, ask your friend to remember what he or she was doing on a specific evening one week earlier and jot down your friend's response. Next, define "autobiographical memory" for your friend and ask him or her to share a memory that fits this definition. Once again, write down your friend's response. Compare the two memories in terms of amount of detail, vividness, emotional content, and evidence of sensory involvement (i.e., sights, sounds, smells).

   B. Ask your friend how old he or she was at the time of the event described. Does your friend have a sense of how much of their memory was actually experienced? How much was influenced by other people's interpretations?

COGNITIVE DEVELOPMENT IN MIDDLE CHILDHOOD

⊙ INFORMATION PROCESSING: Knowledge, Strategies, and New Approaches

Knowledge Base

1. Identify six positive effects of a strong knowledge base.

    A.

    B.

    C.

    D.

    E.

    F.

2. Explain how expert-novice studies with children and adults have been used to understand the importance of knowledge base to cognitive development.

3. Describe at least two differences between experts and novices in regard to their information-processing abilities.

    A.

    B.

COGNITIVE DEVELOPMENT IN MIDDLE CHILDHOOD

Strategy Development

1. As a study aid, try creating a network model for the information in this chapter using appropriate links and nodes. Quickly sketch out your model below. Later, review the chapter and your notes to make your model more complete.

2. Now, write down the three main memory strategies described in your text and discuss how each specific strategy could be used in conjunction with your network model to learn the material in this chapter.

    A.

    B.

    C.

COGNITIVE DEVELOPMENT IN MIDDLE CHILDHOOD

Newer Approaches to Understanding Cognitive Development

1. Explain why production systems and connectionist models are both considered computational models of cognitive development. How are these two types of models similar to and different from one another?

2. Using the basic elements of a connectionist model (i.e., units, nodes, level of activation, and links), explain how these models circumvent the need for cognitive "storage."

3. Discuss the similarities and differences between verbatim traces and fuzzy traces.

         Similarities   Differences

COGNITIVE DEVELOPMENT IN MIDDLE CHILDHOOD

4. Your text authors note that researchers don't yet know why younger children rely on verbatim traces, whereas older children rely more on fuzzy traces. However, they do offer one hypothesis involving knowledge base and script usage that might explain this developmental shift. Explain their hypothesis in your own words.

5. Summarize how researchers believe these new computational models of cognition can be used to more fully understand human cognitive development.

Information-Processing: Where does it stand?

1. Outline the four primary criticisms of information-processing approaches.

   A.

   B.

   C.

   D.

2. Discuss how information-processing researchers have responded to these criticisms.

COGNITIVE DEVELOPMENT IN MIDDLE CHILDHOOD

⊙ LEARNING TO COMMUNICATE: Language in Middle Childhood

> Semantic knowledge-
>
> Phonemic development-
>
> Grammar and syntax-
>
> Pragmatic language skills-

1. Give an overview of language development during middle childhood addressing each of the topics in the bubble.

2. Discuss metalinguistic awareness and note three specific ways it contributes to linguistic skills in middle childhood.

COGNITIVE DEVELOPMENT IN MIDDLE CHILDHOOD

Changes in How Language is Used

1. Describe a personal narrative. How are the following terms linked to the use of a personal narrative?

    A. chronological structure

    B. classic narrative

2. Identify any cultural differences in personal narratives.

Connectionist Models of Language Development

1. Describe the connectionist models of language development and give an example of each.

COGNITIVE DEVELOPMENT IN MIDDLE CHILDHOOD

⊙ COGNITION IN CONTEXT

Development of Mathematical Skills

1. Being the Teacher
   Pretend you are the instructor at a parents' meeting on math skills development. During the pre-meeting social you overhear the comments below. In the space provided near each comment, summarize the information regarding math skills that will update, redirect, and guide the parents at your meeting to provide better support for and ultimately enhance, their children's mathematical skills.

   "...I mean we all know that kids can't even count until they are at least three or four..."

   _____
   _____
   _____
   _____
   _____

   "...I never allow Micah to count on his fingers. It would be too hard for him to change to another way later..."

   _____
   _____
   _____
   _____

   "...Why don't they just teach them all how to count one way and be done with it?..."

   _____
   _____
   _____

   "...What's with all these new concepts and processes? The kids need to focus on memorization and rules. That's the way I was taught..."

COGNITIVE DEVELOPMENT IN MIDDLE CHILDHOOD

2. Summarize current research focused on mathematical word problems.

3. Think back to your own years in elementary math classes. Can you remember experiencing a bug in your understanding of a fundamental math principle? How was this systematic error resolved?

Development of Reading Skills

1. In the first blank, match each example to the most appropriate stage from Chall's Developmental Stages in Reading (Table 11.3). In the second blank, give the person's approximate age.

   ___ ___   Jeremy holds his favorite book, "Pokey Little Puppy," and pretends to read to the family dog.

   ___ ___   Wilhelmina skims over the treatment of continental drift theory in her geology text, and focuses her attention on her main interest, plate tectonics.

   ___ ___   Even though he has heard and read the story several times, Xavier picks up "The Seven Treasure Hunts" and plunges into the story.

   ___ ___   Sitting in his mother's lap, Felix sounds out the letters of an unknown word, then uses the pictures and context to guess at the word meaning.

   ___ ___   Amelia and her aunt are at the bookstore to find a workbook on identifying wildflowers, having just returned from a hiking trip into the mountains.

   ___ ___   Ruth Ann is interested in the work of W.E.B. Dubois, so she is reading books by his contemporaries in order to understand Dubois' life and times.

COGNITIVE DEVELOPMENT IN MIDDLE CHILDHOOD

2. Along with familiarity with the letters of the alphabet, phonemic awareness is a key predictor of success in early reading. Define phonemic awareness and discuss why researchers think it is an important factor in learning to read early and well.

3. Reading is perhaps the single most important academic skill. Below are several quotes extolling the virtues of reading. Using information from your text and other sources, provide support for these authors' statements.

"Reading is to the mind what exercise is to the body."
Richard Steele

"To acquire the habit of reading is to construct for yourself a refuge from almost all of the miseries of life."
W. Somerset Maugham

"The more that you read, the more things you will know. The more that you learn, the more places you'll go."
Dr. Seuss

COGNITIVE DEVELOPMENT IN MIDDLE CHILDHOOD

Development of Writing Skills

1. Writing is a process that begins at an early age and, in some ways, never ends. List the major progressions involved in learning to write well. How are inventive spelling and knowledge telling related to the process of becoming a successful writer?

2. What is meant by the term "recursive revision"?

COGNITIVE DEVELOPMENT IN MIDDLE CHILDHOOD

When You Have Finished

⊙ WORKING THE WEB

1. Take at look at Jill Kerper Mora's work on Spanish/English biliteracy at coe.sdsu.edu/people/jmora/MoraModules/MetalingTransfer.htm. Here you'll find a very interesting web site discussing metalinguistic transfer in Spanish/English biliteracy. The role of teachers in biliteracy development, a comparison of the alphabetic principle in both Spanish and English and approaches to L2 reading instruction are included among other topics. A good list of references and related material sources is found at the end of the article.

2. How might Central Auditory Processing Disorder (CAPD) affect imformation processing and communication? Go to the NYU Child Study Center web site (www.aboutourkids.org/aboutour/articles/capd.html) for details. An overview of the disorder, observable characteristics in the classroom, and treatment are discussed.

3. Visit the Southwest Educational Development Laboratory (SEDL) web site (www.sedl.org) to learn about programs focused on enhancing teaching and learning in math, science, reading and language. Click on the "Programs and Projects" tab and review the offerings. For each program, you'll see a list of current projects. Try clicking the "Electronic Library" tab and take a look at the "Consumer's Guide to Afterschool Science Resources." Information is catalogued by title, subject, grade, and audience.

4. A fun, interactive web site on information processing can be found at www.coe.uga.edu/epltt/InformationProcessing.htm. What differences in information processing are found in students who use English as a second language? Read "Metacognition: One Teacher's Journey." What does Mrs. Smith learn about active and passive learning? What does Mrs. Smith discover about teaching "computers?"

COGNITIVE DEVELOPMENT IN MIDDLE CHILDHOOD

⊙ PRACTICE TEST #1

Multiple Choice Questions
For each question, circle the best answer from the choices given.

1. During which stage of cognitive development can children think logically about real objects? (p. 365)

   a. sensorimotor
   b. preoperations
   c. concrete operations
   d. formal operations

2. What is the major limitation of concrete operational thinking? (p. 365)

   a. Mental operations are still closely tied to real materials and situations.
   b. Logical thinking has not yet emerged.
   c. Chunking of information is limited.
   d. Nodes cannot be activated from internal sources.

3. What model of memory has replaced the stores model in recent years? (p. 366)

   a. chunking
   b. network
   c. scripts
   d. episodic

4. How are working memory and short term store different? (p. 368)

   a. Unlike short term store, working memory has several components.
   b. In short term store information is moved from one place to another.
   c. In working memory, information is simply available for use.
   d. All of the above are differences.

5. Edward was not paying attention when his class reviewed the vocabulary words for their history project. The next day, when there was a surprise quiz, he could not remember what the words meant. His performance on the quiz was due to what memory problem? (p. 370)

   a. lack of encoding
   b. problems with retrieval
   c. difficulty accessing the information
   d. not having a script

COGNITIVE DEVELOPMENT IN MIDDLE CHILDHOOD

6. When you were in elementary school you learned the names of the nine planets. This type of memory is called (p. 372)

a. episodic.
b. semantic.
c. reconstructive.
d. autobiographical.

7. Your sister and you remember the Thanksgiving dinner when you were young and there was a big snowstorm slightly differently. This is because memory is (p. 372)

a. dependent on a knowledge base.
b. scripted.
c. reconstructive.
d. semantic.

8. One of your earliest memories, when you were 4, is that your family got a kitten. This is what type of memory? (p. 373)

a. rehearsal
b. semantic
c. connectionist
d. autobiographical

9. Esmat knows a great deal about plants and trees. When it comes to botany, this is her (p. 376)

a. fuzzy trace.
b. computational model.
c. script.
d. knowledge base.

10. There are two students, Paul and Fred, in your development class who look similar. Your instructor remembers their names this way: Pau*l* has ***light*** hair and Fre*d* has ***dark*** hair. What memory strategy is the instructor using? (p. 379)

a. organization
b. elaboration
c. rehearsal
d. subitizing

COGNITIVE DEVELOPMENT IN MIDDLE CHILDHOOD

⊙ PRACTICE TEST #2

Multiple Choice Questions
For each question, circle the best answer from the choices given.

1. What are the models of cognition that are programmed on computers and then the output is compared to human performance? (p. 380)

a. computational
b. phonemic awareness
c. strategy choice
d. subitizing

2. The neural network models of cognition that view knowledge as based on patterns of activation among interconnected set of individual units is called (p. 382)

a. conservation models.
b. production systems.
c. connectionist models.
d. encoding systems.

3. The theory that memories vary from exact to imprecise and general is the _____ theory. (p. 383)

a. executive processing
b. fuzzy trace
c. production systems
d. stores model

4. Which of the following is NOT a limit of the information processing theory? (p. 384)

a. There is no comprehensive structure for explaining cognitive development.
b. The theory does not take into account how emotions influence thinking.
c. There are no details on how the executive processor works.
d. The emphasis on detailed analysis of cognitive processes.

5. What is the average vocabulary of a typical 10 year old? (p. 385)

a. 20,000 words
b. 40,000 words
c. 60, 000 words
d. 80,000 words

COGNITIVE DEVELOPMENT IN MIDDLE CHILDHOOD

6. Ian knows that "cool" can mean something that is cold or it can mean something that is popular among kids. This understanding is called (p. 386)

a. subitizing.
b. phonemic awareness.
c. metalinguistic awareness.
d. a network model.

7. The strongest support for connectionist models of language development come from (p. 388)

a. computer simulations.
b. observations of children learning to talk.
c. bilingual children.
d. all of the above.

8. Which of the following is NOT a characteristic of subitizing? (p. 390)

a. It only works with small sets.
b. Subitizing requires visible objects.
c. It is an innate perceptual process.
d. It requires retrieval of basic math facts from memory.

9. One of the major sources of difficulty in reading is (p. 392)

a. metalinguistic awareness.
b. a problem decoding written words into speech sounds.
c. syntactical errors.
d. learning classic narrative style.

10. A common writing problem (even in college students!) is adding ideas as they come to mind rather than organizing the writing. This is called (p. 395)

a. knowledge telling.
b. inventive spelling.
c. chunking.
d. fuzzy trace scripts.

COGNITIVE DEVELOPMENT IN MIDDLE CHILDHOOD

⊙ COMPREHENSIVE PRACTICE TEST

Multiple Choice Questions
For each question, circle the best answer from the choices given.

1. Which of the following is NOT a characteristic of concrete operational thinking? (p. 365)

   a. focus on dynamic transformations
   b. ability to mentally reverse operations
   c. decentering
   d. egocentrism

2. Arjun is given squares of varying sizes and asked to put them in order from smallest to largest. This is a test of (p. 365)

   a. subitizing.
   b. seriation.
   c. class inclusion.
   d. episodic memory scripts.

3. Your license plate number is JKY 436. To make it easier to remember you think of it as JERKY 436. This is an example of (p. 367)

   a. chunking.
   b. subitizing.
   c. seriation.
   d. tip of the tongue phenomenon.

4. Both the short term store and working memory (p. 369)

   a. include the idea of activation of concept nodes.
   b. are part of the network model of memory.
   c. have limited capacity and decay over time.
   d. all of the above.

5. In network models of memory, retrieval is the process of (p. 370)

   a. bringing information from the long term store to the short term store.
   b. activating information so that it is part of working memory.
   c. forming a mental image.
   d. placing information in long term memory.

COGNITIVE DEVELOPMENT IN MIDDLE CHILDHOOD

6. Many young children in the U.S. know that when you go to McDonalds you go to a counter and order your food, pay for it, take it to a table and eat. This is an example of a/an (p. 372)

a. autobiographical memory.
b. semantic memory.
c. script.
d. working memory.

7. Children's descriptions of past events become organized and detailed between what ages? (p. 373)

a. 3 and 6
b. 6 and 10
c. 10 and 12
d. after age 14

8. Conscious, intentional and controllable plans used to improve performance are called (p. 377)

a. concept nodes.
b. activation models.
c. knowledge bases.
d. strategies.

9. Research on experts and novices has found that experts have more information than novices and (p. 378)

a. use subitizing more.
b. have larger memory capacity.
c. organize their knowledge differently.
d. have more activation of their short term store.

10. Andrea is given a list of words to memorize. To facilitate her learning, she creates relationships among the words such as "red house" for "house" and "red," two words on the list. This strategy is known as (p. 379)

a. phonemic awareness.
b. rehearsal.
c. elaboration.
d. organization.

COGNITIVE DEVELOPMENT IN MIDDLE CHILDHOOD

11. The two general types of computational models of cognition are (p. 380)

a. production systems and connectionist models.
b. production systems and activation models.
c. activation models and episodic systems.
d. fuzzy trace theory and executive processing systems.

12. You are able to remember what you had for breakfast on Sunday because you know that you went out to breakfast at IHOP after church services. This is an example of which theory of memory? (p. 383)

a. rehearsal
b. fuzzy trace
c. short term store
d. semantic

13. Since the early 1960's, what theory has become the dominant model for understanding cognitive development? (p. 384)

a. fuzzy trace
b. metacognition
c. strategy choice model
d. information processing

14. Deshawn knows that when he tells his mother about what happened at band practice he has to explain the formation the band was doing, since she wasn't there to see it. This shows his _____ language skills. (p. 386)

a. pragmatic
b. semantic
c. phonemic
d. syntactical

15. Krystal knows that bark can mean two different things. This is an example of (p. 386)

a. the rules of social discourse.
b. phonemic awareness.
c. metalinguistic awareness.
d. conccept nodes.

COGNITIVE DEVELOPMENT IN MIDDLE CHILDHOOD

16. Which of the following does NOT have an influence on children's preferred style for personal narratives? (p. 387)

a. age
b. gender
c. culture
d. All of the above influence personal narrative.

17. Karolina is given the arithmetic problem what is 2 + 4? She solves it by counting 2, then 3, 4, 5, 6. She is using (p. 389 - 390)

a. subitizing.
b. a counting strategy.
c. fact retrieval.
d. decomposition.

18. The idea that children solve math problems by choosing the fastest approach they can execute accurately is (p. 391)

a. the decomposition theory.
b. subitizing.
c. debugging.
d. the strategy choice model.

19. Jeff knows that the word "car" is made up of two smaller units, "k" and "ar." This is an example of (p. 392)

a. phonemic awareness.
b. metalinguistic awareness.
c. reconstructive memory.
d. semantic fluency.

20. Jared is writing in social studies. He spells "physical" as "fizzical." His unique spelling is also called (p. 395)

a. phonemic memory.
b. pragmatic use of words.
c. inventive spelling.
d. the strategy choice model.

COGNITIVE DEVELOPMENT IN MIDDLE CHILDHOOD

Short-Answer Questions
Answer each question in the space provided.

1. Describe the concrete operational stage of cognitive development in Piaget's theory. Be sure to include conservation, decentering, dynamic transformation and reversibility, as well as class inclusion and transitive inference in your answer.

2. Compare and contrast the production systems and the connectionist models of information processing.

3. Describe the development of language during middle childhood. Include the connectionist model of language development in your answer.

COGNITIVE DEVELOPMENT IN MIDDLE CHILDHOOD

⊙ CROSSWORD PUZZLE

Across
2. The _____ model of memory views information as moving through a series of storage locations.
3. "neurally inspired" models of cognition
6. _____ trace theory views memory as variable representations on a continuum from exact and literal to imprecise and general.
7. conscious, intentional, and controllable plans used to improve performance
10. The _____ model of memory views information as an interconnected association of concept nodes.

Down
1. A person's explicit knowledge about language itself and about one's use of it is called _____ awareness.
4. _____ awareness is the understanding that words are made up of smaller units of sound.
5. mental representations of the way things typically occur in certain settings or for certain events
8. the process of bringing information from long-term to short-term storage
9. a perceptual process in which people quickly and easily determine the number of objects in a set

Puzzle created with Puzzlemaker at DiscoverySchool.com

12 SOCIAL AND EMOTIONAL DEVELOPMENT IN MIDDLE CHILDHOOD

Before You Read

Social and emotional development in middle childhood (ages 7 to 11) covers a broad array of topics. The chapter begins with an assessment of the social and emotional self, looking at how children evaluate themselves and how this evaluation relates to their sense of self-esteem. Emotional control and the ability to read the emotions of others are critical abilities that begin to develop during this period. In the modern American family, divorce is a reality for many children and the associated problems can be particularly difficult during middle childhood. The effects of divorce and ways that adults can ameliorate associated problems are covered, as are the effects of never-married households and stepfamilies. The next portion of the chapter focuses on play, friends, and peer popularity, with special attention given to rejected children and strategies to improve these children's lives. The chapter concludes by examining the impact of schools and the media, including the effects of classroom climate, video games, computers, and the Internet.

Chapter Learning Objectives

After reading this chapter, you should be able to do the following:

- Outline the developmental progression of self-evaluation and summarize the consequences of positive and negative self-evaluations.

- Describe how the ability to control one's emotions and to correctly read the emotions of others affects relationships.

- Summarize research on the development of gender differences in cognitive skills, emotions, and social behavior.

- Outline Eisenberg's Developmental Levels of Prosocial Reasoning and discuss their cultural universality.

SOCIAL AND EMOTIONAL DEVELOPMENT IN MIDDLE CHILDHOOD

- Summarize research regarding aggressive, destructive, and violent children.

- Identify and discuss two main types of conduct problems.

- Define resilient children and describe the research investigating their developmental outcomes.

- Summarize the social, emotional, and cognitive impacts of divorce and discuss how adults can help children cope better with divorce.

- Describe the effects of living in never-married households and in stepfamilies.

- Discuss the following terms as they relate to peer relationships: best friends, popular children, controversial children, average children, and neglected children.

- Define rejected children and discuss the effects of peer rejection.

- Explain the self-fulfilling prophecy and how it relates to children's achievement.

- Describe the roles played by classroom climate and grouping practices in understanding student achievement.

- Summarize research examining the effects of media on children's cognitive skills, aggression, prosocial behavior, sexual attitudes and behaviors, and stereotyping.

- Discuss the potential impact of video games, computer games, and the Internet on children's development

SOCIAL AND EMOTIONAL DEVELOPMENT IN MIDDLE CHILDHOOD

As You Read

Key terms and concepts are essential to your understanding of the chapter. Your ability to logically discuss and analyze pertinent information is dependent upon your knowledge of these concepts. Terms can be found in boldface throughout the chapter and definitions are listed in a glossary of terms at the end of the chapter. Flashcards may be helpful for memorizing definitions. Begin using the terms as you study, incorporating them into your vocabulary.

ability grouping	master orientation	selection model
achievement motivation	neglected children	self-esteem
attributions	oppositional defiant disorder (odd)	self-evaluations
average children	parentification	self-fulfilling prophecy
classroom climate	peer nomination technique	self-representations
conduct disorder (cd)	popular children	sleeper effect
conduct problems	prosocial reasoning	social cognition model
controversial children	rejected children	social comparison
divorce-stress-adjustment perspective	relational aggression	
helpless orientation	resilient children	

⊙ THE SOCIAL AND EMOTIONAL SELF

Self-Evaluations

1. Identify at least two influences on children's self-evaluation.

    A.

    B.

2. How can the high correlations between children's self-evaluations and physical appearance be explained?

SOCIAL AND EMOTIONAL DEVELOPMENT IN MIDDLE CHILDHOOD

3. Discuss several ways adults can help children develop positive self-evaluations.

Emotional Development

1. For each topic below, summarize the information presented in your text associated with developmental changes in middle childhood.

    A. Ability to empathize:

    B. Ability to read other's emotions:

2. Of the research focused on emotional development, which study was the most interesting to you personally? Why? Which was the most surprising? Why?

SOCIAL AND EMOTIONAL DEVELOPMENT IN MIDDLE CHILDHOOD

Gender Differences

For each of the following gender differences, indicate whether boys or girls score highest.

Girls	Differences	Boys
_____	higher activity levels	_____
_____	engage in outdoor play	_____
_____	relational aggression	_____
_____	likely to seek and receive help	_____
_____	more easily influenced	_____
_____	physical aggression	_____
_____	assertiveness	_____

Moral and Prosocial Reasoning

1. According to Eisenberg (Eisenberg & Fabes, 1998), what types of factors might affect the development and use of prosocial reasoning? Can you think of other factors that might influence prosocial reasoning?

2. Discuss the research in other countries supporting the sequence of levels Eisenberg identified.

SOCIAL AND EMOTIONAL DEVELOPMENT IN MIDDLE CHILDHOOD

3. Using Table 12.2 (page 407), match each of the following examples to the correct level, according to Eisenberg's Developmental Levels of Prosocial Reasoning. Indicate the approximate age at which each level usually emerges.

   _____ "Your party sounds fun, but I'm going to go over and see Angela because she needs my help."

   _____ "My friend Eric has cerebral palsy and I help him with his books at school. If I had a condition like that I'd sure want someone to help me."

   _____ "I help Agnes pick up the toys in her room 'cause then she'll let me come over and swim in her new pool sometimes."

   _____ "I'm a volunteer at the United Way because I feel it's important to give of your time and talents for the good of others."

   _____ "When older people in my neighborhood need help raking leaves I do it for free because that's what good people in our family do."

   Level   Approximate Age

   A. hedonistic orientation

   B. needs-of-others orientation

   C. approval and/or stereotyped orientation

   D. empathic orientation

   E. strongly internalized values orientation

Aggression, Conduct Problems, and Resilient Children

1. Identify three risk factors for aggressive behavior in children.

   A.

   B.

   C.

SOCIAL AND EMOTIONAL DEVELOPMENT IN MIDDLE CHILDHOOD

2. Distinguish between ODD and CD.

3. Describe the phenomenon of resilience in children.

4. Now, identify three characteristics that might protect children from negative conditions. Include social contexts for each.

       A.

       B.

       C.

⊙ FAMILIES

Children and Divorce

1. Describe how the divorce-stress-adjustment perspective and the selection model differentially explain the impact of divorce on children.

SOCIAL AND EMOTIONAL DEVELOPMENT IN MIDDLE CHILDHOOD

2. Fill in the following table to illustrate <u>comparisons</u> between the outcomes for children of divorced and non-divorced parents.

   <u>Child Outcome</u>   <u>Type of Effect</u>

   externalizing problems

   empathy

   teen pregnancy

   physical health effects

   social responsibility

   parentification

   self-esteem

3. Identify and describe three intervening factors that may explain the impact of divorce on children.

   A.

   B.

   C.

4. List at least six ways adults can minimize the negative effects of divorce on children.

   A.

   B.

   C.

   D.

   E.

   F.

SOCIAL AND EMOTIONAL DEVELOPMENT IN MIDDLE CHILDHOOD

Never-Married Households

Compare and contrast the outcomes for children of divorced parents with those for children who live in never-married households.

Stepfamilies

Identify at least four specific challenges that exist within stepfamilies.

      A.

      B.

      C.

      D.

⊙ PLAY, FRIENDS, AND PEER POPULARITY

Logic and Physical Skills in Play

1. How do changes in logical ability affect play during middle childhood?

2. Other than mere enjoyment, what roles do physical skills in play incorporate?

SOCIAL AND EMOTIONAL DEVELOPMENT IN MIDDLE CHILDHOOD

Best Friends

Discuss the category of best friends and list several characteristics important in the designation "best friends."

Peer Popularity

1. Describe the purpose and strategy of the peer nomination technique. Do you feel there are any ethical concerns in using this technique with young children?

2. Complete the following table regarding the five categories of children identified using the peer nomination technique. For each category, identify the relative numbers of positive and negative nominations. Then, identify characteristic social behaviors and cognitions that are associated with each category.

Category	Nomination Pattern	Social Behavior	Social Cognition
A.			
B.			
C.			
D.			
E.			

SOCIAL AND EMOTIONAL DEVELOPMENT IN MIDDLE CHILDHOOD

3. Think for a moment about students you remember from elementary, junior high, and high school. For each age range, identify a student who was popular, rejected, neglected, average, or controversial. Then, indicate specific behavioral, physical, and personality characteristics of each that you believe were associated with that child's status.

Status	Elementary	Junior High	High School
Popular			
Neglected			
Rejected			
Average			
Controversial			

4. How would you describe the causal link between children's social characteristics and their peer status? In other words, which do you believe comes first?

5. Describe three steps that occur in Dodge's social cognition model of peer relations.

   A.

   B.

   C.

SOCIAL AND EMOTIONAL DEVELOPMENT IN MIDDLE CHILDHOOD

6. Being the Teacher
   Imagine that you have been asked to discuss the potential long-term consequences of peer rejection with a group of concerned parents and teachers in your school district. What would you tell this group? You know that you will inevitably be asked, "What can be done to help these children?" How would you respond to this important question?

⊙ SCHOOLS AND THE MEDIA

Children's Beliefs and Teachers' Expectations about Schooling

1. According to your text, which five factors contribute most to children's attributions.

2. To enhance your understanding of the distinctions between the mastery orientation and the helpless orientation toward learning, fill in the missing information below.

		Mastery Orientation	Helpless Orientation
A.	Success Attributions		
B.	Failure Attributions		
C.	Self-Talk		
D.	View of Ability		
E.	Goal Pursuit		
F.	Persistence		

SOCIAL AND EMOTIONAL DEVELOPMENT IN MIDDLE CHILDHOOD

3. Describe the famous Rosenthal and Jacobson (1968) study of the self-fulfilling prophecy.

4. Discuss research questions surrounding the extent to which teacher expectations can affect children's outcomes.

Classroom Climate and Grouping Practices in Schools

1. Identify specific factors that influence classroom climate in each of the following three categories.

Student Factors	Teacher Factors	Environmental Factors

2. Explain why between-class ability grouping is controversial.

SOCIAL AND EMOTIONAL DEVELOPMENT IN MIDDLE CHILDHOOD

Children and the Media

1. *Numerically Speaking* of Children and the Media

   A. Here in the United States, about _____ percent of children under the age of seven have a television in their bedroom and about _____ percent have a VCR or video game player, too.

   B. Hours spent watching TV, viewing movies, and playing video games tend to peak when children are around _____ years of age.

   C. Teen boys spend about _____ minutes per day using the computer and the Internet, whereas teen girls spend about _____ minutes per day.

   D. The average child in the United States leaves his or her elementary school years having watched over _____ murders and _____ other violent acts on television.

   E. Video games are most popular among boys between the ages of _____ and _____ years.

   F. Even during this age range of peak use, _____ percent of boys play video games less than one hour per day.

SOCIAL AND EMOTIONAL DEVELOPMENT IN MIDDLE CHILDHOOD

2. Summarize the effects of TV on children's outcomes using the following table.

	Educational TV	Entertainment TV
Effects on Cognitive Skills		
School Grades		
School Attitudes		
Reading		
Aggression		
Prosocial Behavior		
Sexual Attitudes		
Stereotyping		

SOCIAL AND EMOTIONAL DEVELOPMENT IN MIDDLE CHILDHOOD

3. Describe the results of classic longitudinal research examining the relationship between boys' viewing of TV violence during childhood and their aggressive behavior in adulthood.

4. Now explain the primary limitation of this type of research.

5. Review Albert Bandura's social learning theory in Chapter 1. Now, explain how Bandura experimentally examined the effects of TV violence on children's aggression using the concepts of modeling, imitation, and reinforcement.

6. Clearly, not every child who watches many hours of violent TV becomes an aggressive adult. Describe factors that seem to mediate the effects of TV violence on children's behavior.

7. Watch a show that children are likely to watch consistently. As you watch, consider how it might influence children's cognitive schemas. Is there content that might affect how children perceive interactions with people who are different from themselves? Is there content that might alter how children think about resolving certain kinds of situations? Is there content relevant to how men and women are supposed to behave in certain contexts?

SOCIAL AND EMOTIONAL DEVELOPMENT IN MIDDLE CHILDHOOD

Video Games, Computers, and the Internet

1. Identify the potential benefits and concerns with children's use of video games such as Nintendo and PlayStation.

    Potential Benefits   Potential Concerns

2. Identify the potential benefits and concerns with children's use of computer games and CD-ROMs.

    Potential Benefits   Potential Concerns

SOCIAL AND EMOTIONAL DEVELOPMENT IN MIDDLE CHILDHOOD

When You Have Finished

⊙ WORKING THE WEB

1. Here is an excellent place to get a quick overview of social, physical, and cognitive development in middle childhood (www.mc.maricopa.edu/dept/d46/psy/dev/middle_child/index.html). Look particularly at the "school" section, which describes the "psychology behind elementary education." In the section on "Becoming an Individual," click on "Self-esteem is a key factor in development throughout life" and take the Self-Esteem Test.

2. For an interesting insight into how children look for and find friends, go to www.nncc.org/Guidance/dc26_wo.friends1.html, a web site of the National Network for Child Care. Click on "Children Without Friends" and read about the problems of and reasons for peer rejection. You will also find information on ways to improve a child's social skills.

3. To evaluate children's social skills and behavior, examine the "Social Attributes Checklist" at www.athealth.com/consumer/disorders/childsocialskills.html. The research contained here "suggests that a child's long-term social and emotional adaptation, academic and cognitive development, and citizenship are enhanced by frequent opportunities to strengthen social competence during childhood." Written especially for teachers, the authors note their responsibility to being "proactive in creating a classroom community that accepts and supports all children."

4. The American Academy of Pediatrics web site (www.aap.org/healthtopics/stages.cfm#middle) has a variety of information and links on the topic of middle childhood. Take a look at "Childhood Friendships," "Fostering Self-Esteem in Boys and Girls," and "Stress and Your Child" for an in-depth view of friends and peer popularity. Audio files are available for several subjects pertaining to middle childhood.

5. Visit the Center for Disease Control and Protection at www.cdc.gov/ncbddd/child/middlechildhood.htm and check out the descriptions of emotional and social changes in middle childhood. In a separate link you'll find a discussion of middle childhood from nine to eleven years of age. A discussion of positive parenting for children is also helpful. How might the goals of positive parenting differ for those of other cultures?

6. A great web site (kidshealth.org/kid/watch/house/homealone.html) developed particularly for children offers information on dealing with feelings and staying healthy. A section called "Kids Talk" offers the answers to interesting questions such as "Why do feet stink?", "Why do I have a belly button?", and "Somebody in my friend's family died. What should I do?"

SOCIAL AND EMOTIONAL DEVELOPMENT IN MIDDLE CHILDHOOD

7. If you are looking for ways to introduce more serious topics, including sexual activity, HIV/AIDS, violence, terrorism, and drugs and alcohol, look at the Talk With Your Kids web site (www.talkwithkids.org). The organization offers free copies of several booklets and 10 helpful tips to guide the discussions.

8. "40 Developmental Assets for Middle Childhood" presented by the Search Institute at www.search-institute.org/assets//MiddleChildhood.html is based on an "extensive review of the theory, research, and practice base for childhood development." Asset categories include support, empowerment, constructive use of time, and positive identity. Explore several of the links to further your understanding of how parents and other adults can provide assistance during this critical period of development.

SOCIAL AND EMOTIONAL DEVELOPMENT IN MIDDLE CHILDHOOD

⊙ PRACTICE TEST #1

Multiple Choice Questions
For each question, circle the best answer from the choices given.

1. Measuring your own qualities and performance and judging them against one's peers is called (p. 402)

a. self-esteem.
b. social comparison.
c. the me-self.
d. self-representations.

2. Another term for self-concept is (p. 402)

a. self-representation.
b. self-evaluation.
c. self-esteem.
d. the I-self.

3. Blair's parents modeled positive emotional skills and talked about her feelings in ways that helped her to understand herself. In middle childhood, Blair is likely to (p. 405)

a. show relational aggression.
b. be a lower level of prosocial reasoning.
c. be successful in making friends.
d. have conduct problems.

4. Which group of children is more likely to engage in relational aggression? (p. 406)

a. preschoolers
b. toddlers
c. boys
d. girls

5. Ameneh is 12. She sees a classmate fall on the stairs. Ameneh goes over to help, and thinks "My teacher will be very proud of me helping that girl." What stage of Eisenberg's levels of prosocial reasoning is she MOST LIKELY at? (p. 407)

a. hedonistic orientation
b. needs-of-others orientation
c. approval/stereotyped orientation
d. empathic orientation

SOCIAL AND EMOTIONAL DEVELOPMENT IN MIDDLE CHILDHOOD

6. Choose the TRUE statement below. (p. 408 - 409)

a. There is no evidence of a genetic predisposition towards aggressive behavior.
b. Aggressiveness is a characteristic that tends to change over time.
c. Cultural conditions have not been found to have an effect on aggressive behavior.
d. Aggressive children are more likely to live in a coercive home environment.

7. Since Heather's parents divorced, Heather's mother has depended on Heather, who is 12, to take care of her younger brothers after school. Heather is supposed to help them with their homework and cook dinner so it's ready when her mother gets home from work. Before she goes to bed, Heather reads to her brothers and supervises them brushing their teeth. Heather's responsibilities for her siblings may be a form of (p. 413)

a. emotional parentification.
b. instrumental parentification.
c. child neglect.
d. the sleeper effect of divorce.

8. Which of the following is a POSITIVE outcome of divorce? (p. 414 - 415)

a. Some children develop a very close relationship with their mothers after divorce.
b. Because of guilt feelings, fathers place less demands on their children after divorce.
c. Parenting often becomes more authoritarian after divorce.
d. Divorce may lead to children and their custodial parent moving.

9. Which ethnic group has the highest rate of childbearing outside of marriage? (p. 417)

a. Asian-American
b. Caucasian
c. African-American
d. Latino

10. Why is the quality of parenting often lower in step-families than in single mother households? (p. 417)

a. Family members take on different roles.
b. Stepfathers tend to be less involved than biological fathers who are in the home.
c. There may be competition between the children and stepfather for the mother's attention.
d. All of the above.

SOCIAL AND EMOTIONAL DEVELOPMENT IN MIDDLE CHILDHOOD

⊙ PRACTICE TEST #2

Multiple Choice Questions
For each question, circle the best answer from the choices given.

1. Which of the following popular middle childhood activities reflects these children's new sense of logic, order and organization? (p. 419)

a. Barbies
b. horseback riding
c. a baseball card collection
d. skateboarding

2. The number of best friends a child reports increases until what age? (p. 420)

a. 7
b. 11
c. 13
d. 17

3. Marc is actively disliked by many of his classmates. He is physically aggressive at times and he threatens and bullies others. His peer nomination category is most likely to be (p. 422)

a. rejected.
b. neglected.
c. controversial.
d. average.

4. The model that explains how different children perceive, interpret and respond to information in social settings is the (p. 423)

a. connectionist model.
b. popularity model.
c. peer nomination model.
d. social cognition model.

5. Charles is not accepted by his peers in school. According to research, he is more likely to (p. 424)

a. get lower grades.
b. be anxious and fearful.
c. be depressed.
d. all of the above.

SOCIAL AND EMOTIONAL DEVELOPMENT IN MIDDLE CHILDHOOD

6. Choose the example of an EXTERNAL attribution from the following children's remarks. (p. 426)

a. "I failed the math test because I didn't study."
b. "I only passed the science quiz because it was so easy."
c. "I've always gotten A's in Phys. Ed. because I'm a natural athlete."
d. "After taking that SAT prep course, I got a high score because I knew all the test taking strategies."

7. Which of the following is NOT a factor that affects classroom climate? (p. 427)

a. teacher characteristics
b. number of students in the class
c. whether the school is in an urban or suburban setting
d. student behaviors

8. Watching TV or movies and playing video games all peak at what age? (p. 428)

a. 13
b. 16
c. 21
d. 10

9. Which of the following statements about TV and aggression is FALSE? (p. 430 - 431)

a. TV violence has a moderately negative impact on children's behavior.
b. Children who are aggressive prefer violent TV.
c. Bandura's studies conclusively proved that violence does not causes aggressive behavior.
d. Children's cartoon and late-afternoon and early-evening TV shows have the highest rates of violent acts.

10. What group are the most frequent users of video games? (p. 431)

a. 6 to 8 year old boys
b. 8 to 12 year old boys
c. 14 to 16 year old boys
d. 7 to 10 year old girls

SOCIAL AND EMOTIONAL DEVELOPMENT IN MIDDLE CHILDHOOD
⊙ COMPREHENSIVE PRACTICE TEST

Multiple Choice Questions
For each question, circle the best answer from the choices given.

1. Taylor, who is 7, describes herself as a tall girl with long brown hair who is a good soccer player. This is an example of (p. 402)

a. self representation.
b. self evaluation.
c. self-esteem.
d. the I-self.

2. What was the finding of recent research on children's ability to read emotions expressed by people of different ethnic backgrounds than their own? (p. 405)

a. Children of all ethnicities had the most difficulty interpreting emotions expressed by Asian actors.
b. African American children were the most proficient of any ethnic group in interpreting emotions expressed by others.
c. Ethnicity had no effect on children's accuracy of reading emotions.
d. Children sometimes have difficulty interpreting the emotions expressed by individuals of a different ethnic background than their own.

3. Withdrawing friendship or in some way disrupting or threatening social relationships to hurt others is called (p. 406)

a. empathic orientation.
b. social comparison.
c. relational aggression.
d. oppositional defiant disorder.

4. Ryan, a second grader, hears at his church about a food drive that is being sponsored for a local shelter. He tells his mother that they should give some cans of food to it. When she forgets to bring the cans to church, Ryan doesn't seem to be bothered. He is MOST LIKELY in which stage of prosocial reasoning? (p. 407)

a. hedonistic orientation
b. needs-of-others orientation
c. approval/stereotyped orientation
d. empathic orientation

SOCIAL AND EMOTIONAL DEVELOPMENT IN MIDDLE CHILDHOOD

5. Which of the following has been associated with a higher level of aggression in children? (p. 409)

a. high socioeconomic status
b. parents' reinforcement of prosocial behavior
c. coercive home environment
d. parental supervision and appropriate limits placed on children

6. Which of the following disorders is most common among children? (p. 409)

a. oppositional defiant disorder
b. conduct disorder
c. emotional parentification
d. multiple personality disorder

7. Niusha was born into a poor family that had recently immigrated to the U.S. Her parents had little education and worked long hours at their low wage jobs. Children at Niusha's school did not perform well on state tests. In spite of this start, Niusha did well in school and eventually became a doctor. She would be described as (p. 410)

a. oppositionally defiant.
b. resilient.
c. having a sleeper effect.
d. having an empathic orientation.

8. A child who has a negative effect after his parents' divorce may do so because the divorce starts a chain of events leading to stressors for him. This reflects which view of divorce? (p. 411)

a. the selection model
b. instrumental parentification
c. the externalizing model
d. divorce-stress-adjustment perspective

9. The belief that there are subtle effects of parental divorce that may not be apparent until the child is an adolescent or adult is referred to as (p. 413)

a. the sleeper effect.
b. instrumental parentification.
c. internalizing problems.
d. the selection model.

SOCIAL AND EMOTIONAL DEVELOPMENT IN MIDDLE CHILDHOOD

10. Which of the following is FALSE about never married single parents? (p. 417)

a. They have fewer parenting resources.
b. They show less effective parenting.
c. They generally receive child support from the other parent of the child.
d. They tend to move frequently.

11. Terence's parents are divorced. His mother has re-married and he gets along well with his stepfather. Terence's father sees him every weekend and Terence stays with his father for 6 weeks in the summer. Despite the divorce, all of the adults maintain good relationships for Terence's sake. What conclusion could be made about Terence? (p. 417 - 418)

a. Terence is likely to experience a sleeper effect from the divorce.
b. Terence may have more parenting resources than if his biological parents had remained married.
c. Terence will probably fare worse than if his mother had never re-married.
d. The quality of parenting Terence receives will probably decline as he grows older.

12. Which of the following is very important in middle childhood play? (p. 419)

a. fantasy and make believe
b. using skills acquired during early childhood
c. playing sports just to win
d. acquiring and improving physical skills

13. In Bigelow's study of children's friendships, eighth graders reported the most important trait in a best friend was (p. 420)

a. common activities.
b. an admirable character.
c. psychological intimacy.
d. physical attractiveness.

14. The method most frequently used by developmental researchers to identify children's social status is the (p. 421)

a. selection model.
b. peer status method.
c. friendship inventory.
d. peer nomination technique.

SOCIAL AND EMOTIONAL DEVELOPMENT IN MIDDLE CHILDHOOD

15. Which of the following is NOT one of the steps in Dodge's social cognition model? (p. 423)

a. positive emotional bias
b. perceiving social information
c. interpreting social information
d. considering potential responses

16. Choose the statement that is FALSE. (p. 424)

a. Childhood peer relations are one of the most powerful predictors of mental health problems.
b. Compared to popular children, rejected children are 7 times more likely to fail a grade.
c. Peer rejection leads to murder or suicide quite often.
d. Children who are withdrawn in elementary school are at higher risk for depression in later school years.

17. Children who have which type of orientation tend to attribute their success to external and uncontrollable factors and their failure to internal, stable factors? (p. 426)

a. helpless
b. mastery
c. achievement
d. self-fulfilling

18. Placing children in instructional groups based on their ability levels, either in different classes or within a single class is also known as (p. 427)

a. classroom climate.
b. tracking.
c. a self-fulfilling prophecy.
d. resiliency.

19. Beginning in middle childhood, girls spend more time than boys (p. 428)

a. playing video games.
b. watching TV.
c. on the computer.
d. reading print media and listening to the radio.

SOCIAL AND EMOTIONAL DEVELOPMENT IN MIDDLE CHILDHOOD

20. For boys, at age 8, what is the best predictor of aggressiveness at age 18? (p. 430)

a. heavy use of video games
b. having a TV in their bedroom
c. watching violent TV
d. participating in sports

Short-Answer Questions
Answer each question in the space provided.

1. Your older sister and her husband are separated and going to divorce. She asks you how she can prevent the divorce from having negative effects on her two children. Based on what you've learned in Chapter 12, what advice would you give her?

2. According to Dodge's social cognition model, how are popular and rejected children different in how they process social information? What are the likely outcomes of long-term peer rejection?

3. What have researchers found about the effects of media on children?

SOCIAL AND EMOTIONAL DEVELOPMENT IN MIDDLE CHILDHOOD
⊙ CROSSWORD PUZZLE

Across
5. role reversal in which a child assumes responsibilities usually taken care of by parents
8. _____ grouping places children in instructional groups based on their performance level.
9. _____ aggression is withdrawing friendship or otherwise disrupting social relationships to hurt others.
10. _____ orientation is the tendency to attribute success to external and uncontrollable factors.

Down
1. _____ children are actively disliked by their peers.
2. _____ comparison is the process of comparing your own qualities and performances to others.
3. describes children who succeed, achieve, and have positive developmental outcomes despite negative conditions
4. The peer _____ technique is a poll used to identify categories of popular and unpopular children.
6. individuals' beliefs about why they or others succeed or fail
7. _____ disorder involves consistent violations of other people's basic rights or the breaking of societal rules

Puzzle created with Puzzlemaker at DiscoverySchool.com

13 PHYSICAL DEVELOPMENT IN ADOLESCENCE

Before You Read

In this chapter, you'll find a description of physical development during the teenage years or adolescence. The adolescent body enters puberty, and growth and maturation continue into adulthood. Impulse control and personal behavior management are immature and may be related to ongoing brain development. Growth and maturation body and brain lead new concerns regarding sexual activity. Your text examines contraceptive use and the status of sexual knowledge and education in the adolescent population. Sexually transmitted diseases, pregnancy, and forced sexual behavior (rape, sexual assault, and sexual harassment) are addressed. Nutrition and exercise are vitally important to growing minds and bodies, as well as to the development of healthy habits for adulthood. Unfortunately, as your text describes, adolescents are less likely to follow a healthy diet due to busy schedules and the availability of quick meals. Finally, your authors look at the impacts of sleep deprivation, substance use and abuse, and depression.

Chapter Learning Objectives

After reading this chapter, you should be able to do the following:

♦ Describe the typical sequence of events during puberty.

♦ Discuss how body image and early or late maturation may affect outcomes for adolescents.

♦ Summarize the research on brain development during adolescence.

♦ Outline the major patterns of early sexual activity and explain the difficulties in estimating sexual activity.

PHYSICAL DEVELOPMENT IN ADOLESCENCE

- Discuss the reasons why a teenager might become sexually active at an early age or at a later age.

- Identify the major trends in contraceptive use among teenagers.

- Summarize the state of sex education in the U.S.

- Compare and contrast chlamydia, gonorrhea, and human papillomavirus (HPV).

- Summarize the risks for teenage pregnancy and teen fatherhood.

- Discuss the impacts of teen parenthood.

- Distinguish between rape, sexual assault, and sexual harassment.

- Describe the typical eating and exercise habits of teenagers.

- Compare and contrast anorexia nervosa and bulimia nervosa.

- Describe the status of sleep among the general teen population including the reasons for lack of sleep.

- Summarize the main risk factors for drug use among adolescents.

- Discuss the prevalence of depression in teenagers.

- Describe the leading causes of death among adolescents.

PHYSICAL DEVELOPMENT IN ADOLESCENCE

As You Read

Key terms and concepts are essential to your understanding of the chapter. Your ability to logically discuss and analyze pertinent information is dependent upon your knowledge of these concepts. Terms can be found in boldface throughout the chapter and definitions are listed in a glossary of terms at the end of the chapter. Flashcards may be helpful for memorizing definitions. Begin using the terms as you study, incorporating them into your vocabulary.

adolescent growth spurt	delayed phase preference	puberty
androgens	early maturation	rape
anorexia nervosa	estrogens	sexual assault
binge drinking	gateway drugs	sexual harassment
body image	gonorrhea	sexually transmitted diseases (STDs)
ublimia nervosa	human papillomavirus (HPV)	spermarche
chlamydia	late maturation	substance abuse
clinical depression	menarche	substance use
contraception	prefrontal cortex	

⊙ GROWTH OF THE BODY AND BRAIN DURING ADOLESCENCE

Puberty and Maturation

1. Listed below are the primary changes in reproductive system development and secondary sexual characteristics for each sex. For each list, rank the items in chronological order, labeling the earliest change with a "1."

   MALES
   ____ facial hair begins to grow
   ____ voice begins to deepen
   ____ penis and testicles increase in size
   ____ spermarche occurs
   ____ pubic hair appears
   ____ hair grows in the armpits

   FEMALES
   ____ menstruation begins
   ____ breasts begin to enlarge
   ____ hair grows in the armpits
   ____ pubic hair appears

2. At what age does menarche begin for most young women? Has the age increased or decreased in the last century? What might be the main causes for this change?

PHYSICAL DEVELOPMENT IN ADOLESCENCE

3. Each of the following statements regarding puberty and maturation is FALSE. Your job is to change some part of each statement in order to make it TRUE.

   A. Increased sexual attraction and subtle changes in secondary sex characteristics begin around the age of 13.

   Change(s):

   B. Testosterone and estradiol are examples of androgens.

   Change(s):

   C. Adrenarche occurs after Gonodarche and leads to the development of primary sex characteristics.

   Change(s):

   D. The adolescent growth spurt peaks at about age 14 for girls and age 16 for boys.

   Change(s):

   E. Late-maturing girls tend to engage in more delinquency and have more problems with depression and substance abuse.

   Change(s):

   F. Enlargement of the breasts, appearance of pubic hair, and increased output of oil-producing glands are all examples of primary sex characteristics.

   Change(s):

   G. Water pollution and global warming are thought to be the main causes of the decreasing average age of menarche.

   Change(s):

   H. Early-maturing girls tend to have more positive body images than early-maturing boys.

   Change(s):

PHYSICAL DEVELOPMENT IN ADOLESCENCE

Brain Development

1. Discuss the main changes in the adolescent brain for each of the areas or topics listed.

Synaptogenesis and synaptic pruning

Prefrontal cortex

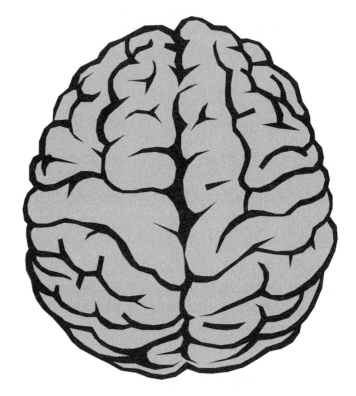

Neurotransmitters

PHYSICAL DEVELOPMENT IN ADOLESCENCE

2. How do the changes seen in the adolescent brain affect the general health and well-being of these young people?

⊙ SEXUAL ACTIVITY DURING ADOLESCENCE

Patterns of Sexual Activity

1. *Numerically Speaking* of Sexual Activity
   Fill in the blanks with the correct numbers.

   A. In one study, only _____ percent of adolescents believed there was a risk for contracting a sexually transmitted disease through oral sex.

   B. Among all high school students, _____ percent of males and _____ percent of females reported sexual intercourse before the age of 13.

   C. In 2002, _____ percent of girls and _____ percent of boys between the ages of 15 and 19 had sex before the age of 15.

   D. Available studies indicate that between 20 percent to 30 percent of high school students and about _____ percent of teens between the ages of 12 and 15 have engaged in oral sex at least once.

   E. According to a nationwide survey of high school students, more than _____ percent of adolescents have had intercourse by the ninth grade and nearly _____ percent had engaged in intercourse by the twelfth grade.

331

PHYSICAL DEVELOPMENT IN ADOLESCENCE

Reasons for Becoming Sexually Active

1. List the main factors associated with both earlier and later sexual activity among teens.

   <u>Earlier Sexual Activity</u>   <u>Later Sexual Activity</u>

2. Of those teens who abstain from sexual activity, what are the three reasons most cited for their decision?

   A.

   B.

   C.

3. Describe the study by Roche & Ramsbey (1993) and its findings regarding sexual behaviors at given stages of dating.

PHYSICAL DEVELOPMENT IN ADOLESCENCE

Contraceptive Use in Adolescence

1. Describe the overall trends in contraceptive use among teens.

2. What are the main reasons for inconsistent contraceptive use among adolescents?

Sexual Knowledge and Sex Education

Give an overview of the sex education classes you received in high school. Ask an older or younger person about the programs they attended or currently attend. Compare their experience(s) with yours.

PHYSICAL DEVELOPMENT IN ADOLESCENCE

⊙ SPECIAL CONCERNS ABOUT TEENAGE SEXUAL ACTIVITY

Sexually Transmitted Diseases and Adolescents

1. For each detail on the left, mark the sexually transmitted disease(s) with which it is associated.

   Chlamydia = C
   Gonorrhea = G
   Human papillomavirus = HPV

Detail	Sexually transmitted disease		
	C	G	HPV
caused by a bacteria			
commonly reported			
risk factor for cervical cancer			
a "silent" disease			
currently incurable			
cured with antibiotics			
can lead to infertility			
can be passed to a baby during birth			
spread vaginally, orally, and anally			
increased risk for other infections			
increased risk for PID			
produces few or no symptoms			
may lead to serious blood or joint problems			

2. Summarize the main risk factors for sexually transmitted diseases among teens.

PHYSICAL DEVELOPMENT IN ADOLESCENCE

Teenage Pregnancy

1. Fill in the blanks to make each of the following statements regarding teenage pregnancy correct.

    A. Approximately _____ U.S. teenage girls become pregnant each year.

    B. Before they turn _____ years old, about 34 percent of U.S. teens will become pregnant at least once.

    C. The U. S. teenage pregnancy rates are twice as high as in the countries of _____ and _____, and 8 times as high as those in _____.

    D. Adolescent girls account for about _____ percent of all pregnancies and approximately _____ percent of all births each year.

2. Place an X in the blank if teenage pregnancy has been correlated with the following risk factors.

    _____ poverty   _____ lower self-efficacy

    _____ family instability   _____ depression

    _____ AD/HD   _____ early age of first intercourse

    _____ increased risk-taking   _____ overweight

    _____ ODD   _____ lack of parental supervision

    _____ social withdrawal during childhood   _____ aggression

    _____ previous pregnancy

3. Discuss the risk factors for becoming a teenage father.

PHYSICAL DEVELOPMENT IN ADOLESCENCE

4. List and discuss three negative outcomes with which teenage pregnancy is associated.

   A.

   B.

   C.

5. Being the Teacher
   Imagine you have been asked to present an after-school in-service program for a group of high school teachers on teenage pregnancy and forced sexual behavior. You will have approximately one hour to give these teachers an overview of the information in Chapter 13 that would be most relevant to their everyday interactions with teenagers. What information would you cover? Why would you include it with this particular audience? What types of questions would you anticipate receiving from your audience?

PHYSICAL DEVELOPMENT IN ADOLESCENCE

⊙ HEALTH ISSUES IN ADOLESCENCE

Nutrition and Exercise

1. Interview several teenagers and note their eating habits for a day. Combining all of the information you receive, describe a typical menu for the teens with whom you talk.

   Breakfast -

   Snacks -

   Lunch -

   Snacks -

   Dinner/Supper -

   Additional Items -

2. Regular exercise and physical activity have many benefits. List three positive effects teenagers report most.

   A.

   B.

   C.

PHYSICAL DEVELOPMENT IN ADOLESCENCE

3. List three occasions when both teen boys and girls are more likely to exercise.

   A.

   B.

   C.

Eating Disorders

For each of the following factors, place an X in the column of the eating disorder with which it is most closely related.

Factor	Eating Disorder		
	Anorexia Nervosa	Bulimia Nervosa	Both
distorted body image			
uncontrolled eating binges			
most common among female adolescents			
use of laxatives and enemas			
intense guilt			
very restricted diet			
appears between the ages of 14 to 18			
mild genetic link			
intense fear of gaining weight			

PHYSICAL DEVELOPMENT IN ADOLESCENCE

Adolescents Need More Sleep

1. Describe five problems associated with lack of sleep in adolescents.

2. Define delayed phase preference and discuss how it affects sleeping patterns in teenagers.

Substance Use and Abuse

1. Using Figure 13.7 as your guide, answer each of the following questions.

    A. Which two substances were <u>tried</u> more often by 9th graders than by 12th graders?

    B. Which substance is <u>used</u> more often by both ages, tobacco or marijuana?

2. List four negative behaviors or outcomes with which teen alcohol use is related.

    A.

    B.

    C.

    D.

3. Discuss why alcohol, tobacco, and marijuana are called "gateway drugs."

PHYSICAL DEVELOPMENT IN ADOLESCENCE

4. Describe the risk factors for drug use associated with each of the following topics.

   Being an adolescent -

   Individual characteristics -

   Beliefs, values, and experiences -

   Family factors -

   Parenting practices -

   Friends and associates -

Depression

1. List the symptoms most often linked with clinical depression.

2. Discuss the gender differences connected to depression.

PHYSICAL DEVELOPMENT IN ADOLESCENCE

Causes of Death

1. In a recent national study it was found that unintentional injury was the leading cause of death for all adolescents, except for two groups. Give the age range, ethnicity, and leading cause of death for those two groups.

   <u>Age Range</u>   <u>Ethnicity</u>   <u>Leading Cause of Death</u>

   A.

   B.

2. Summarize what is known about the increased numbers of fatal automobile accidents among the adolescent population.

3. What can be done to reduce the frequency of teen vehicle accidents?

   Legislation -

   Parents -

PHYSICAL DEVELOPMENT IN ADOLESCENCE

4. Discuss the factors associated with teenage suicide.

5. Identify the gender differences related to suicide attempts.

6. How has the rate of suicide deaths changed since 1960?

PHYSICAL DEVELOPMENT IN ADOLESCENCE

When You Have Finished

⊙ WORKING THE WEB

1. A good overview of puberty can be found at The Psi Café – A Psychology Resource Site (www.psy.pdx.edu/PsiCafe/Areas/Developmental/Puberty/index.htm). You'll find links to web sites with information on precocious and delayed puberty, as well as resources for both male and female teens and for parents.

2. A variety of health information for teens and their parents can be located at www.plannedparenthood.org. Sections on emergencies, pregnancy, and sexuality are up-to-date and easy to read. The site also has a health center locator.

3. An "award-winning Planned Parenthood web site," teenwire.com is available in both English and Spanish. Here you'll find material on masturbation myths, dealing with dating abuse, and articles such as "Vulva: An Owner's Manual." Geared toward teens with questions, this site offers quizzes on pregnancy and its causes and animated educational items including "Am I Normal?" and "How to Use a Condom."

4. At the National Youth Violence Prevention Resource Center (www.safeyouth.org), choose the "Browse Topics" folder and scroll through the list of subjects. Choose two or three of interest, then review the national, state, and local data collected by researchers and various governmental agencies. Additional information on rate of teen deaths by accident, homicide, and suicide can be found at www.acef.org/kidscount/kc2000/sum_6.htm.

5. Dr. Aaron White, an alcohol researcher at the Duke University Medical Center, discusses adolescent brain development, including the effects of alcohol and other substances at www.duke.edu/~amwhite/Adolescence/. A downloadable fact sheet on brain development is also available. For a look inside the teenage brain, visit www.pbs.org/wgbh/pages/frontline/shows/teenbrain/work/. Interviews with neuroscientists and an interactive illustration of the teenage brain highlight this web site.

6. Check out the report on "Eating Disorders during Adolescence: National Problems and Interventions" at faculty.washington.edu/jrees/adolescentnutrition1.html. The web site acts as a "reference for healthcare professionals, students, and educators" and provides a thorough discussion of anorexia nervosa.

7. Need for sleep and lack of sleep among adolescents are the main topics at www.stanford.edu/~dement/adolescent.html. A good conversation on adolescent sleep and a pointed description of teenagers' need for sleep can be found here, as well as tips for "sleep hygiene," aimed especially at teens. There is also a good set of links for additional, related information.

PHYSICAL DEVELOPMENT IN ADOLESCENCE

⊙ PRACTICE TEST #1

Multiple Choice Questions
For each question, circle the best answer from the choices given.

1. During puberty, the first ejaculation happens for males. What is this called? (p. 442)

   a. menarche
   b. androgens
   c. spermarche
   d. delayed phase preference

2. Kyra is 11 and is already experiencing puberty. As an early maturing girl, what type of body image is she likely to have? (p. 445)

   a. Good - - she will be happy to be ahead of her peers.
   b. Poor - - she is likely to see herself as too fat.
   c. Negative - - she is likely to believe she is too thin.
   d. Good - - she will feel more self-confident.

3. What area in the brain that grows in adolescence is important for planning, judgment, decision making, and inhibiting impulsive responding? (p. 447)

   a. prefrontal cortex
   b. hippocampus
   c. parietal lobes
   d. hypothalamus

4. In recent years the overall rate of sexual intercourse among adolescents has decreased. What is believed to be the cause of this decline? (p. 449)

   a. Teens have a better understanding of the health risks of unprotected sex.
   b. The increased emphasis on abstinence in sex education programs.
   c. Teens often only consider vaginal intercourse as "sex."
   d. All of the above may be reasons for the decline.

5. The most frequent place teens reported having sex was (p. 451)

   a. at school.
   b. their own home.
   c. in a park.
   d. at parties.

PHYSICAL DEVELOPMENT IN ADOLESCENCE

6. Which of the following is NOT a reason teens don't use contraceptives consistently? (p. 453)

a. Many teens are not mature enough to admit to themselves that they are sexually active.
b. Some teens are afraid if they use contraceptives their parents will find out that they are sexually active.
c. Teens who talk to their partners about contraceptives are less likely to use them.
d. Not using contraceptives is part of some teens' patterns of risk taking behavior.

7. Choose the statement about sex education that is FALSE. (p. 454)

a. Most teens are very knowledgeable about STDs , how they are spread and how to prevent them.
b. Almost all public school systems provide sex education programs.
c. Recent research has found teens have better knowledge of how to prevent pregnancy.
d. In general, teens' knowledge of sex and contraception is increased by participating in sex education programs.

8. A common STD caused by a bacteria that often produces no symptoms can cause infertility in females and health problems in babies born to women with it. This STD is (p. 457)

a. gonorrhea
b. human papillomavirus
c. syphilis
d. chlamydia

9. Which group of teenagers has the highest pregnancy rate? (p. 459)

a. Whites
b. Blacks
c. Hispanics
d. Asians

10. How is sexual assault different from rape? (p. 462)

a. Sexual assault is contact due to physical or psychological coercion that may or may not involve penetration.
b. Rape is sexual contact that is a result of physical force and/or use of a weapon.
c. Sexual assault is any type of unwanted sexual remarks or jokes.
d. Sexual assault and rape are two terms for the same act.

PHYSICAL DEVELOPMENT IN ADOLESCENCE

⊙ PRACTICE TEST #2

Multiple Choice Questions
For each question, circle the best answer from the choices given.

1. What percentage of teenagers consumes too much saturated fat? (p. 464)

   a. 40%
   b. 50%
   c. 75%
   d. 90%

2. Which teen is LEAST LIKELY to get regular physical exercise? (p. 464)

   a. Lindsay, who is Caucasian.
   b. Shanae, who is African American.
   c. Dave, who loves to play basketball.
   d. Edwin, who runs track with his best friend.

3. What is the estimated prevalence rate for anorexia in adolescent girls? (p. 465)

   a. 10 out of 100
   b. 5 out of 100
   c. 3 out of 100
   d. 1 out of 100

4. Which of the following has NOT been associated with lack of sleep in teens? (p. 466)

   a. decreased microsleep
   b. greater levels of depression and anxiety
   c. increased risk of accidents
   d. slower reactions

5. Which group of teens has the LOWEST reported use of alcohol and tobacco? (p. 469)

   a. Non-Hispanic Whites
   b. Hispanics
   c. African Americans
   d. All of the above groups have about equal use.

PHYSICAL DEVELOPMENT IN ADOLESCENCE

6. Choose the teen *most likely* to use drugs from the descriptions below. (p. 470)

a. Emily, who believes drugs can cause long term health consequences.
b. Kyle, who has been physically abused and has witnessed domestic violence in his family.
c. Brian, who is well supervised by his parents.
d. Maya, who is very involved in activities at her church.

7. How is clinical depression different from normal grief and loss? (p. 471)

a. The symptoms of clinical depression last longer.
b. Those with clinical depression tend to have low self esteem.
c. Teens with clinical depression have negative thoughts about themselves and their environment.
d. All of the above are differences

8. The heritability index for clinical depression has been found to be as high as (p. 472)

a. 60.
b. 75.
c. 90.
d. less than 15.

9. The leading cause of death for 15 to 19 year old African American males is (p. 472)

a. motor vehicle accidents.
b. homicide.
c. cancers.
d. suicide.

10. Which group of teens has the highest suicide rate? (p. 473)

a. Caucasian girls
b. African American girls
c. Latino boys
d. Caucasian boys

PHYSICAL DEVELOPMENT IN ADOLESCENCE

⊙ COMPREHENSIVE PRACTICE TEST

Multiple Choice Questions
For each question, circle the best answer from the choices given.

1. Michelle's body is changing. She has her first menstruation, followed by pubic hair appearing and then her breasts enlarging. Michelle is (p. 442)

   a. having an abnormal sequence of pubertal changes.
   b. a normal 12 year old.
   c. is experiencing puberty.
   d. both b and c.

2. What physical system regulates the levels of sex hormones? (p. 443)

   a. the hippocampus
   b. the HPG axis
   c. the prefrontal cortex
   d. the adrenal glands

3. Colleen is 20. She is short and stocky in her build. Which type of puberty did she MOST LIKELY experience? (p. 445)

   a. on time
   b. late
   c. early
   d. The type of puberty cannot be determined by a girls' height and build.

4. During adolescence, the changes in the prefrontal cortex and the limbic system combine with changes in levels of what neurotransmitter to make teens more emotional and reactive to stress? (p. 447)

   a. adrenaline
   b. dopamine
   c. serotonin
   d. noradrenaline

5. Data from national surveys indicate that by the ninth grade, what percentage of teens have had intercourse? (p. 449)

   a. one fourth
   b. one third
   c. one half
   d. two thirds

PHYSICAL DEVELOPMENT IN ADOLESCENCE

6. Girls from which ethnic group reported experiencing pressure to both become sexually active and to conform to traditional norms not to be sexually permissive? (p. 451)

a. Caucasians
b. Latinas
c. African Americans
d. both b and c.

7. Choose the teen who is MOST LIKELY to have early sexual activity. (p. 451)

a. Travis, who lives with his biological mother and father and is an honor roll student.
b. Lucas, who is from an upper class family and is planning a career as a lawyer, like his parents.
c. Mollie, whose single mother often works late, and who uses alcohol and marijuana.
d. Emma, who is religious; her parents and church youth group friends disapprove of early sexual activity.

8. The best predictor of contraceptive use among teens is (p. 453)

a. age.
b. ethnicity.
c. availability of condoms.
d. whether or not the teen lives in a two parent family.

9. What recent statistic indicates teens may be using their knowledge of contraception more now than in the past? (p. 454)

a. Rates of abortions for teens have declined.
b. Fewer teens are becoming infected with HPV.
c. Teens are less likely to get a STD than 10 years ago.
d. Teen pregnancy rates are declining.

10. Prevalence rates for both gonorrhea and chlamydia are highest in which group? (p. 458)

a. Asian Americans
b. African Americans
c. Caucasians
d. Hispanics

PHYSICAL DEVELOPMENT IN ADOLESCENCE

11. Which of the following is NOT one of the risk factors for teenage pregnancy? (p. 458)

a. popularity
b. living in poverty
c. lack of parental supervision
d. lower expectations about educational achievement

12. Choose the statement about teen pregnancy and parenting that is TRUE. (p. 460 - 461)

a. Most teenage parents never achieve stability in their lives.
b. Babies with teen mothers are less likely to be born prematurely or with low birthweight.
c. Pregnant teens are less likely to receive consistent prenatal care.
d. Nowadays, teenage parents are just as likely to finish high school as their peers.

13. Faith has an after-school job working at a grocery store. The boys that stock shelves often make sexual remarks to her and make comments about her body. Faith hates this unwanted attention. She is experiencing (p. 462)

a. sexual assault.
b. sexual harassment.
c. normal adolescent behaviors.
d. none of the above.

14. What percentage of teens report engaging in regular vigorous physical activity? (p. 464)

a. one-fourth
b. one-third
c. one-half
d. two-thirds

15. The serious eating disorder that is characterized by binge eating followed by purging, fasting, or excessive exercise is (p. 465)

a. anorexia.
b. delayed phase preference.
c. bulimia.
d. excessive body mass index.

PHYSICAL DEVELOPMENT IN ADOLESCENCE

16. What percentage of high school students get at least 8 hours of sleep on school nights? (p. 466)

a. 20%
b. 35%
c. 50%
d. 60%

17. Binge drinking is defined as consuming how many alcoholic drinks during a single occasion? (p. 469)

a. 2
b. 4
c. 5 or more
d. All of the above would be considered binge drinking.

18. Raza's parents have recently separated, and it seems likely they will divorce. Because of the separation, Raza and his mother have moved and he had to change high schools. Raza's mother has noticed her son is having problems sleeping and is not interested in eating his favorite foods. She is having a hard time getting him involved in soccer, which he played at his old high school. Most likely, Raza is (p. 471)

a. suffering from clinical depression.
b. experiencing delayed phase preference.
c. becoming anorexic.
d. having a sleeper effect from his parents' divorce.

19. When driving, teenagers are less likely than adults to (p. 473)

a. take risks.
b. wear seatbelts.
c. drive too fast.
d. all of the above.

20. The estimate of suicide attempts among teens is (p. 473)

a. 35%
b. 20 to 25%
c. 15 to 18%
d. 3 to 11 %

PHYSICAL DEVELOPMENT IN ADOLESCENCE

Short-Answer Questions
Answer each question in the space provided.

1. What are the typical outcomes of early vs. late pubertal maturation for boys? For girls?

2. Which teens are at greatest risk of becoming pregnant? What are the likely outcomes for children of teenage mothers?

3. Outline the risk factors for substance use among adolescents. What is the role of "gateway drugs" in the development of substance abuse?

PHYSICAL DEVELOPMENT IN ADOLESCENCE

⊙ CROSSWORD PUZZLE

Across
2. _____ depression involves sadness, loss of interest, feelings of worthlessness, and changes in appetite that persist for an unusually long time.
3. _____ use refers to the ingestion on more than a few occasions of any substance that alters psychological functioning.
5. _____ nervosa is an eating disorder with binge eating, followed by purging, fasting, or exercise.
6. sexual intercourse as a result of physical force or psychological coercion
7. Body _____ is the way a person thinks about his or her own form and the way it looks to others.
8. the process of physical maturation that leads to the physical capability to reproduce
9. Alcohol, tobacco, and marijuana are called _____ drugs.

Down
1. the first menstrual period for females
2. methods, such as condoms and birth control pills, used to prevent pregnancy
4. a common STD caused by a bacteria that often produces no symptoms, but can lead to infertility

Puzzle created with Puzzlemaker at DiscoverySchool.com

14 COGNITIVE DEVELOPMENT IN ADOLESCENCE

Before You Read

In this chapter, you'll learn about the final level of Piaget's classic stage theory of cognitive development. Your authors include a discussion of the current state of Piaget's theory, significant criticisms of his work based on contemporary research, and an accounting of Piaget's contributions to developmental psychology. Recent sociocultural views of cognitive development building on the work of Vygotsky are also introduced. Then, you'll explore the major theories of intelligence, including the original psychometric approach, Sternberg's triarchic theory, and Gardner's theory of multiple intelligences. The chapter offers a brief history of intelligence testing and looks at the concerns associated with ethnic differences and cultural biases associated with intelligence testing. The adolescent register, genderlects, and dialects are explored in their connections to language development during the teenage years. Finally, your text presents information on adolescent decision making and career choice.

Chapter Learning Objectives

After reading this chapter, you should be able to do the following:

♦ Describe the basic changes that occur during Piaget's stage of formal operational thought.

♦ Summarize the main criticisms and contributions of Piaget's theory.

♦ Discuss the ways situated cognition, guided participation, and socially shared cognition build upon Vygotsky's theory.

♦ Define intelligence.

♦ Explain the psychometric approach to intelligence.

COGNITIVE DEVELOPMENT IN ADOLESCENCE

- Summarize Spearman's two-factor theory of intelligence.

- Discuss the differences between fluid ability and crystallized ability.

- Note the key characteristics of Sternberg's triarchic theory of intelligence and of Gardner's theory of multiple intelligences.

- Compare and contrast reliability and validity.

- Outline a brief history of intelligence assessment, then identify the main elements of the Stanford-Binet and Wechsler intelligence scales.

- List the three components to the formal definition of mental retardation.

- Identify three characteristics typical of gifted and talented children.

- Describe the common arguments for and against intelligence testing with ethnic minorities.

- Give an example of words from the adolescent register.

- Discuss and give examples of genderlects.

- Describe the origins of social dialects and the potential implications of speaking a dialect.

- Outline the decision making process in adolescents and how this ability may affect their career choices.

- Discuss ways of improving the school-to-work transition.

COGNITIVE DEVELOPMENT IN ADOLESCENCE

As You Read

Key terms and concepts are essential to your understanding of the chapter. Your ability to logically discuss and analyze pertinent information is dependent upon your knowledge of these concepts. Terms can be found in boldface throughout the chapter and definitions are listed in a glossary of terms at the end of the chapter. Flashcards may be helpful for memorizing definitions. Begin using the terms as you study, incorporating them into your vocabulary.

abstract thought	formal operational thought	psychometric approach
adolescent egocentrism	general intelligence (g)	reliability
adolescent register	gifted (or talented) children	situated cognition
combinational logic	guided participation	socially shared cognition
componential subtheory	hypothetico-deductive reasoning	specific intelligence (s)
contextual subtheory	imaginary audience	theory of multiple intelligences
crystallized ability	intelligence	triarchic theory of intelligence
dialect	mental retardation	validity
experiential subtheory	mentoring	
fluid ability	personal fable	

⊙ PIAGET'S STAGE 4: FORMAL OPERATIONAL THOUGHT (12 Years +)

What is Formal Operational Thought?

1. Discuss what is meant by "formal operational thought."

2. Define hypothetico-deductive reasoning.

COGNITIVE DEVELOPMENT IN ADOLESCENCE

3. Piaget used several different tasks to examine adolescents' deductive reasoning abilities. One of the tasks he created was the famous "pendulum problem." Describe this task, then, compare and contrast the likely responses of children in the concrete and formal operations stages.

4. Describe the first conversation you can remember having regarding an abstract idea or thought. At what age did the conversation occur? What was the topic?

5. Give an example of combinational logic you have experienced while using this text and your study guide.

Adolescent Egocentrism

1. Think back to your own teenage years for a moment or two. Then, consider Piaget's description of "adolescent egocentrism." Using your own behavior, can you describe two examples of the "imaginary audience" form and two examples of the "personal fable" form of adolescent egocentrism?

COGNITIVE DEVELOPMENT IN ADOLESCENCE

2. Discuss the three components of postformal reasoning proposed by (Kaplan, 2004; Labouvie-Vief, 2006).

   A.

   B.

   C.

Piaget's Theory: Review, Evaluation, and Legacy

1. In the second column, fill in the appropriate Piagetian process or concept. In the third, identify the child's most likely stage of development.

Example	Process or Concept	Stage
Tamika understands that pouring juice from a small, wide cup into a tall, narrow cup doesn't change the amount of juice.		
John writes in his journal frequently and believes that he is the only one who truly knows how he feels.		
Four-year-old Terri knows that she has a sister, but doesn't understand that her sister has a sister.		
Fourteen-month-old Henry tries to move the blanket to find the toy that his mother hid beneath it.		
Orlando calls every farm animal she sees a "doggie."		
When Tashanda walks into a room, she is extremely self-conscious and sure that everyone is watching her every move.		
Carolyn thinks that the eyes of the pretty woman in the painting in her bedroom follow her as she moves around the room.		
Everything that Ella gets her hands on ends up in her mouth.		
Tony enjoys dropping different things from his high chair and laughs with glee as they hit the ground.		
Sheila quickly forgets the keys her uncle has just taken from her and isn't upset that they are gone.		
Juanita says "Bad truck!" when she trips over her toy and skins her knee.		
Amos gets mad when Josh gets the taller glass of soda even though his mother explains that she poured the same amount in each glass.		

COGNITIVE DEVELOPMENT IN ADOLESCENCE

2. Identify the two main weaknesses of Piaget's theory.

   A.

   B.

3. Describe what is least criticized about Piaget's constructivist view of development.

4. Summarize the contributions of Piaget's theory of cognitive development to the field of developmental psychology.

   A.

   B.

   C.

   D.

COGNITIVE DEVELOPMENT IN ADOLESCENCE

⦿ RECENT SOCIOCULTURAL VIEWS OF COGNITIVE DEVELOPMENT

In the following outline, list the three newer sociocultural perspectives on cognitive development that are described in your text. Then, summarize the main emphasis or points of agreement regarding cognition that the three perspectives share. Next, describe one way in which each perspective differs from Vygotsky's theory. Finally, give a specific example of how each perspective increases our understanding of the impact of culture on children's cognitive development.

Three new sociocultural perspectives:

1.   2.   3.

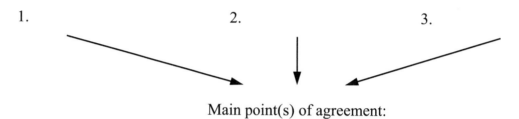

Main point(s) of agreement:

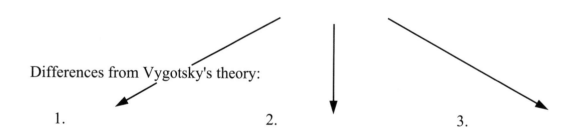

Differences from Vygotsky's theory:

1.   2.   3.

COGNITIVE DEVELOPMENT IN ADOLESCENCE

⊙ INTELLIGENCE

Theories of Intelligence

1. For each intelligence theory, component, or assessment listed on the left, select the person on the right with whom it is most closely related. Place the associated letter in the blank. Names may be used more than once.

   ___ psychometric approach
   ___ two-factor theory
   ___ specific intelligence
   ___ triarchic theory
   ___ 150 abilities to define intelligence
   ___ theory of multiple intelligences
   ___ WISC-IV
   ___ seven mental abilities
   ___ Stanford – Binet scale
   ___ fluid and crystallized ability

   A. Charles Spearman
   B. David Wechsler
   C. J. P. Guilford
   D. Howard Gardner
   E. Lewis Terman
   F. Robert Sternberg
   G. Louis Thurstone
   H. Raymond Cattell and John Horn

2. Underline the word(s) in parentheses that will make each statement correct.

   A. Culture has a (significant/negligible) impact on how intelligence is defined.

   B. Intelligence is often described as the ability to learn, think logically about (concrete/abstract) concepts, and adapt to the environment.

   C. Known as the father of mental testing, (Galton's/Spearman's) research was key in establishing the psychometric approach.

   D. In order to use the psychometric approach in identifying psychological skills and abilities, researchers employ (paper-and-pencil tests/magnetic resonance imaging).

   E. Crystallized ability, unlike fluid ability, is a culturally-based, acquired set of skills and abilities which tend to (increase/decrease) throughout adulthood.

COGNITIVE DEVELOPMENT IN ADOLESCENCE

2. Continued

   F. In Spearman's two-factor theory of intelligence, general intelligence or g, refers to a (broad/limited) skill that is utilized to some extent on all intellectual tasks.

   G. Sternberg's triarchic theory of intelligence is based on (historical psychometric data/information processing data).

   H. Within Sternberg's triarchic theory of intelligence, the contextual subtheory describes an individual's ability to exhibit intelligent behavior in (make-believe/real-life) contexts.

   I. According to (Sternberg/Gardner), cultural values, opportunities, and individual choice are all involved in shaping intelligence.

   J. Gardner's theory of multiple intelligences is based on (intuitive/psychometric) data, research on brain damage, evolutionary history, and the existence of exceptional people.

   K. (Interpersonal/Intrapersonal) intelligence refers to the ability to understand and regulate your own emotions.

   L. The experiential subtheory of Sternberg uses the concept of (automaticity/meta components).

   M. According to Gardner, the abilities to perceive, transform, and recreate information about the size and shape of objects is related to (logical-mathematical intelligence/spatial intelligence).

COGNITIVE DEVELOPMENT IN ADOLESCENCE

3. Complete the following chart by filling in the blanks with missing information.

Sternberg's Triarchic Theory of Intelligence

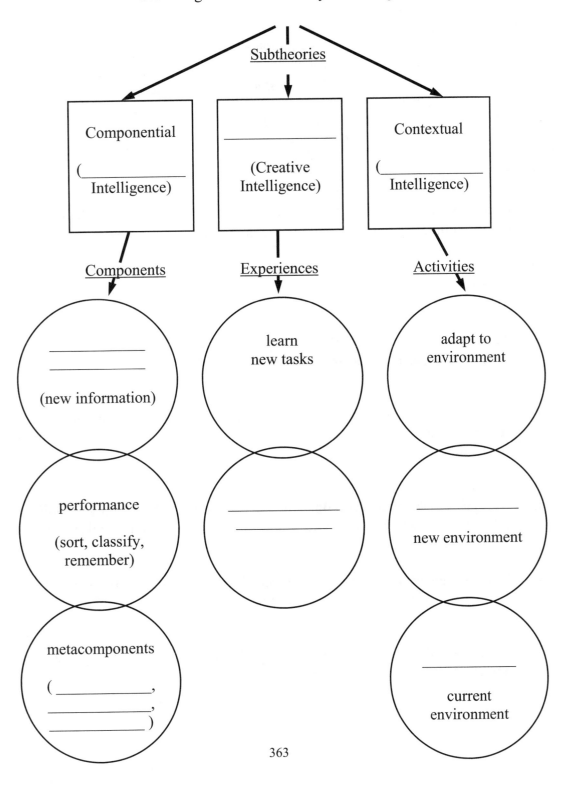

COGNITIVE DEVELOPMENT IN ADOLESCENCE

4. Many students have learned to name and order the planets in our solar system by using the mnemonic below (left). Construct your own mnemonic to remember Gardner's eight intelligences using the blanks next to each.

My	Mercury	Linguistic	**L**_____
Very	Venus	Logical-mathematical	**L**_____
Educated	Earth	Musical	**M**_____
Mother	Mars	Bodily-kinesthetic	**B**_____
Just	Jupiter	Spatial	**S**_____
Served	Saturn	Interpersonal	**I**_____
Us	Uranus	Intrapersonal	**I**_____
Nine	Neptune	Naturalist	**N**_____
Pizzas	Pluto		

5. Read the description of each individual below. In the blank provided, which of Gardner's multiple intelligences is probably most prevalent in the person.

   A. Kenny enjoys rebuilding vintage cars with his dad and plans to major in computer engineering.

   _____

   B. Mayim is fluent in English, Hebrew, and Japanese and has published poetry in a national young artist's magazine.

   _____

   C. Starfish is the president of her sixth-grade class. She coordinates all of the art projects for the school play and would like to campaign for mayor of her city when she is older.

   _____

   D. Caedmon's rock collection is on exhibit at the county fair. He enjoys classifying each of his new acquisitions by testing their hardness, cleavage, and streak.

   _____

   E. Sinead is quite accomplished on bassoon, oboe, and English horn. She writes jigs and reels for the Celtic society in her town.

   _____

   F. Mahalia won the state championship in hurdles and long jump. She practices yoga on a regular basis and teaches tai chi at the YWCA.

   _____

COGNITIVE DEVELOPMENT IN ADOLESCENCE

Assessing Intelligence

1. Why are the terms "reliability" and "validity" NOT interchangeable?

2. Compare and contrast the Stanford-Binet Intelligence Scale and the Wechsler Scales in terms of design, reliability, and validity.

Extremes of Intelligence: Mental Retardation and Giftedness

1. Identify the three components of the formal definition of mental retardation (MR).

    A.

    B.

    C.

2. Complete the following table with information regarding the four levels of MR.

Level of MR	Approximate IQ	Percentage of people at each level

COGNITIVE DEVELOPMENT IN ADOLESCENCE

3. Describe how the terms "gifted" and "talented" are typically used by researchers and educators.

4. Distinguish globally gifted from unevenly gifted.

5. Identify the three characteristics of gifted and talented children that have been described by Winner (1996).

   A.

   B.

   C.

6. Using the names of the primary researchers associated with each project, identify and briefly describe two longitudinal studies of gifted and talented individuals.

   A.

   B.

COGNITIVE DEVELOPMENT IN ADOLESCENCE

Ethnic Differences and Questions About Cultural Bias

Ethnic differences in test scores and cultural bias in testing are important issues in the intelligence field. Provide an argument or example to support each of the views listed.

View	Supporting Argument or Example
Intelligence tests are culturally biased.	
Minorities have less test-taking skill and experience.	
Most examiners are white.	
Test results lead to inadequate and inferior educational placements.	
Tests are useful in evaluating present functioning.	
The tests are beneficial in obtaining special programs.	
Intelligence tests are effective in evaluating programs.	
Tests are advantageous in indicating future functioning.	

⊙ LEARNING TO COMMUNICATE: Language in Adolescence

The Adolescent Register

1. Define adolescent register.

2. Identify three or more slang words from your adolescent years, then ask a teenager if he or she knows the "meaning" of the word(s). What is his or her favorite slang word?

COGNITIVE DEVELOPMENT IN ADOLESCENCE

Genderlects

1. Contrast the genderlects for boys and girls by identifying four features of each language.

   Language of Boys   Language of Girls

   A.   A.

   B.   B.

   C.   C.

   D.   D.

2. Why do language theorists believe genderlects develop?

Social and Cultural Dialects

1. Indicate which of the following statements are true and which are false. If false, alter the statement in some way to make it true.

   A. A dialect consists of audible speech characteristics or differences in how words are pronounced.   T/F

   B. Dialects develop in response to social and cultural conditions.   T/F

   C. Ebonics is not a distinct dialect of English.   T/F

   D. The most studied social dialect of Standard American English is Hispanic English.   T/F

   E. Speaking a dialect has no relationship to intelligence, ambition or success.   T/F

   F. Dialect is one component of accent.   T/F

COGNITIVE DEVELOPMENT IN ADOLESCENCE

⊙ COGNITION IN CONTEXT: ADOLESCENTS MAKING DECISIONS

How Well Do Adolescents Make Decisions?

1. Fill in the parts of the chart below to create a map of the decision making process.

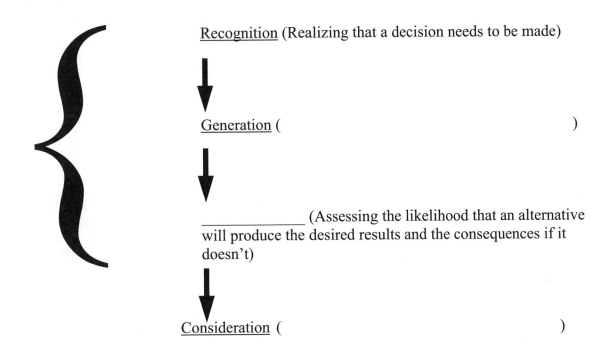

2. Emily Ann has received an invitation to a party. She knows her parents would not approve of the host or of the underlying reasons for the get-together. How might her decision making process vary depending on Emily Ann's age?

At 13 Years of Age   At 17 Years of Age

COGNITIVE DEVELOPMENT IN ADOLESCENCE

Making Vocational Choices

1. Read each vignette below. Then, identify at least two occupational categories which best fit each person. Suggest two career choices using Holland's Six Occupational Categories (1997) as your guide.

   A. As the president of her school art club, Venus is out-going and competent. She has succeeded in gaining access for herself and several of her talented friends to the local art gallery. Their work is being presented at an evening reception featuring the artwork of local artisans. Venus designed the flyer advertising the celebration and has distributed them to area businesses.

Occupational Category	Possible Career Path
a.	a.
b.	b.

   B. Aloysius is the star of the school debate team. Punctual and efficient, he is always prepared and well-versed in the subject matter. Aloysius has a meeting scheduled with the principal of the school to discuss the possibility of developing a chess club. He and his fellow enthusiasts would like to offer instruction to interested students in the area elementary schools.

Occupational Category	Possible Career Path
a.	a.
b.	b.

   C. Quiet and retiring, Ambrosia enjoys reading, writing, and computers. She is interested in post-apocalyptic novels that she buys at thrift stores and is designing a computer program that will explore Earth's readiness to endure the future. Ambrosia's favorite movies are *Blade Runner*, *Soylent Green*, and *The Postman*.

Occupational Category	Possible Career Path
a.	a.
b.	b.

COGNITIVE DEVELOPMENT IN ADOLESCENCE

2. How does research on work values pertain to adolescents' vocational choices?

3. List at least three factors, other than an individual's characteristics, that may be involved in vocational decisions.

   A.

   B.

   C.

The Forgotten Third: Improving the Transition from School to Work

1. Identify and discuss four school or work settings that tend to facilitate the transition from school to work.

   A.

   B.

   C.

   D.

COGNITIVE DEVELOPMENT IN ADOLESCENCE

2. Describe how mentoring enables the school-to-work experience to be more beneficial and successful.

3. What effects does working for pay have on adolescents?

COGNITIVE DEVELOPMENT IN ADOLESCENCE

When You Have Finished

⊙ WORKING THE WEB

1. At the Knowledge Loom, educators worldwide gather to share information. To find out more about "Adolescent Literacy in the Context Areas," go to knowledgeloom.org/adlit/index.jsp. Click on "Investigate" and you'll find both English and Spanish versions discussing the four key components of the "Adolescent Literacy Support Framework." An excellent bibliography of resources for adolescent literacy can be found at this site.

2. At www.advocatesforyouth.org/youth/index.htm, visit the Youth Action Center to learn how one organization is trying to create community partnerships between adults and adolescents. Check out the section on "Today's News," then look at the topics in "Health and Well-Being." How are the young people involved in the Youth Activist Network working to provide access to accurate sexual health information and services?

3. The award winning web site at www.hoagiesgifted.org/index.htm is a great resource for parents, educators, kids, and teens. There is an excellent bibliography of resources on giftedness and an interesting list of "acronyms, terms, and other things we need to know." For an overview of the site, look at "Gifted 101: A Guide for First Time Visitors."

4. Formed to "bring attention to the unique emotional needs of gifted children," SENG (Supporting Emotional Needs of the Gifted) provides information for families, schools, workplaces and communities. Go to www.sengifted.org and click on the Articles and Resources tab. In the articles library, you'll find reading on emotional needs and social issues, as well as tips on parenting and counseling gifted individuals.

5. A very readable paper on "How Linguists Approach the Study of Language and Dialect" can be found at www.stanford.edu/~rickford/papers/l73_reading_1.doc. If you have questions about the variation in languages and dialects or have ever wondered about regional and social approaches to the study of human language, this article may offer some answers.

6. Take a look at this lesson plan for grade 8 English Language Arts (www.learnnc.org/lessons/barbaragroome4212004693). In what ways are students being asked to learn about dialect and "lingo"? Search the Web for the poems and novel being studied and read the excerpts you find. Can you think of other ways to immerse students in an investigation of dialects?

COGNITIVE DEVELOPMENT IN ADOLESCENCE

7. If you are interested in hearing examples of different dialects, go to students.csci.unt.edu/~kun/link.html, where you'll find a fascinating collection of links to web sites offering recordings and descriptions of many English dialects.

8. "A Parent's Guide: Your Teen in the Working World" gives an overview of how teens choose a career and the influences upon those choices (www.oberlin.edu/faculty/ndarling/transition/group27/career.htm). This is a good web site for parents pondering the pros and cons of teenagers who work.

COGNITIVE DEVELOPMENT IN ADOLESCENCE

⊙ PRACTICE TEST #1

Multiple Choice Questions
For each question, circle the best answer from the choices given.

1. Danielle's social studies class is given an essay assignment to write about what the world would be like today if Germany and Japan had won World War II. This assignment requires what kind of reasoning skills? (p. 481)

   a. reflective thinking
   b. abstract thinking
   c. adolescent egocentrism
   d. postformal reasoning

2. What the information processing theorists call "metacognition" is equivalent to _____ in Piaget's theory. (p. 482)

   a. reflective thinking
   b. combinatorial logic
   c. postformal reasoning
   d. hypothetico-deductive reasoning

3. During the night an acne pimple popped up on Sarah's nose. In the morning she tells her mother, "I can't go to school like this! Everyone will be staring at my huge zit!" This is an example of (p. 482)

   a. adolescent egocentrism.
   b. personal fable.
   c. imaginary audience.
   d. both a and c.

4. 16 year old Galen has heard all the horror stories about the dangers of drinking and driving. In his driver's ed. class they even saw video footage of actual drunk driving crash scenes. Nonetheless, he has four beers with friends and then gets behind the wheel. He tells himself, "I know you're not supposed to drink and drive, but I'm a better driver than most kids. Nothing can happen to me because I've got everything under control." Galen's thinking demonstrates (p. 483)

   a. imaginary audience.
   b. combinatorial logic.
   c. personal fable.
   d. situated cognition.

COGNITIVE DEVELOPMENT IN ADOLESCENCE

5. Recent research based on Piaget's theory finds that he may have underestimated the cognitive abilities of (p. 484)

a. infants.
b. preschoolers.
c. elementary school aged children.
d. adolescents.

6. Which of the following is NOT one of the applications of Piaget's theory to the field of education? (p. 485)

a. Piaget's stages and concept of cognitive readiness have shaped guidelines for when to introduce topics into the curriculum.
b. Piaget's views of the child have led to the design of interactive and hands-on curricula.
c. Piaget's theory led to the development of guided participation in a community of practice.
d. For older students, teachers encourage reflective abstraction to think about the implications and limitations of their ideas.

7. Renata is given an algebra problem: 8X = 400. She is not able to solve it. Her teacher then says, "If you and 7 of your friends were given $400, how would you divide it up evenly?" Renata is quickly able to deduce the answer. The teacher's example demonstrates the importance of (p. 487)

a. guided participation.
b. situated cognition.
c. socially shared cognition.
d. combinatorial logic.

8. A view of cognition that children are involved in sociocultural activities to the degree that their level of cognitive development allows is called (p. 487 - 488)

a. the theory of multiple intelligences.
b. triarchic theory.
c. socially shared cognition.
d. guided participation.

COGNITIVE DEVELOPMENT IN ADOLESCENCE

9. The guided participation view differs from Vygotsky's theory in that guided participation emphasizes (p. 488)

a. that children's thinking cannot be understood without considering the sociocultural context.
b. how a person's social roles or shared interactions with others change as the person develops.
c. that individuals have multiple intelligences that operate relatively independently.
d. how mental processes work together to produce intellectual thought.

10. Mr. Seo puts the 11th graders in his American Government class into groups to come up with a campaign plan for their fictional presidential candidates. Michael's group had some creative ideas. Mr. Seo asks "Who came up with these ideas?" Michael says, "We all did together." This demonstrates (p. 488)

a. socially shared cognition.
b. guided participation.
c. combinatorial logic.
d. adolescent egocentrism.

COGNITIVE DEVELOPMENT IN ADOLESCENCE

⊙ PRACTICE TEST #2

Multiple Choice Questions
For each question, circle the best answer from the choices given.

1. Although she is only in high school, Ariel has had several of her poems and short stories published. According to Gardner's theory, she would likely score high in what type of intelligence? (p. 493)

a. musical
b. spatial
c. interpersonal
d. linguistic

2. The consistency of scores when a test is repeated under the same conditions is called (p. 495)

a. validity.
b. reliability.
c. standardization.
d. norms.

3. The most severe forms of mental retardation usually result from (p. 499)

a. lack of stimulation during infancy.
b. head injuries.
c. genetic disorders.
d. living in poverty.

4. Which of the following is NOT one of Sattler's arguments for using intelligence tests with minority children? (p. 501)

a. Minority children may have less test taking experience.
b. Tests help students get access to special programs.
c. Tests are useful in evaluating present functioning.
d. Tests help families, educators and communities evaluate the effectiveness of programs.

5. What is the purpose of the adolescent register? (p. 504)

a. to show who is popular and who is not
b. to minimize dialects among teens
c. identify peer groups and exclude those outside the peer group
d. to learn the current slang

COGNITIVE DEVELOPMENT IN ADOLESCENCE

6. Genderlects of boys usually include more _____ than those of girls. (p. 505)

a. verbal conflict and coercion
b. collaborative suggestions
c. communication about emotions
d. attempts to control and manage interactions

7. A teen says "After school, I walk home. I no tired." This is an example of which dialect? (p. 506)

a. African American English
b. Hispanic English
c. Asian English
d. none of the above

8. Which of the following is NOT part of the process of decision making? (p. 507)

a. generating alternatives
b. evaluating the likelihood that an alternative will produce the desired results
c. taking contexts into consideration
d. All of the above are part of decision making.

9. Theories of vocational choices tend to focus on either the person's interests or (p. 509)

a. work values.
b. parental values.
c. gender appropriateness of jobs.
d. peer choices of occupations.

10. Research has found that working more than how many hours per week during the school year is associated with poorer grades and negative behaviors? (p. 510)

a. 10
b. 15
c. 20
d. 25

COGNITIVE DEVELOPMENT IN ADOLESCENCE

⊙ COMPREHENSIVE PRACTICE TEST

Multiple Choice Questions
For each question, circle the best answer from the choices given.

1. What kind of thinking skill is essential for solving problems in chemistry, physics and other sciences? (p. 482)

   a. reflective
   b. combinatorial logic
   c. adolescent egocentrism
   d. socially shared cognition

2. What part of the personal fable is correlated with better mental health and psychological adjustment? (p. 483)

   a. invulnerability
   b. imaginary audience
   c. personal uniqueness
   d. omnipotence

3. Which of the following statements about Piaget's theory is FALSE? (p. 484 - 485)

   a. Piaget's research has not had widespread applications in education.
   b. Piaget may have overestimated the abilities of most adolescents and adults.
   c. Cross cultural studies show that children pass through Piaget's stages in the same order.
   d. Recent research shows that children may in fact be in 2 stages at the same time.

4. Which of the following concepts is part of recent sociocultural views of cognitive development? (p. 487)

   a. guided participation
   b. situated cognition
   c. metacognition
   d. both a and b

5. A high school engineering club is set up to use guided participation. New members prepare the materials to be used while the more experienced students actually perform the tests. In the club, the new members are (p. 488)

   a. central participants.
   b. using the triarchic theory of intelligence.
   c. legitimate peripheral participants.
   d. building up their fluid intelligence.

COGNITIVE DEVELOPMENT IN ADOLESCENCE

6. The idea that thought is a shared group activity derived, at least in part, from interactions occurring between people in a group is called (p. 488)

a. situated cognition.
b. socially shared cognition.
c. crystallized intelligence.
d. multiple intelligences.

7. Which of the following conceptions of intelligence are believed to be biologically based? (p. 490)

a. general intelligence and fluid ability
b. specific intelligence and fluid ability
c. general intelligence and crystallized ability
d. specific intelligence and crystallized ability

8. Which part of Sternberg's theory is similar to the concept of automaticity in information processing theory? (p. 491)

a. logico-mathematical reasoning
b. combinatorial logic
c. the componential sub-theory
d. the experiential sub-theory

9. Although Jacob didn't have a high score on an intelligence test taken at school, he has "street smarts" and knows how to survive in his environment. For Sternberg, this would be part of which sub-theory? (p. 492)

a. experiential
b. contextual
c. componential
d. hypothetico-deductive

10. How many types of intelligences are included in Gardner's theory? (p. 492)

a. 3
b. 5
c. 8
d. 10

COGNITIVE DEVELOPMENT IN ADOLESCENCE

11. Gardner emphasizes that all of his types of intelligences exist to some degree in everyone. What makes us unique is our (p. 494)

a. profile of intelligences.
b. amount of intrapersonal intelligence.
c. experiential component.
d. socially shared cognition.

12. Which of the following is NOT a legitimate use of intelligence tests by professionals? (p. 495)

a. identify people who have cognitive deficits
b. screen children for entry into special educational programs
c. determine if a child has a brain disorder
d. make a diagnosis of mental retardation

13. Both the Stanford Binet and the Wechsler Scales have reliability correlations around (p. 496)

a. .50.
b. .75.
c. .90.
d. .99.

14. Chima is tested using the Wechsler Scales of intelligence. His IQ score is 69. This would put him in what category? (p. 499)

a. average
b. mildly mentally retarded
c. moderately mentally retarded
d. profoundly mentally retarded

15. Recent studies have found all of the following to be true of gifted and talented adolescents EXCEPT (p. 500)

a. They are more likely to come from rural areas.
b. Their parents tend to have more education.
c. Their families are supportive and they have a positive home environment.
d. They rate their family interactions as affectionate and happy.

COGNITIVE DEVELOPMENT IN ADOLESCENCE

16. Why might minority children score lower than Caucasian children on intelligence tests? (p. 501)

a. Their genetics limit their intelligence.
b. Ethnic minorities focus less on oral skills.
c. They have been told that they should expect to do well.
d. Test items may require knowledge that is specific to the middle class whites who design the tests.

17. Audible speech characteristics or differences in how words are pronounced is called a/an (p. 505)

a. accent.
b. dialect.
c. genderlect.
d. adolescent register.

18. By what age are adolescents able to evaluate options and defend their decisions? (p. 507)

a. 13
b. 14
c. 16
d. 18

19. The personality characteristics persistent, practical and efficient are included in which of Holland's general occupational categories? (p. 509)

a. investigative
b. enterprising
c. social
d. conventional

20. Which type of school/work alternative provides paid work experience with specific skill goals as part of the student's schooling? (p. 510)

a. internships
b. youth apprenticeships
c. cooperative educational programs
d. service learning experiences

COGNITIVE DEVELOPMENT IN ADOLESCENCE

Short-Answer Questions
Answer each question in the space provided.

1. Describe the 5 important higher level cognitive abilities that comprise formal operational thought. What is the most significant limitation of adolescents' cognitive abilities?

2. Describe the psychometric approach to intelligence. Be sure to include the definitions for general and specific intelligences, fluid and crystallized abilities. How is the psychometric approach linked to intelligence testing?

3. What are the 3 main characteristics of gifted and talented children? Differentiate between globally gifted and unevenly gifted teens.

COGNITIVE DEVELOPMENT IN ADOLESCENCE

⊙ CROSSWORD PUZZLE

Across
2. False beliefs that adolescents have about their own thoughts, influence, and risks are called personal _____.
3. _____ logic is the ability to generate and systematically consider all possible arrangements of a set of elements.
8. the ability of a test to measure what it intends to measure
10. a consistent and systematic variety of a single language that is shared by a certain subgroup of speakers

Down
1. the consistency of scores when a test is repeated
4. the process of taking responsibility for teaching and advising students to ensure learning
5. _____ ability is a biologically-based ability to think and perceive relations among elements.
6. the ability to learn, think logically, and adapt to the environment
7. _____ cognition is the idea that we cannot fully understand children's thinking without considering the context.
9. _____ thought refers to things that are not real or things that are only possibilities.

Puzzle created with Puzzlemaker at DiscoverySchool.com

15 SOCIAL AND EMOTIONAL DEVELOPMENT IN ADOLESCENCE

Before You Read

Adolescents moving from childhood to adulthood face major developments in identity, autonomy, and intimacy. This chapter begins with an examination of self-definition and the skills, interests, and characteristics that constitute one's identity. Sexual orientation and the development of morality are addressed as a part of this self-definition. Within families, adolescents are challenged with resolving conflicts with parents; in addition, some deal with issues involving adoption, and sexual and ethnic diversity. You'll read about peer relationships and their associated trials, tribulations, and pleasures, from cliques and crowds to dating and use of leisure time. Finally, the chapter focuses on school climate and structure, and the relationships of culture and poverty to adolescent development.

Chapter Learning Objectives

After reading this chapter, you should be able to do the following:

- Identify the major changes in adolescent identity development.

- List the four possible identity statuses during adolescence according to Marcia (1966).

- Discuss Phinney's Three-Stage Model of Ethnic Identity Development.

- Describe the factors contributing to the development of sexual orientation.

- Explain Kohlberg's third level of moral reasoning.

- Summarize the main criticisms of Kohlberg's theory.

SOCIAL AND EMOTIONAL DEVELOPMENT IN ADOLESCENCE

- Define autonomy and discuss how its development affects families.

- Outline the academic, social, and emotional outcomes for children raised by lesbian or gay parents.

- Explain why certain family practices and parenting styles are helpful in promoting strength and resilience in ethnic families.

- Describe the development of friendships during adolescence.

- Summarize the role of cliques and crowds in the development of an adolescent.

- Discuss the progress from gender segregation to dating during adolescence.

- Define stage-environment fit and its relationship to school structure.

- Give an overview of the differences in academic achievement among students in the U. S. and those in other countries.

- Compare and contrast individualism and collectivism.

- Explain ways parents and schools can help prevent problems with schooling.

- List several ways in which poverty can affect adolescent development.

- Define acculturation and discuss its relevance to adolescent development in immigrant families.

SOCIAL AND EMOTIONAL DEVELOPMENT IN ADOLESCENCE

As You Read

Key terms and concepts are essential to your understanding of the chapter. Your ability to logically discuss and analyze pertinent information is dependent upon your knowledge of these concepts. Terms can be found in boldface throughout the chapter and definitions are listed in a glossary of terms at the end of the chapter. Flashcards may be helpful for memorizing definitions. Begin using the terms as you study, incorporating them into your vocabulary.

acculturation	ethnic identity	intimacy
autonomy	homosexual experience	life-course persistent pattern
biculturalism	homosexual orientation	postconventional level
child cultural brokers	identity	psychological autonomy granting
cliques	identity achievement	sexual orientation
collectivism	identity diffusion	stage-environment fit
crowds	identity foreclosure	strength and resilience perspective
cultural deficit perspective	identity moratorium	
culture	individualism	

⊙ WHO AM I? Adolescents Understanding of Themselves

Identity

1. Fill in the blanks to complete the following statements regarding James Marcia's theory of identity development.

    A. Marcia's theory is an extension of _____ theory of psychosocial development.

    B. According to Marcia, the two main aspects of identity development in adolescence are _____ and _____.

    C. The relative influence of these two main aspects of identity development determine the following four possible identity statuses during adolescence:

    1.   3.

    2.   4.

SOCIAL AND EMOTIONAL DEVELOPMENT IN ADOLESCENCE

2. Now, summarize parallels between Marcia's model of identity development and Phinney's model of ethnic identity development.

3. All of the following statements regarding ethnic or racial identity are FALSE. Make appropriate changes that will create TRUE statements.

   A. Children of minority groups do not identify themselves as members of specific ethnic groups until they are teenagers.

   Change(s):

   B. Children as young as three years of age understand differences between themselves and those of majority groups.

   Change(s):

   C. Children of minority groups typically do not prefer other children of their own ethnicity until they are ready to date.

   Change(s):

   D. Minority teens with a foreclosed identity status do not have clear feelings about their own ethnicity.

   Change(s):

   E. The second stage of ethnic identity search involves identity diffusion and foreclosure.

   Change(s):

   F. A personal experience with prejudice might lead an ethnic minority teen to the resolution of conflict stage.

   Change(s):

SOCIAL AND EMOTIONAL DEVELOPMENT IN ADOLESCENCE

Sexual Orientation

1. Describe the four stages of homosexual identity development (Rub et al., 2006, Troiden, 1988).

    Stage 1:

    Stage 2:

    Stage 3:

    Stage 4:

2. Describe biological and environmental factors that may play a role in the development of sexual orientation.

    Biological Factors					Environmental Factors

3. Explain how the recent "exotic becomes erotic" account of sexual orientation (Bem, 1996) attempts to integrate biological and environmental influences on both homosexual and heterosexual orientation.

SOCIAL AND EMOTIONAL DEVELOPMENT IN ADOLESCENCE

4. Explain how researchers distinguish between a homosexual orientation and homosexual experiences.

5. Define what is meant by "the heterosexual assumption" and explain why it is a myth.

6. Summarize the difficulties experienced by many gay and lesbian youth.

Morality

1. Review Kohlberg's Stages and Levels of Moral Reasoning on page 297 of your text. Identify the six stages and three levels, give the typical age ranges, and note an example of each type of reasoning.

Level	Stage	Typical Age Range	Example of Reasoning

SOCIAL AND EMOTIONAL DEVELOPMENT IN ADOLESCENCE

2. Identify the specific aspects of Kohlberg's theory that have been supported by research.

3. Identify specific criticisms of Kohlberg's theory of moral development.

⊙ SOCIAL RELATIONSHIPS: FAMILY

Teens Developing Autonomy: Conflict with Parents

1. List at least five positive effects that may result from adolescent-parent conflict.

   A.

   B.

   C.

   D.

   E.

2. Define psychological autonomy granting and discuss the positive outcomes with which this style of parenting is associated.

SOCIAL AND EMOTIONAL DEVELOPMENT IN ADOLESCENCE

Family Structures

1. Identify at least four unique challenges facing adopted children.

2. Summarize research regarding outcomes for children who have lesbian or gay parents when compared to children whose parents are heterosexual. Make sure that you include information regarding sexual identity, sexual orientation, peer relations, sociability, intelligence, and emotional and behavioral problems.

3. As your textbook's authors note, courts often require that a lesbian or gay parent not live with his or her partner in order to retain custody of their children. Describe three research findings indicating that this practice is not in the children's best interest.

   A.

   B.

   C.

SOCIAL AND EMOTIONAL DEVELOPMENT IN ADOLESCENCE

4. Place a check if researchers have identified the following family resilience factors within the indicated ethnic minority groups.

Cultural Traditions	African American	Latino American	Asian American	Native American/ Alaskan
Sense of ethnic pride				
Group cooperation				
Fluid household boundaries				
Emphasis on strict discipline				
Respect for elders				
Traditional gender roles				
Obedience and loyalty to parents				
la familia				
System of mutual aid				
Chiao shun and *guan* discipline styles				
Frequent interaction with relatives				
Extended family systems				

⊙ SOCIAL RELATIONSHIPS: PEERS

Friends and Peers in Adolescence

1. Discuss the research on close and supportive friendships during adolescence.

SOCIAL AND EMOTIONAL DEVELOPMENT IN ADOLESCENCE

2. According to Sullivan (1953), what function(s) do *chumships* serve during adolescence?

3. Distinguish between the characteristics of adolescent cliques and those of crowds.

Cliques	Crowds

4. Think for a moment about your own experiences during middle school, junior high school, or high school. Now create a network model (see Chapter 11) of the crowds at your particular school.

SOCIAL AND EMOTIONAL DEVELOPMENT IN ADOLESCENCE

Peer Pressure, Delinquent Behavior, and Aggression

1. Identify at least five concerns that adults have regarding adolescent peer pressure.

   A.

   B.

   C.

   D.

   E.

2. Discuss the extent to which these concerns seem valid.

From Gender Segregation to Dating

Describe the process through which adolescents move from gender segregation to involvement in cross-sex relationships as identified in Dunphy's (1963) classic study.

SOCIAL AND EMOTIONAL DEVELOPMENT IN ADOLESCENCE

Leisure Time in Adolescence

1. What are the most common leisure activities for adolescents?

2. Other than enjoyment, what roles do leisure activities play in the lives of young people?

⊙ CONTEXTS OF DEVELOPMENT

Adolescents in School

1. In what ways may schoolwide practices affect school climate?

2. Identify at least four ways school structures can be modified to be more "adolescent-appropriate."

    A.

    B.

    C.

    D.

SOCIAL AND EMOTIONAL DEVELOPMENT IN ADOLESCENCE

Differences in Academic Performance

1. Summarize the information on differences in academic performance in relationship to ethnicity and gender.

2. Being the Teacher
   You have been asked to lead a roundtable discussion on preventing problems with schooling. Parents, administrators, teachers, and students will be involved with the project. Using the information in Table 15.4, prepare a brief handout setting the stage for the discussion. What possible projects and tangible results might issue from this meeting?

SOCIAL AND EMOTIONAL DEVELOPMENT IN ADOLESCENCE

Cultural Contexts for Development

1. Define culture.

2. Differentiate between individualism and collectivism.

3. Fill in the following table to help you distinguish between individualism and collectivism.

		Individualism	Collectivism
A.	Belief System		
B.	Examples of Countries		
C.	Parenting Practices		
D.	Attachment		
E.	Academics		
F.	Self-Concept		
G.	Social Behaviors		

SOCIAL AND EMOTIONAL DEVELOPMENT IN ADOLESCENCE

4. Describe recent questions and controversies regarding the distinctions between individualism and collectivism.

5. Summarize the effects of living in poverty in the following areas:

   Effects of Living in Poverty

   A. Life Domain

   B. Physical Health

   C. Mental Health

   D. Academic Achievement

   E. Child Care/ Schooling

   F. Parenting Quality

   G. Stability of Home

SOCIAL AND EMOTIONAL DEVELOPMENT IN ADOLESCENCE

6. Describe similarities and differences in the experiences of being poor in the United States.

Specific to Inner-City Poor	Specific to Rural Poor	Common to Both

7. Describe the characteristics of community-bridging families.

   A.

   B.

   C.

   D.

   E.

8. Describe two strategies used by immigrants to help themselves adapt to a new country.

   A.   B.

9. Explain the role of a child cultural broker and identify the benefits and difficulties of this position within the family.

401

SOCIAL AND EMOTIONAL DEVELOPMENT IN ADOLESCENCE

When You Have Finished

⊙ WORKING THE WEB

1. Developed by a group of education, health, mental health, and religious organizations sharing a concern for school students, the web site at www.apa.org/pi/lgbc/publications/justthefacts.html posts factual material on sexual orientation. One of the missions is to ensure that students receive an opportunity for learning and healthy development in a safe and supportive environment, making it a good resource for principals, educators, and school personnel.

2. For a discussion of autonomy and teens, read "Development of Autonomy in Adolescence" at www.ianrpubs.unl.edu/epublic/pages/publicationD.jsp?publicationId=54. You'll find definitions of autonomy and an explanation of why it's important. Family problems are addressed and guidelines given for adults to help teens develop autonomy and positive social values.

3. We hear about peer pressure in the news, but how much do parents really know about their children's friends? Read the brief article for parents, "The Power of Peers," at www.youthdevelopment.org/articles/fp109901.htm. A short exercise helping parents to examine how much they know about their children's friends is included.

4. The Center for Research on Education, Diversity, and Excellence reports on a research project, entitled "Peer Group Influence and Academic Aspirations Across Cultural/Ethnic Groups of High School Students," at crede.berkeley.edu/research/sfc/intro3_5.html. The main aim of the study is to "provide critical knowledge about how ethnically diverse adolescents come to make critical decisions about their schooling and their futures." The report also looks at the role of families, peers, and communities on the decisions these adolescents make.

5. Take a look at the intriguing web site, "The Psychology of Cyberspace," at www.rider.edu/~suler/psycyber/psycyber.html. Explore the "hypertext book" and see if you can answer the following questions:
    What is the "online disinhibition effect"?
    What is a "palace"?
    What is an "avatar"?
    Who are the "bad boys of cyberspace"?
    What do teenagers do on the internet?

6. The Society for Research on Adolescence focuses on the "theoretical, empirical, and policy research issues of adolescence." One interest group within the society studies "emerging adulthood." Skim through the list of publications at www.s-r-a.org/easigpubabc.html.

SOCIAL AND EMOTIONAL DEVELOPMENT IN ADOLESCENCE

⊙ PRACTICE TEST #1

Multiple Choice Questions
For each question, circle the best answer from the choices given.

1. A person's self definition, including the knowledge and understanding of the combination of skills, interests and characteristics that make one unique is called (p. 518)

a. moratorium.
b. foreclosure.
c. identity.
d. the me-self.

2. According to Phinney, how many stages are there for a person to achieve an ethnic identity? (p. 520)

a. 2
b. 3
c. 4
d. 5

3. How is a homosexual experience different from a homosexual orientation? (p. 521)

a. They are the same thing.
b. Orientation refers to a sexual encounter with a same sex person, an experience refers only to attraction to others of same sex.
c. An experience is an encounter with someone of the same sex and orientation is when a child feels different from his or her same sex peers.
d. An experience is a same sex sexual encounter, an orientation refers to same sex attractions.

4. Which of the following conclusions about sexual orientation has NOT been found by recent research? (p. 524 – 525)

a. The suicide rate is the same for heterosexual and homosexual adolescents.
b. Homosexual men and women report higher levels of childhood cross-gender play and preferences.
c. Twin studies have found a higher concordance for homosexuality among identical twins as compared to fraternal twins.
d. Compared to heterosexual peers, homosexual teens have a higher likelihood of failing a grade or dropping out of school.

SOCIAL AND EMOTIONAL DEVELOPMENT IN ADOLESCENCE

5. What is the highest level in Kohlberg's theory of moral reasoning? (p. 525)

a. Conventional
b. Postconventional
c. Formal operational
d. Postformal

6. The leaders of the Civil Rights movement of the 1960's believed that all people should be treated equally, regardless of their race. They staged actions, such as lunch counter sit-ins and Rosa Parks' famous refusal to give up her bus seat. Although they broke laws for their cause, what level of moral development would they be considered to be in according to Kohlberg's theory? (p. 526)

a. Preconventional
b. Conventional
c. Postformal
d. Postconventional

7. 17 year old Josh had an argument with his parents about how many hours he can work at his part-time job. Who, according to research, is most likely to be upset and consider the argument to be very important and meaningful? (p. 531)

a. Josh's mom
b. Josh's dad
c. Josh
d. all of them are likely to be equally upset

8. What is the dimension of parenting that involves encouraging adolescents to develop their own individual opinions and beliefs? (p. 531)

a. moratorium granting
b. authoritarian parenting
c. psychological autonomy granting
d. strength and resilience perspective

SOCIAL AND EMOTIONAL DEVELOPMENT IN ADOLESCENCE

9. Recent research on the outcomes for children raised by lesbian or gay parents has found (p. 532)

a. no disturbances in gender identity as compared to children raised by heterosexuals.
b. these children were no more likely to become homosexual than children raised by heterosexuals.
c. advantages for children whose gay or lesbian parent lives with a committed partner, compared to those whose parent lived alone with the child.
d. all of the above.

10. Deidre is African-American. Although her family had little money, she had a warm supportive family, and her grandmother and aunts and uncles were very involved with her life. Deidre is about to graduate from college and plans to go to law school, with a concentration in civil rights and equal employment law. Which research perspective would predict this outcome for Deidre? (p. 533)

a. autonomy perspective
b. cultural deficit perspective
c. strength and resilience perspective
d. None of the above would have predicted such a positive outcome.

SOCIAL AND EMOTIONAL DEVELOPMENT IN ADOLESCENCE

⊙ PRACTICE TEST #2

Multiple Choice Questions
For each question, circle the best answer from the choices given.

1. When does intimacy in friendships emerge for girls? (p. 536)

   a. late childhood
   b. early adolescence
   c. mid-adolescence
   d. late adolescence

2. A group of adolescent peers who have similar reputations or share attitudes or activities are referred to as a (p. 537)

   a. clique.
   b. collective.
   c. crowd.
   d. chumship.

3. At what age does conformity to peer pressure peak? (p. 538)

   a. 14
   b. 15
   c. 16
   d. 12

4. Dunphy's classic study of the transition form same-sex peer groups to opposite-sex dating found (p. 540)

   a. teens tended to select romantic partners from outside their crowd.
   b. opposite sex relationships tended to be between teens with different attitudes and economic status.
   c. intimacy among opposite sex friends decreased during adolescence.
   d. cross-sex interactions occurred almost exclusively between cliques from the same larger crowd.

5. Why is it difficult to estimate media usage by adolescents today? (p. 542)

   a. Adolescents say they are doing homework on the computer when they're really not.
   b. Teens tend to overestimate the time they spend listening to music.
   c. Teens tend to use media while they are also doing other tasks.
   d. All of the above.

SOCIAL AND EMOTIONAL DEVELOPMENT IN ADOLESCENCE

6. Lindsay has just moved from middle school to high school. Her grades are lower than in middle school, although she says she is working just as hard as she did in middle school. Lindsay feels like she is just a number in this huge regional high school. She misses the guidance counselor and English teacher she had all through middle school. Lindsay is probably experiencing (p. 544)

a. poor stage-environment fit.
b. acculturation shock.
c. the school's zero tolerance policy.
d. the top dog phenomenon.

7. If schools do not take into account their students' home cultures, the result may be (p. 545)

a. students are less likely to put in extra effort.
b. students will not seek academic help.
c. students don't care as much about how well they do.
d. all of the above.

8. The cultural orientation in which people are believed to be independent of each other, and emphasis is on self-fulfillment and personal accomplishments is known as (p. 546)

a. collectivism.
b. individualism.
c. biculturalism.
d. acculturation.

9. What proportion of African American and Hispanic children lives in poverty? (p. 548)

a. 20%
b. 30%
c. 40%
d. 50%

10. Zil's parents were born in India, and immigrated to the U.S. in their 20's. Zil was born in the U.S. While she follows her parents' Hindu traditions and celebrates holidays such as Diwali, she also enjoys American customs and holidays. Zil would be considered to be (p. 552)

a. individualistic.
b. a child cultural broker.
c. bicultural.
d. not acculturated.

SOCIAL AND EMOTIONAL DEVELOPMENT IN ADOLESCENCE

⊙ COMPREHENSIVE PRACTICE TEST

Multiple Choice Questions
For each question, circle the best answer from the choices given.

1. Keyona is 16. When she was in elementary school she wanted to be an actress. In middle school, she thought about being a veterinarian. Now, as a junior in high school Keyona is learning about a career in biochemistry. According to Marcia, what stage of identity formation is Keyona MOST LIKELY in? (p. 519)

   a. identity achievement
   b. identity foreclosure
   c. identity moratorium
   d. identity diffusion

2. Emily was born in China, but was adopted and brought to the U.S. Her adoptive parents are Caucasian. Although she knows that she looks Chinese to others, she feels that she is White American girl. She doesn't speak Chinese or really know much about Chinese traditions or customs. What stage of Phinney's model of ethnic identity development is Emily most likely in? (p. 520)

   a. unexamined ethnic identity
   b. ethnic identity search
   c. blended bicultural identity
   d. alternating bicultural identity

3. Which of the following statements about sexual orientation is TRUE? (p. 521 - 524)

   a. There is no evidence of a genetic basis for sexual orientation.
   b. No differences have been found at autopsy in the brains of heterosexual and homosexual men.
   c. All adolescents are heterosexual at first and become homosexual only after having failed relationships with members of the opposite sex.
   d. In an national survey, 22% of men and 17% of women reported having had some type of homosexual experience at some point in their lives.

4. In Kohlberg's later work on moral development, he concluded that (p. 526)

   a. there are actually 8 stages of moral development.
   b. stage 6 is rarely reached in adults.
   c. all aspects of moral development are universal, regardless of the individual's culture.
   d. Adolescents never reach stage 5.

SOCIAL AND EMOTIONAL DEVELOPMENT IN ADOLESCENCE

5. Who is most likely to have conflicts with their parents? (p. 530)

a. teenage girls
b. teenage boys
c. pre-teen girls
d. pre-teen boys

6. The majority of people who were adopted report (p. 532)

a. good adjustment and normal functioning.
b. feeling emotionally attached to their adoptive parents.
c. being satisfied with their adoptive status.
d. all of the above.

7. For which ethnic group have researchers noted a strong sense of family, fluid household boundaries and mutual aid among family members? (p. 533)

a. Native American
b. Caucasian
c. African American
d. Arab American

8. Compared to the amount of time spent with parents, siblings and other adults, adolescents spend how much time with their friends outside of the classroom? (p. 536)

a. the same amount
b. twice
c. three times
d. four times

9. A small group of between 3 and 9 friends who voluntarily spend together is called a (p. 537)

a. crowd.
b. chumship.
c. clique.
d. collective.

SOCIAL AND EMOTIONAL DEVELOPMENT IN ADOLESCENCE

10. Teens at greatest risk for following a life course persistent pattern of delinquency are those who are (p. 538)

a. aggressive.
b. unpopular.
c. rejected by non-aggressive peers.
d. all of the above.

11. Intimacy among same sex friends _____ across adolescence, but intimacy among opposite sex friend _____ over adolescence. (p. 540)

a. remained constant, increased substantially
b. increased slightly, decreased dramatically
c. decreased substantially, increased slightly
d. increased dramatically, remained constant

12. 15 to 18 year olds spend how much time per day listening to CDs, radio and other media, on average? (p. 542)

a. 1.5 hours
b. 2.75 hours
c. 4. 25 hours
d. 5 or more hours

13. The degree to which the setting is successful in meeting the cognitive, social and emotional needs of a particular child's environment is called (p. 544)

a. acculturation.
b. biculturalism.
c. collective-individual match.
d. stage-environment fit.

14. How does the U.S. high school drop out rate for Hispanic students compare to that of white students? (p. 545)

a. It is twice as high for Hispanic students.
b. Hispanic students' drop out rate is 3 times higher than whites.
c. Hispanic students drop out almost 4 times more often than white students.
d. The drop out rate for Hispanics is 6 times higher than whites'.

SOCIAL AND EMOTIONAL DEVELOPMENT IN ADOLESCENCE

15. The system of shared customs and meanings that allow individuals to participate as a member of a group, and that are transmitted from one generation to the next is the definition of (p. 546)

a. individualism.
b. culture.
c. collectivism.
d. acculturation.

16. How does the rate of poverty for children from birth to age 18 compare to the poverty rate for all age groups? (p. 548)

a. The children's poverty rate is 1 ½ times higher than the rate for all ages.
b. The rate of poverty for children is 3 times as high as it is for all other age groups.
c. The elderly have a higher poverty rate than children.
d. Children are less likely to be in poverty than other age groups.

17. What proportion of the homeless population in the U.S. is comprised of families with children? (p. 550)

a. 2/3
b. 1/2
c. 1/3
d. 10%

18. How does the poverty rate of children in inner cities compare with that of children in rural areas? (p. 551)

a. Inner city children have twice the poverty rate of rural children.
b. Rural children have 3 times the poverty rate of inner city children.
c. The poverty rates are different, with 33% in inner cities and 10% in rural areas.
d. They are very close, 24% in inner cities vs. 19% in rural areas.

19. The process of learning the language, values, customs and social skills of a new culture is called (p. 551)

a. biculturalism.
b. acculturation.
c. collectivism.
d. none of the above.

SOCIAL AND EMOTIONAL DEVELOPMENT IN ADOLESCENCE

20. Ashok's family has only been in the U.S. for 2 years. Although Ashok is only 11, his parents rely on him to interpret for them and explain American social customs. Ashok's role in his family is that of (p. 552)

a. child cultural broker.
b. biculturalism mediator.
c. culture-environment match.
d. all of the above.

Short-Answer Questions
Answer each question in the space provided.

1. Describe the 3 stages in Phinney's model of ethnic identity development. What theory does Phinney's have similarities to?

2. What has the most recent research discovered about the outcomes for children raised by gay or lesbian parents?

3. Discuss the effects that immigration has on the children in a family. What processes have to occur? What role are children often put in by their parents? How do children who were born in the U.S. of immigrant parents adapt?

SOCIAL AND EMOTIONAL DEVELOPMENT IN ADOLESCENCE

Crossword Puzzle

Across
1. groups of adolescent peers who have similar reputations or share primary attitudes and activities
2. _____ orientation is the tendency to be attracted to another.
5. an emotional attachment to another that involves sharing and trusting
7. self-definition
8. the process of learning the language, values, customs, and social skills of a new culture
9. emphasizes individual rights, self-fulfillment, and personal accomplishments
10. the ability to be independent in thought and action, control impulses, and accept responsibility for one's behavior

Down
1. emphasizes duty to others and group goals, values, and well-being
3. a system of share customs and meanings that allow individuals to participate as a member of a group
4. adopting two cultural orientations simultaneously
6. small groups who spend time together on a voluntary basis

Created by Puzzlemaker at DiscoverySchool.com

APPENDIX
Chapter 1

CHAPTER ANSWERS
Practice Tests 1, 2, and Comprehensive

Item Number	Practice Test 1	Practice Test 2	Comprehensive
1	a	d	b
2	b	d	a
3	d	b	c
4	d	c	a
5	a	a	b
6	c	d	b
7	b	b	c
8	b	b	d
9	d	a	a
10	c	a	b
11			c
12			b
13			a
14			b
15			b
16			c
17			a
18			b
19			d
20			c

Short-Answer Questions:

1. The id lies completely below the level of conscious awareness and represents the primitive sexual and aggressive instincts that humans inherited in evolution. The ego is the rational branch of personality; it tries to negotiate realistic ways to satisfy the id's impulses. The superego represents the moral branch of personality and contains our ethical principles, ideals, and conscience. (page ref: 9)

2. Students' answers will vary depending upon which of the theories that they choose to describe. A summary of all of the major developmental theories and theorists is located on page 10 in the text. (page ref: 10)

3. Descriptive research methods attempt to describe something about a behavior, such as how often and under what conditions it occurs. The book lists three examples of descriptive research types. One is naturalistic observation, where researchers watch children in their natural environments and record what they do, when, with whom, and other details. Another type of descriptive research method is structured observation, where the researcher creates a suitable situation (often in a laboratory), arranges for children to be placed in it, and observed their behavior. Finally, the text describes case studies, which are intensive studies of one child or a small number of children to create a detailed description of the some particular behaviors. (page ref: 23)

APPENDIX
Chapter 2

CHAPTER ANSWERS
Practice Tests 1, 2, and Comprehensive

Item Number	Practice Test 1	Practice Test 2	Comprehensive
1	d	d	c
2	d	c	b
3	c	b	c
4	b	b	a
5	a	c	b
6	c	c	b
7	b	a	c
8	c	b	c
9	d	d	d
10	a	c	a
11			b
12			d
13			b
14			b
15			d
16			a
17			c
18			b
19			a
20			b

Short-Answer Questions:

1. Mitosis, also known as "copy division," is the type of cell division that occurs when chromosomes are copied into each new cell. Meiosis, also known as "reduction division," is the type of cell division that occurs during the formation of gametes. (page ref: 51)

2. GxE interaction: the interacting effects of genetics and the environment on the development of traits and characteristics. Students' answers will vary depending upon which of the ways that they choose to define; however, students should choose from range of reaction, canalization, niche-picking, and probabilistic epigenesis. (page ref: 65)

3. Heritability: a mathematical estimate of the degree of genetic influence for a given trait or behavior. Heritability estimates range from 0.00 to 1.00. Higher values mean that there is a stronger genetic influence on the trait. (page ref: 71)

APPENDIX
Chapter 3

CHAPTER ANSWERS
Practice Tests 1, 2, and Comprehensive

Item Number	Practice Test 1	Practice Test 2	Comprehensive
1	c	d	b
2	b	c	d
3	a	c	b
4	b	d	b
5	c	c	c
6	c	d	a
7	a	c	d
8	b	a	b
9	d	b	c
10	c	c	b
11			b
12			a
13			b
14			b
15			a
16			d
17			c
18			b
19			c
20			b

Short-Answer Questions:

1. Cephalocaudal pattern: areas in the head and upper body tend to form and grown before the areas in the lower body grow; proximodistal pattern: areas closer to the center of the body tend to form and grow before the areas toward the extremities grow. (page ref: 88)

2. Cesarean section: surgical procedure in which the baby is removed through an incision made through the mother's abdomen and into the uterus; acceptable uses for this procedure include attempting to reduce a baby's exposure to a maternal virus or birthing complications. (page ref: 96, 103)

3. Students' answers will vary depending upon which of the birthing options that they choose. Birthing options are covered on pages 106-110 in the text. (page ref: 106-110)

APPENDIX
Chapter 4

CHAPTER ANSWERS
Practice Tests 1, 2, and Comprehensive

Item Number	Practice Test 1	Practice Test 2	Comprehensive
1	b	c	c
2	c	b	a
3	a	a	a
4	d	b	d
5	c	a	b
6	c	c	a
7	a	a	c
8	d	b	b
9	b	b	c
10	a	c	c
11			b
12			c
13			b
14			a
15			b
16			c
17			a
18			c
19			c
20			d

Short-Answer Questions:

1. Preterm birth: birth that occurs before 37 weeks of gestation; low birth weight: weight less than 5½ pounds at birth; very low birth weight: weight less than 3½ pounds at birth; small for gestational age: born below the tenth percentile of birth weight for gestational age. (page ref: 123)

2. Synaptogenesis: dendrites and axons branch out to form an enormously large number of connections with neighboring neurons; Myelination: the fatty insulation (myelin sheath) grows around the axons. (page ref: 134)

3. Gross motor development is the process of coordinating movements with the large muscles in the body. An example of gross motor development in moving the larger parts of the body, such as the head, neck, torso, arms, and legs (such as crawling). Fine motor development is the process of coordinating intricate movements with smaller muscles. An example of fine motor development would be finger movements (such as grasping a small object). (page ref: 142-143)

APPENDIX
Chapter 5

CHAPTER ANSWERS
Practice Tests 1, 2, and Comprehensive

Item Number	Practice Test 1	Practice Test 2	Comprehensive
1	d	a	b
2	a	d	c
3	b	c	b
4	c	b	d
5	d	a	a
6	a	d	b
7	a	d	c
8	b	a	d
9	d	c	c
10	b	b	b
11			a
12			b
13			b
14			a
15			b
16			d
17			b
18			c
19			d
20			b

Short-Answer Questions:

1. Preferential looking technique: Using a looking chamber, researchers can determine if infants consistently look longer at some patterns than at others. Researchers can then infer that the infants can see a difference between the patterns. Habituation-dishabituation technique: Infants are shown a stimulus repeatedly until they habituate to it. Then, a new stimulus is presented. This technique capitalizes on infants' tendency to look longer at new stimuli than familiar stimuli. (page ref: 155, 157)

2. Constructivist view believed that young infants are not aware that what they see is related to what they hear, so they need to learn through experience to coordinate their sensory systems. Separatist view believed that infants initially confuse input from their senses and have to learn to separate their sensory impressions. (page ref: 158)

3. Semanticity: language represents thoughts, objects, and events through specific and abstract symbols. Productive: there is no limit to the number or types of utterances that humans can create. Displacement: people can communicate about things that are distant in time or space or even about things that are physically or logically impossible or nonexistent. (page ref: 172)

APPENDIX
Chapter 6

CHAPTER ANSWERS
Practice Tests 1, 2, and Comprehensive

Item Number	Practice Test 1	Practice Test 2	Comprehensive
1	b	d	b
2	c	a	a
3	a	c	c
4	d	b	d
5	c	c	a
6	a	a	d
7	d	b	b
8	b	d	d
9	a	b	c
10	c	d	a
11			b
12			c
13			d
14			a
15			c
16			b
17			d
18			a
19			b
20			c

Short-Answer Questions:

1. Ainsworth's research demonstrated stranger and separation anxiety in infants and toddlers. Bowlby's theory was the dominant framework for the study of attachment. Bowlby's ethological theory says that infants' traits and behaviors developed over time to increase their chances of survival. Infants are wary of strangers, who might be harmful to them. Their preference for a known caregiver to a stranger can help ensure their safety and survival. By protesting separation from a primary caregiver, infants attempt to keep the caregiver close by, also increasing the chances they will be safe and cared for. (page ref: 190 -194)

2. The general description of a child with a slow to warm up temperament is a child who shows mildly negative responses to new stimuli and situations, but with repeated exposures gradually develops a quiet, positive interest. The answer should include 4 of the following 9 dimensions of temperament: activity level, regularity, approach/withdrawal, adaptability, threshold of responsiveness, intensity of reaction, quality of mood, distractibility and attention span/persistence. (page ref: 204 – 205)

3. By the age of 2, toddlers engage in coordinated imitation, which are interactions where the children take turns imitating each other and are aware that they are being imitated. Common toddler games are: throwing and catching; putting toys into a container and "pouring" them out; running and chasing; stacking and toppling blocks or other objects; climbing and jumping; and requesting, receiving and returning items. Conflicts are common among toddlers, usually over toys. Between age 2 and 3, toddlers pretend an object is something else. For example, a wooden block could be a car or a stick a gun. (page ref: 215 – 216)

APPENDIX
Chapter 7

CHAPTER ANSWERS
Practice Tests 1, 2, and Comprehensive

Item Number	Practice Test 1	Practice Test 2	Comprehensive
1	b	c	c
2	d	b	a
3	a	a	b
4	c	d	d
5	a	a	a
6	d	a	c
7	b	c	d
8	c	b	b
9	a	d	c
10	d	b	a
11			d
12			b
13			c
14			d
15			a
16			a
17			c
18			b
19			c
20			d

Short-Answer Questions:

1. Experience-expectant development is the development of basic experiences or activities that all humans share. During this type of development, excess synapses are pruned. Experience-dependent development is the development of specific motor skills, a particular language, and culturally specific behaviors. New synapses are formed to code these experiences. A stimulating environment is important both types of development. Synapses will be pruned in young children according to the environmental experiences, and new synapses will form in older children in response to the environment. (page ref: 230 - 232)

2. The effects of neglect include: language delays, lower intelligence, poor impulse control, and social withdrawal. Children who suffer from neglect have lower cognitive performance and academic achievement than even physically abused children. They tend to be more withdrawn than physically or sexually abused children. (page ref: 247 - 248)

APPENDIX
Chapter 8

CHAPTER ANSWERS
Practice Tests 1, 2, and Comprehensive

Item Number	Practice Test 1	Practice Test 2	Comprehensive
1	b	a	b
2	d	c	c
3	a	b	a
4	c	d	d
5	d	c	c
6	b	b	b
7	a	a	a
8	c	d	d
9	d	b	c
10	b	c	d
11			a
12			b
13			b
14			c
15			a
16			d
17			a
18			d
19			c
20			b

Short-Answer Questions:

1. Piaget and Vygotsky both had theories of how children's thinking develops, and both theories have influenced educational practices. Piaget focused more on the child as an individual, active learner, while Vygotsky looked at children's learning within the context of social interactions. Piaget didn't give language a special role in learning, whereas Vygotsky gave language, especially the internalization of private speech, a significant emphasis. Piaget postulated universal stages of cognitive development; Vygotsky focused on an individual child's zone of proximal development. (page ref: 256 - 266)

2. In the information processing approach, executive processes are compared to a computer's central processing unit (CPU) because both direct and monitor activity. The sensory memory is analogous to input devices such as the keyboard, a diskette or CD-ROM. Short-term memory is compared to RAM (Random Access Memory) because both hold a limited amount of information which is currently being used. Long-term memory is comparable to computer storage devices such as the hard drive, because both allow information to be stored relatively permanently. Information can be retrieved from long-term memory or the hard drive to use as needed. (page ref: 267 - 269)

3. Bilingualism is simply fluency in two languages. A child can learn both languages *simultaneously* or *sequentially.* In *additive bilingualism*, the child learns a second language while maintaining their first language. In *subtractive bilingualism,* the child loses fluency in the first language as a result of learning a second language. The rate of language acquisition is slightly slower for bilingual children, but research has found advantages such as more cognitive flexibility, higher creativity and logical thinking, and more advanced language awareness than their monolingual peers. (page ref: 277 – 279)

APPENDIX
Chapter 9

CHAPTER ANSWERS
Practice Tests 1, 2, and Comprehensive

Item Number	Practice Test 1	Practice Test 2	Comprehensive
1	d	b	a
2	a	a	c
3	c	c	b
4	b	d	d
5	a	a	b
6	c	c	d
7	d	b	a
8	b	d	c
9	c	a	d
10	a	b	b
11			c
12			a
13			b
14			d
15			c
16			a
17			d
18			a
19			c
20			b

Short-Answer Questions:

1. The self is the characteristics, emotions, and beliefs people have about themselves. The two basic aspects are the "I-self", or the conscious awareness that one exists as a separate and unique person who can affect others, and the "me-self", which is what one knows about oneself and how one describes oneself.
Psychologists do not believe infants are born with a sense of self. The "me-self" emerges around 2 years old and is initially very concrete. With age, children's self-descriptions become more abstract and realistic. (page ref: 290 - 291)

2. Parenting Styles: Authoritarian: firm control, but rejecting or unresponsive; Authoritative: parents are warm and exert firm control; Permissive: parents are warm but have little control; Neglecting/rejecting: don't set limits and are unresponsive to children's needs.
Outcomes: Authoritarian: children feel trapped and angry, lower school performance, hostile and aggressive, less popular and dependent; Authoritative: good academic achievement and self esteem, independent, accurate in understanding their parents' values; Permissive: more impulsive, poor school performance, dependent and lack confidence; Neglecting/Rejecting: poor school performance, disruptions in peer relations and cognitive development. (page ref: 298 - 302)

3. The two components of quality day care are structural quality (objective aspects of the environment such as child-adult ratio, caregivers' education, size of the facility) and process quality (the subjective, actual experiences of the children). Research has found high quality care associated with positive social and cognitive outcomes. The cognitive benefits are greatest for those children from the most disadvantaged backgrounds. (page ref: 316 - 318)

APPENDIX
Chapter 10

CHAPTER ANSWERS
Practice Tests 1, 2, and Comprehensive

Item Number	Practice Test 1	Practice Test 2	Comprehensive
1	c	d	b
2	b	c	c
3	d	a	a
4	a	b	a
5	b	c	d
6	c	a	c
7	a	b	b
8	d	d	d
9	c	a	c
10	b	b	b
11			a
12			d
13			a
14			c
15			d
16			b
17			c
18			d
19			a
20			b

Short-Answer Questions:
1. Factors: Sedentary lifestyle, cost of participation and transportation to organized sports (esp. poor families), lack of opportunities and unsafe neighborhoods, diet, esp. processed and fast foods, too much food (portion size), AAP recommendations: limit TV/videos to 2 hours per day, encourage more physical activity, be a good role model for healthy eating and exercise, limit children's food choices, offer nutritious meals and snacks.
(page ref: 329 – 330, 334 - 336)

2. Communication disorders are conditions in which children have significant difficulty producing speech sounds, using spoken language or understanding what others say. Learning disorders are difficulties with specific skills such as reading, math or writing. Both types of disorders are "invisible" disabilities that often go undiagnosed and untreated. Together they make up the largest percentage of children receiving special educational services. (page ref: 350 - 353)

3. Autism has been changed to autistic spectrum disorders to reflect the fact that the disorder can range from mild to severe. It is believed to affect 1 to 6 children out of every 1,000 in the U.S. Although the exact cause of ASDs is unknown, they do have a strong genetic component and have also been linked to brain abnormalities. These abnormalities include immaturity of the limbic system and in the frontal and midbrain areas as well as increased neuron density in the hippocampus and higher than normal brain weight. (page ref: 353 – 355)

APPENDIX
Chapter 11

CHAPTER ANSWERS
Practice Tests 1, 2, and Comprehensive

Item Number	Practice Test 1	Practice Test 2	Comprehensive
1	c	a	d
2	a	c	b
3	b	b	a
4	d	d	c
5	a	b	b
6	b	c	c
7	d	a	a
8	c	d	d
9	d	b	c
10	b	a	d
11			a
12			b
13			d
14			a
15			c
16			b
17			b
18			d
19			a
20			c

Short-Answer Questions:

1. In the concrete operational stage, children can think logically about real objects and situations. Their thought is decentered; that is, they can consider multiple aspects of the problem. They focus on the dynamic transformations in the problem and they are able to mentally reverse processes. In concrete operations, children can solve class inclusion problems. This means they know that objects can be classified in different ways and at different levels. They are also able to do transitive inference, or mentally drawing inferences by comparing relations among objects. (page ref: 364 – 365)

2. Both models are computational in that they are implemented in a computer simulation and focus on cognitive processes. Both models seek to understand humans' developmental changes. Connectionist models hypothesize that knowledge is not stored but is reconstructed based on patterns of activation among individual components.
(page ref: 381 – 382)

3. Vocabulary development continues, more abstract words are learned and children's skill in the use of passive voice, making inferences, referential communication and the social rules of discourse improve.
The connectionist model posits that language acquisition results from changes in the strengths of connections between units based on how closely the language produced matches external criteria.
(page ref: 385 - 388)

APPENDIX
Chapter 12

CHAPTER ANSWERS
Practice Tests 1, 2, and Comprehensive

Item Number	Practice Test 1	Practice Test 2	Comprehensive
1	b	c	a
2	a	b	d
3	c	a	c
4	d	d	b
5	c	d	c
6	d	b	a
7	b	c	b
8	a	a	d
9	c	c	a
10	d	b	c
11			b
12			d
13			b
14			d
15			a
16			c
17			a
18			b
19			d
20			c

Short-Answer Questions:

1. Table 12.4 lists 11 suggestions for how adults can minimize the negative effects of divorce on children. (page ref: 416)

2. Popular children tend to have a positive bias in that they perceive and interpret social situations as friendly and comfortable. Rejected children tend to have a negative bias that leads to negative interpretations of situations as threats, even when they are not. Rejected children are 7 times more likely to fail a grade, 4 times more likely to drop out of school, and are rated by teachers as anxious, fearful and depressed. There are also correlations between peer rejection and delinquency, violent behavior and substance abuse. (page ref: 423 - 424)

3. The media have mixed effects on children. Educational TV can improve academic skills and prosocial behavior in young children (under 7). Watching violence on TV causes more aggressive thinking and behavior in the short term and is correlated with higher levels of aggression long-term. Video games can improve spatial skills, but their violent content increases aggression. (page ref: 429 – 432)

APPENDIX
Chapter 13

CHAPTER ANSWERS
Practice Tests 1, 2, and Comprehensive

Item Number	Practice Test 1	Practice Test 2	Comprehensive
1	c	c	a
2	b	b	b
3	a	d	c
4	d	a	d
5	b	c	b
6	c	b	d
7	a	d	c
8	d	a	a
9	b	b	d
10	a	c	b
11			a
12			c
13			b
14			d
15			c
16			a
17			c
18			a
19			b
20			d

Short-Answer Questions:

1. <u>Early maturation for boys</u>: gain muscle mass and height, leading to greater body satisfaction; enhanced self image; advantage in sports; seen as attractive; affiliate with older adolescents, which is associated with delinquent behavior; <u>Late maturing boys</u>: embarrassed about lack of development; may be teased; <u>Early maturing girls</u>: add more fat leading to heavier build, and less body satisfaction; usually shorter; receive more attention from boys which leads to dating at a younger age and older friends; higher risk for delinquency, problems in school, depression and substance abuse; lower self esteem; alienation from slower developing peers; <u>Late maturing girls</u>: negative body image; see themselves as too thin; less attention from boys (page ref: 444 -445)

2. <u>Teens at greatest risk are</u>: living in poverty; earlier age of first intercourse; lack of parental supervision; lower self efficacy and educational expectations; higher external locus of control, perception of few and/or negative life options; already have a child; <u>Likely outcomes for children of teenage mothers</u>: as infants, more likely to be premature, low birthweight, have birthing complications and higher infant mortality; as children they are at higher risk for accidents, illnesses, child abuse and neglect; teen parents are more likely to have an unresponsive parenting style and unrealistic expectations for their children; teen parents are less empathetic towards their children, less patient, less verbal and provide less stimulating environments for their babies (page ref: 458 – 461)

3. Risk factors for substance abuse: sensation seeking, aggressive, impulsive and has poor behavioral control; history of antisocial behavior; believe drug use is not risky and is fun; high stress level; family history of substance abuse; harsh, inconsistent or permissive discipline; lack of parental supervision; substance-using friends
Gateway drugs, such as alcohol, tobacco and marijuana are typically used prior to harder drugs such as cocaine or heroin. Earlier and more frequent use of gateway drugs is associated with a greater chance of using harder illegal drugs.
(page ref: 468 - 470)

APPENDIX
Chapter 14

CHAPTER ANSWERS
Practice Tests 1, 2, and Comprehensive

Item Number	Practice Test 1	Practice Test 2	Comprehensive
1	b	d	b
2	a	b	d
3	d	c	a
4	c	a	d
5	a	c	c
6	c	a	b
7	b	b	a
8	d	d	d
9	b	a	b
10	a	c	c
11			a
12			d
13			c
14			b
15			a
16			d
17			a
18			b
19			d
20			c

Short-Answer Questions:

1. <u>5 cognitive abilities</u>: 1) Hypothetico-deductive reasoning = the use of deductive reasoning to systematically manipulate several variables, test the effects in a systematic way and reach correct conclusions in complex problems; 2) Logical reasoning about abstract concepts; 3) Separating reality from the possible; 4) Combinatorial logic = the ability to generate and systematically consider all possible combinations of a set of elements; 5) Reflective thinking = metacognition
<u>Limitation of adolescent thinking</u>: egocentrism, the inability to distinguish between their own abstract reasoning and thoughts and the reasoning and thoughts of others. (page ref: 480 - 482)

2. The psychometric approach tries to quantify individuals' psychological skills and abilities. General intelligence is broad thinking ability that underlies all intellectual tasks and functions. Specific intelligence is ability in a particular area. Fluid ability is a biologically based ability to think and perceive relations among elements. Crystallized ability is a body of knowledge and skills acquired in a particular culture. The psychometric approach uses paper and pencil tests to measure ability; intelligence tests come from early attempts to quantify intelligence. (page ref: 490, 495)

3. <u>3 characteristics of gifted and talented children</u>: 1) Precocity, 2) Rage to master their favorite topic, 3) They march to their own drummer - - they have unique ways of learning. Globally gifted refers to children who show exceptional talent in all areas. Unevenly gifted children are exceptional in 1 or 2 areas but are at or below average in other areas. (page ref: 500)

APPENDIX
Chapter 15

CHAPTER ANSWERS
Practice Tests 1, 2, and Comprehensive

Item Number	Practice Test 1	Practice Test 2	Comprehensive
1	c	b	c
2	b	c	a
3	d	a	d
4	a	d	b
5	b	c	a
6	d	a	d
7	a	d	c
8	c	b	b
9	d	b	c
10	c	c	d
11			a
12			b
13			d
14			c
15			b
16			a
17			c
18			d
19			b
20			a

Short-Answer Questions:

1. Table 15.1 lists the three stages in Phinney's model:
Unexamined ethnic identity; Ethnic identity search; and Achieved ethnic identity
Phinney's model parallels that of Marcia in identity development which considers crisis and commitment in the formation of identity. (page ref: 520 -521)

2. As many as 14 million children and teens in the U.S. have gay or lesbian parents. Most were born while their parents were in heterosexual marriages. Not a single study has found these children to be significantly disadvantaged compared to the children of heterosexual parents. Children and teens raised by homosexual parents showed no disturbances in gender identity and were no more likely to be homosexual than their peers raised by heterosexual couples.
(page ref: 532 - 533)

3. All family members undergo the process of acculturation. This process may take several generations and can cause conflict and stress. When the children speak a different language than their parents, they report less communication and closeness with their parents. U.S. born teens in immigrant families tend to change their values and beliefs more rapidly than their parents, creating a bigger difference in values between children and parents in these families. The more differences in the acculturation of parents and children, the more there is family conflict. Teens and even children often are put into the role of child cultural brokers who interpret not only the language for their parents, but also the cultural customs and norms. Many children develop bicultural identities that include both their family's identity and that of the country to which they immigrated.
(page ref: 551 -553)

APPENDIX

CHAPTER ANSWERS
Crossword Puzzles

Chapter 1
Across
1. hypotheses
7. ethology
8. scientific
10. nature

Down
2. socioemotional
3. social
4. theory
5. cognitive
6. physical
9. nurture

Chapter 2
Across
2. heritability
4. phenotype
9. fertilization
10. allele

Down
1. chromosomes
3. gene
5. genotype
6. amniocentesis
7. meiosis
8. mitosis

Chapter 3
Across
2. dilation
5. afterbirth
8. apgar
9. germinal
10. malpresentation
11. ovulation

Down
1. prenatal
3. teratogen
4. organogenesis
6. germinal
7. implantation

Chapter 4
Across
3. locomotor
5. postural
6. colostrum
7. acuity
8. fine
9. neurons
10. programmed

Down
1. mortality
2. myelination
4. gross
5. primitive

Chapter 5
Across
1. holophrases
3. habituation
7. assimilation
9. scheme
10. telegraphic

Down
2. accommodation
4. perception
5. sensorimotor
6. language
8. intermodal

Chapter 6
Across
1. symbolic
4. mutual
5. sensitive
7. attachment
8. separation

Down
1. social
2. contagion
3. temperament
6. stranger
8. strange

Chapter 7
Across
2. compulsive
5. palmar
7. palsy
9. expectant

Down
1. synaptic
3. malnutrition
4. glial
6. amnesia
8. dependent
10. neglect

Chapter 8
Across
1. mediation
3. private
5. animism
7. egocentrism
10. scaffolding

Down
2. operations
4. processing
6. bilingual
8. metacognition
9. automaticity

Chapter 9
Across
9. discipline
11. morality
12. permissive
13. parental

Down
2. nonparental
3. segregation
4. authoritative
6. conscience
8. punishment
10. constancy

APPENDIX

CHAPTER ANSWERS
Crossword Puzzles

Chapter 10
Across
5. comorbidity
9. prevalence
10. iep

Down
1. exceptional
2. sensitization
3. autism
4. cortisol
6. overweight
7. organized
8. sexual

Chapter 11
Across
2. stores
3. connectionist
6. fuzzy
7. strategies
10. network

Down
1. metalinguistic
4. phonemic
5. scripts
8. retrieval
9. subitizing

Chapter 12
Across
5. parentification
8. ability
9. relational
10. helpless

Down
1. rejected
2. social
3. resilient
4. nomination
6. attributions
7. conduct

Chapter 13
Across
2. clinical
3. substance
5. bulimia
6. rape
7. image
8. puberty
9. gateway

Down
1. menarche
2. contraception
4. chlamydia

Chapter 14
Across
2. fables
3. combinational
8. validity
10. dialect

Down
1. reliability
4. mentoring
5. fluid
6. intelligence
7. situated
9. abstract

Chapter 15
Across
1. crowds
2. sexual
5. intimacy
7. identity
8. acculturation
9. individualism
10. autonomy

Down
1. collectivism
3. culture
4. biculturalism
6. cliques

NOTES

NOTES

NOTES

NOTES

NOTES

NOTES

NOTES

ND

NOTES

NOTES

NOTES